We have been conditioned to think of Extra-Terrestrials in terms of science-fiction fantasy, as easily controlled as a television set. The 'serious' news media leans over backwards to avoid mentioning the subject in any way except facetiously. The tabloids operate a censorship in reverse: by exaggerating and sensationalising the facts of the case histories, they reduce them to absurdity. Yet overwhelming evidence has accumulated, which is contained in this book, that humanity as a whole must prepare itself for the historically unprecedented shock of confrontation with non-human intelligent beings from elsewhere in the cosmos.

This is no science-fiction fantasy. The stakes in the game are real, and it is being played for keeps. Our survival as the dominant species on this planet may depend on our ability to recognise, differentiate between and communicate with the variety of intelligent extra-terrestrial life-forms at present hovering above us. Continuing to pretend that they do not exist after they have unmistakably signaled their presence would be suicidal insanity. Simplistic beliefs that they are all benevolent Space Brothers, or all demonic invaders intent on enslaving us, fail to correlate with the known facts of the numerous case histories. The available evidence indicates that we have a wide variety of visitors, with different types of motivation for being here and different ways of interacting with us. Some have had us under surveillance since deep antiquity, periodi-cally stimulating our development. Others are more recent arrivals, apparently alerted to the presence of intelligent life on Earth by our first nuclear explosions, after which UFO activity suddenly began being reported on a large scale world-wide.

During the last few years, incidents in Russia, China, France, Aus-tralia, England, Brazil and the suburbs of New York City have demonstrated that their previously covert presence is becoming undeniably overt. It is time to face the facts instead of evading them, as we have for nearly forty years. This book is an attempt to bridge the gap in understanding be-tween the children of the Earth and the children of the stars, to prepare the way for mutually beneficial communication instead of disastrous antagonistic confrontation, to renew the alliance which existed in deep antiquity as we cross the threshold of the Space Age.

Extra-Terrestrials Among Us is an excellent anthology and erudite overview of the UFO question. It weaves together the best that has been written or recorded from the past to the present, and the reader is treated to a feast of bedizening projections into the future. Issues are joined and controversies are neither ignored nor scorned. For the curious, George Andrews has linked an anchor of facts to a sometimes highly original and tantalizing fabric of intriguing data and speculations. All who love true mysteries should be richly rewarded.

Berthold E. Schwarz, MD
Fellow American Psychiatric Association

About The Author

GEORGE CLINTON ANDREWS has previously published several books, and is a careful researcher. He enjoys a rustic life style in rural Drury, Missouri, where he is a self-employed farmer besides being a writer. He has an extraordinary lineage of famous ancestors, which includes George Clinton (first Governor of New York, and also Vice President under Jefferson), DeWitt Clinton (builder of the Erie Canal), and through his mother's ancestry traces a double link to Goethe. He has been an active member in many professional UFO organizations throughout the world. He witnessed an unforgettable UFO sighting which led to the decade of research that culminated in the writing of *Extra-Terrestrials Among Us*.

To Write to the Author

We cannot guarantee that every letter written to the author can be answered, but all will be forwarded to him. Both the author and the publisher appreciate hearing from readers, learning of your enjoyment and benefit from this book. Llewellyn also publishes a bi-monthly news magazine with news and reviews of practical esoteric studies and articles helpful to the student, and some readers' questions and comments to the author may be answered through this magazine's columns if permission to do so is included in the original letter. The author sometimes participates in seminars and workshops, and dates and places are announced in the *Llewellyn New Times*. To write to the author, or to ask a question, write to:

George Andrews
c/o THE LLEWELLYN NEW TIMES
P.O. Box 64383-010, St. Paul, MN 55164-0383, U.S.A.
Please enclose a self-addressed, stamped envelope for reply, or
$1.00 to cover costs.

ABOUT LLEWELLYN'S PSI-TECH SERIES

We live within a Universe that is immense—every attempt to measure it merely extends our awareness of its size still further. Yet the Universe also reaches to the amazingly small—and the further we penetrate into its structure the more we find. A Universe of Planets, Stars and Galaxies, of Particles and Forces, and of Consciousness—for we are part of the Universe and we know we are Conscious, that we have Awareness. And every effort to study Conscioiusness likewise reveals that the Universe in this dimension is also immense and complex.

Our Awareness of this forces the conclusion that *we are not alone!* Just as the material Universe extends far beyond the sky we see —so we realize does the Universe of Consciousness extend far beyond our small selves, and must include Beings and Intelligences of which we presently know little, or nothing!

Or do we know more than we think? Our history, and our mythology, is filled with "reports" of other Beings and Intelligences: Gods and Goddesses, Angels and Archangels, and also (at the smaller side) Fairies, Elves, and Gnomes *And of Visitors from other Places!*

Why presume that because our perceptions are so limited that none, or only some, of this is true? Why limit ourselves to seeing with only partially opened vision? **Where the Mind of Man goes, so goes Man.**

Now we are reaching out, seeking to make *Contact.* We send our space probes, we listen to space noise hoping for an intelligent message. We speculate about reports of prior contacts—UFOs through the ages, and we wonder about sightings now of Objects in the Sky and Messages through Psychic Channels.

Yes, we also reach within, for we know that the Human Psyche has potential that is only vaguely perceived and little developed. We seek to extend our Awareness and Consciousness not only through material instruments and tools, but through enriching our perceptions with training, understanding and application.

Perhaps we must now reach for the Sky with our imagination and acceptance of the many contacts reported in history, myth, *and religion.* In this book, we review the panorama of these contacts, and explore our reluctance to accept that "someone may be knocking at the door". That it may only be a sudden leap in our Awareness—our ability to communicate with more Advanced Intelligences—that we can resolve *soon enough* the serious crises of Global Conflict, Environmental Abuse, and Personal Violence: new names for the dread Four Horseman of *Apocalypse Now!*

We are NOT alone: it is time to answer the knocking at the door and to see with greater vision and acceptance the immensity and unity of the Greater Universe within which we have our being. Reach out with your mind and be one with the Consciousness of the Universe. **Before it is too late!**

Carl Llewellyn Weschcke, Publisher

Other Books by George Andrews

The Book of Grass, Peter Owen Ltd., London, 1967; Grove Press,
    New York, 1968; Fayard, Paris, 1970; Penguin, London, 1971.
Burning Joy (early poems), Trigram Press, London, 1968.
Drugs and Sexuality, Panther, London, 1973.
Drugs and Magic, Panther, London, 1976.
The Coca Leaf and Cocaine Papers, Harcourt Brace Jovanovich, New
    York and London, 1976.

Llewellyn's PSI·TECH Series

EXTRA-TERRESTRIALS AMONG US

by
George C. Andrews

1990
Llewellyn Publications
St. Paul, Minnesota, 55164-0383

International Standard Book Number: 0-87542-010-9
Library of Congress Catalog Number: 85-45279

First Edition, 1986
First Printing, 1986
Second Printing, 1987
Third Printing, 1987
Fourth Printing, 1987
Fifth Printing, 1988
Sixth Printing, 1990

Library of Congress Cataloging-in-Publication Data
Andrews, George Clinton, 1926—
    Extra-terrestrials among us.

    1. Unidentified flying objects.   1. Title.
TL789.A58   1986   001.9'42   85-45279
ISBN 0-87542-010-9

Cover Photo: Wyoming Department of Tourism

Produced by Llewellyn Publications
Typography and Art property of Chester-Kent, Inc.

Published by
LLEWELLYN PUBLICATIONS
A Division of Chester-Kent, Inc.
P.O. Box 64383
St. Paul, MN 55164-0383, U.S.A.
Printed in the United States of America

Acknowledgements

I wish to thank Tom Adams, Ella Alford, Philippe d'Arschot, Tom Ashcraft, Nicole Beaufume, Simone Benmoussa, Fiona Brewster, Tania Brunell, Larry Bryant, Ray and Irene Buckwalter, Dorothy Burrow, Jocelyn Burton, Kanai Callow, Ken Campbell, Dr. Hasan Choudhury, Lindsey and Bobbie Clennell, Carol Clivio, Tony and Rowena Crerar, Jessie Deer-in-Water, Georgie Downes, Martin and Solange Doyle, Gail Duke, P. M. H. Edwards, Lucius Farish, Larry Fenwick, Elly Fithian, Phyllis Galde, Lyn Gambles, Gloria Goltz, Richard Gregory, Jimmy Guieu, Teresa and Julia Gurney, Dr. Ronnie Hawkins, Richard Heiden, Peter and Andrea Hill, John Hunt, Natasha Jackson, Julian and Bonnie Joyce, Ida Kannenberg, Gail Kuric, Marie-Francoise Lepeltier, Rick and Carol Lovejoy, Joseph Mangini, Clarity Martin, Olga Matthews, Rollo and Serena Maughling, James Allen McCarty, Dr. James and Wendy McClenon, John "Pee Wee" Michael, John Michell, Roxandra Moissiu, J. "Nosh" Neil, Neil Oram, Gwilym and Judy Owen, Jill Purce, Dr. John T. and Elaine Richards, Robert J. M. Rickard, Michael Roll, Dr. Alice Rose, Sue Rose, Christopher Rudman, Dr. Harley Rutledge, Eero Ruuttila, Nicholas Saunders, Frank and Maureen Scherer, Nancy Schiraldi, Dr. Michael and Cynthia Schlosser, Dr. Berthold E. Schwarz, Zapata Seal, Paul Sieveking, Harry Smith, Dr. Leo Sprinkle, Shirley Starke, Marie Steinwachs, Dennis Stillings, Le Estria Tatum, Michael Taylor, Alice Thompson, Eugenia Victoria del Tola, David Tomlin, Walter and Mary Jo Uphoff, Robert Warth, Carl Weschcke, Eve Weston-Lewis, Ion Will, Lavinia Wittenberg, Thomas Woodruff, William Young, Dhyani Fisher Ywahoo, Lionel Ziprin, and my wife, children and family, for the help they gave me while I was working on this book.

PERMISSIONS

Paris-Match, issue of Oct. 26, 1984, interview with Professor Jean-Pierre Petit.

Project Identification: the First Scientific Field Study of UFO Phenomena by Dr. Harley D. Rutledge, published by Prentice-Hall in 1981.

UFO-Dynamics: Psychiatric and Psychic Aspects of the UFO Syndrome by Dr. Berthold E. Schwarz, Rainbow Books, 2299 Riverside Drive, Moore Haven, FL 33471 in 1983.

Ancient Mysteries by Peter Haining, Taplinger, New York, 1977.

The Songs of the South, translated by David Hawkes, Penguin Classic, 1985.

3 Enoch or the Hebrew Book of Enoch, translated by Hugo Odeberg, Cambridge University Press, 1928.

Djanggawul by Roland M. Berndt, Routledge & Kegan Paul, Ltd., London, 1952.

UFOs From Behind the Iron Curtain by Ion Hobana and Julien Weverbergh, Souvenir Press, London, 1964.

Enochian Magic by Gerald Schueler, Llewellyn 1985.

Sun of Beatrice, Nebraska (Nov. 13, 1985) and Betty Loudon of the Nebraska State Historical Society for her article about the UFO incident in Nebraska of June 7-10, 1884.

Lumieres Dans La Nuit, 30250 Sommieres, France for the article by Antonio Ribera.

Secrets of the Great Pyramid by Peter Tompkins, Harper & Row, 1973.

Destiny Mars by M. W. Saunders and Duncan Lunan, Downs Books. Caterham, Surrey, England, 1975. Serious researchers can contact M. W. Saunders at 7 Leazes Avenue, Chaldon, Surrey CR3 5AG, England.

The Case for the UFO by Morris K. Jessup, 1955, Lyle Stuart Inc.

Almost the entire sixth chapter of this book is based on material from *Stigmata*, P.O. Box 1094, Paris, TX 75460. Thomas R. Adams now publishes both *Stigmata* (the Project Stigma report on the continuing investigation into the occurrence of animal mutilations) and *Crux* (strange phenomena, singular events, UFOs, quirky notions and goofball ideas) annually from this address.

The Invisible Landscape by Terence and Dennis McKenna, Seabury Press, 1975.

Clear Intent by Lawrence Fawcett and Barry J. Greenwood, Prentice-Hall, 1984.

The UFO Crash/Retrieval Syndrome: Status Report II by Leonard Stringfield, published by the Mutual UFO Network in 1980. Mr. Stringfield's privately published *Status Report III* is available from his home address: 4412 Grove Avenue, Cincinnati, Ohio 45227, at $11 per copy. He wishes to communicate with anyone having information relevant to UFO crashes or retrievals.

Ida Kannenberg of Hillsboro, Oregon, for her statement and Hweig's dictation, which were published in the *Proceedings of the Rocky Mountain Conference on UFO Investigation*, Laramie, Wyoming, 1981.

Michael Roll of Bristol, England, for portions of "Normalizing the Paranormal", an article on which we collaborated, which appeared in *Pursuit*, Vol. 17, No. 3, Whole No. 67, p. 120, Third Quarter, 1984.

Thomas E. Bearden of Huntsville, Alabama, for the quotation from his unpublished "Free Stream Creation".

"The Westchester Wing—Part II", an article by R. Perry Collins, appeared in *Pursuit*, Vol. 18, No. 4, Whole No. 72, pp. 166-172, Fourth Quarter, 1985. *Pursuit* is a quarterly published by the Society for the Investigation of the Unexplained (SITU), P.O. Box 265, Little Silver, NJ 07739.

Abduction of British policeman: *Sunday Mirror*, London, Nov. 29, 1981.

Concerning the luminous phenomena associated with the Welsh revival: summarised from *Stars and Rumours of Stars*, written and published by Kevin McClure, 8 Scotland Road, Little Bowden, Market Harborough, Leics., England, 1980.

The Varo annotated edition of Morris K. Jessup's *The Case for the UFO* was reprinted in 1973 by Gray Barker, a pioneer researcher who died recently, a loss deeply mourned by his colleagues.

Concerning the Kerr-McGee operation in Shiprock, New Mexico: "Terata" by Christopher Norwood in *Mother Jones*, Jan. 1985.

Concerning the Kerr-McGee operation in Gore, Oklahoma: Native Americans for a Clean Environment (N.A.C.E.), P.O. Box 212, Marble City, OK 74945.

Concerning sudden appearance of large brain after human/E.T. interbreeding: *On Tiptoe Beyond Darwin* by Max H. Flindt, published by the author in 1967 at 1526 Stafford Street, Redwood City, CA. Also *Flying Saucers Are Watching Us* by Otto O. Binder, Belmont Books, New York City, 1968.

Concerning UFO/psychic experiences of the Sunderland family: article by Tony Wilmot in *Weekend*, Jan. 2-8, 1985, London, England.

Concerning prehistoric war in heaven: summarised from "The War of the Gods" by Michael Cohen in *UFO Annual*, New York, 1978.

Statement by nuclear physicist Stanton Friedman from *Post-Dispatch*, St. Louis, MO, June 30, 1985.

May 29, 1986, sighting of the Westchester Wing from *News-Times*, Danbury, CT, May 30, 1986.

Swedish cloud-emitting UFO case from *Ostersunds-Posten*, Ostersund, Sweden, May 6, 1986. Translation credit: Erik Fredricksson.

Brazilian UFO incidents during, before and after May 19, 1986: *O Globo*, Rio de Janeiro, May 22 and 23, 1986 (credits: Robert Pratt and Alberto do Carmo, translation credit: Wendelle Stevens); Reuter News Agency, May 23, 1986; United Press International, May 24, 1986.

Case no. 99 of the Italian UFO wave of 1978: "La Vague Italienne de 1978" by Maurizio Verga, translated by M. Le Gourrierec, in issue # 215-216 (May-June 1982) of *Lumieres Dans la Nuit*, 30250 Sommieres, France.

Contents

Chapter One

FLYING DRAGON
IN THE HEAVENS

Government authorities all over the world continue to deny the reality of UFO phenomena, in spite of obvious evidence which they deliberately ignore or actively suppress. Humanity is not being prepared by its leaders for the shock of confrontation with non-human intelligent beings.

Although two major motion pictures (*Close Encounters* and *E.T.*) have increased public awareness of the subject, they have also paradoxically generated public apathy, since people tend to put them in the same category as *Star Wars* and *Return of the Jedi*: fiction in which danger is vicariously experienced for its thrill value to provide entertainment. The public therefore thinks of UFOs in terms of fantasy as easily controlled as a television set, without even the foggiest notion that the stakes in this game are real, and it is being played for keeps.

This type of complacent know-nothing attitude is encouraged and perpetuated by those in charge of the news media, who systematically disparage UFOs and those who report them as unworthy of anything but ridicule. The 'serious' news media leans over backwards to avoid mentioning the subject in any way except facetiously. The tabloids tend to operate a censorship in reverse: by exaggerating and sensationalising the facts of the case histories, they reduce them to absurdity.

However, the support system for this complacent know-nothing attitude has recently been shattered once and for all. The cover-up has been cracked wide open. Humpty Dumpty has just taken his great fall. Never again will government 'experts' be able to explain away UFO phenomena in conventional terms with even superficial credibility. The release of a book named *Clear Intent*, by Lawrence Fawcett and Barry J. Greenwood (Prentice-Hall, 1984), provides massive, overwhelming and irrefutable evidence based on the *government's own documents* that our highest public officials and the elite of our security and intelligence organisations have been deliberately and persistently lying to tax-paying citizens on the subject of UFOs for the last 39 years. The authors of the book and their associates succeeded in liberating over 4,000 pages of documents relevant to UFO activity from the CIA, FBI, National Security Agency, Air Force Intelligence, and other government agencies through astute use of the Freedom of Information Act. The cat is now out of the bag. The evidence is on the table for all to see.

UFO phenomena have been classified *above* 'top secret' since 1950, classified even above the category for nuclear weaponry. Jets that attempted to fire on UFOs have been vaporised along with their pilots, disintegrating in mid-air without smoke or flame. UFOs have penetrated our most heavily guarded off-limits Strategic Air Command missile sites and other highly sensitive installations time after time with impunity. Usually when jets were sent up after them, the UFOs would leave the jets behind as if they were standing still. On one occasion the UFOs just blinked out like lights switched off, vanishing as the jets approached, then as the jets went over the horizon the UFOs switched themselves back on again, reappearing as suddenly as they had disappeared. On several occasions after UFOs flew over missile sites, the targeting of the missiles changed, and the warheads all had to be replaced. On June 22, 1980, a senior airline pilot reported a UFO about ten miles in diameter over the Kuwait oil fields.

Clear Intent does such a masterful job of using the government's own documents to prove that UFO phenomena are real that no open-minded person who inspects the assembled evidence is likely to have any further doubt about it. Faced with these disclosures, a complacent facetious attitude can be maintained only by idiots, as the support system for it has eroded away to nothing.

Clear Intent focuses on UFOs as aircraft, not on the entities that pilot them, so in that sense this book begins where "Clear Intent" leaves off.

A recent development not covered by *Clear Intent* took place in Russia, where a Soviet government official made an unprecedented landmark of a public statement: that a UFO incident had actually happened.

The city of Gorki is strictly off-limits to anyone without a special Soviet government pass. It also happens to be the city in which the KGB keeps outspoken physicist Andrei Sakharov confined. On March 27, 1983, a cigar-shaped UFO about the size of a Boeing 747 hovered over Gorki Airport at low altitude for about 40 minutes. No jets were scrambled. After 40 minutes, it disappeared over the horizon without incident. During the furor that followed this event, the Soviet government appointed cosmonaut Pavel Popovich to be the head of a Commission on Abnormal Atmospheric Phenomena. Upon taking charge of the Commission, the first thing Popovich did was to issue a public statement that the UFO incident had definitely taken place.

It was reported in the *Sunday Times* of London, England, on March 10, 1985, that this special Commission of the Soviet Academy of Sciences had officially announced that a domestic Aeroflot airliner, traveling from Tblisi to Tallinn at an altitude of 30,000 feet and a speed of 300 miles per hour, had been followed by a UFO for approximately 800 miles, during which the UFO changed shape several times. Besides the crew and the passengers of the airliner, ground control at several different airports along the flight path observed the presence of the UFO right behind the airliner.

The release of this official report by the Soviet Academy of Sciences confronts us with the paradox of the totalitarian, tight-lipped, severely censored Russians volunteering information of a type that our supposedly democratic free press systematically distorts or suppresses. The U.S. government responded unofficially with a typical paranoid reaction: NASA 'expert' James Oberg attempted to explain away the incident as a test of a secret Soviet weapon that violated the 1963 outer space treaty, the fiery return to Earth of a dummy warhead. Mr. Oberg did not attempt to explain how this particular dummy warhead managed to change from a star-shape to a cone, to a double cone, to a cloud, to a plum-shape, to a square, and then to a giant needle-nosed wingless aircraft which followed close behind the Aeroflot airliner for 800 miles, during which the Aeroflot changed the direction of its flight several times. What I find difficult to explain is how the U.S. news media managed to almost totally ignore this particular official announcement by the Soviet Academy of Sciences.

On July 30, 1985, the *Japan Times* of Tokyo reported that on June 11 a Chinese jumbo jet making a Peking to Paris flight had encountered a UFO over Mongolia, which the jetliner's captain described in these terms: "Its brilliance extended from forty to fifty kilometers, and it was about ten kilometers wide. An extremely bright spot radiated from the center. The object traveled extremely fast, pacing the aircraft in a southerly direction for about two minutes." Once again, the U.S. news media responded to this incident by almost totally ignoring it.

After 29 years of service, Police Lieutenant George Lesnick of Fairfield, Conn., retired from duty, and felt free to speak out publicly about the UFO sightings in his district during the course of his career. He was interviewed by James Lomuscio in an article entitled "UFO COP", which was published in *Fairpress*, Yorktown Heights, New York, on July 17, 1985, from which the following statements are summarised:

The incidents began on March 24, 1976, when Lesnick and another officer saw six luminous ball-shaped objects in the sky over Fairfield. They were moving at extremely high speed, but would come to instantaneous dead stop in the sky, then go off in different directions. Two police officers in the nearby town of Easton also saw the objects, as well as hundreds of other witnesses. They checked the airports. There were no aircraft in the area. It was a clear night. Hundreds of normally reliable people had all seen the same thing. Lesnick began to investigate the subject of UFOs. He teamed up with an astronomer who is chairman of the Science Department at Windward School. Their research indicates that usually nine out of ten reports turn out to be misidentification of natural phenomena, and one in ten is worth investigating. The standard official explanation for the intense UFO activity over that borderline area of New York and Connecticut is that hoaxers flying small planes are shining lights down at people in order to frighten them. Lesnick lets drop the hard fact that "despite four years of sightings, nobody has ever been able to track down any planes or any pilots, or any airports they could be coming from." Furthermore, there have been no sounds of any aircraft engines during the sightings. Hundreds of citizens witnessed a UFO larger than a football field hover for ten minutes only 500 feet above the ground. Sightings were also reported on that same night from Putnam and Dutchess counties in New York. The authorities gave the usual explanation of pilots perpetrating a hoax. If such pilots existed, they would have had to have been in many different places simultaneously, with an unlimited supply of fuel, and be capable of performing maneuvers the Air Force Blue Angels would be unable to duplicate. Wind velocity on that night was up to 32 miles per hour, too high for silent light aircraft to operate. UFO sightings in that region have been so abundant during the last four years that the standard official explanation has lost all local credibility, and the sightings continue to occur. In Lesnick's opinion, it is the extra-terrestrial hypothesis which fits best with the recorded facts.

On Sept. 5, 1985, Premier Wran of Australia, accompanied by Minister of Agriculture Hallam, reported seeing a UFO from their government jet, which they described as "extremely bright and spherical". Pilots of another aircraft in the area confirmed the sighting, as did the crew of their jet. One crew member photographed the object. The Sydney Meteorological Bureau reported contact at that time with an object hovering overhead at an altitude of approximately a hundred thousand feet. Premier Wran stated the object was "quite eerie, quite spooky" and had a large oblong shape, very bright and shiny, like nothing he had ever seen before.

On Sept. 9-12, a sudden brief flurry of UFO incidents erupted in the Oxford area of England. Seven separate incidents were reported during those four days.

On Feb. 3, 1986, a huge fireball left a blazing trail across the sky over Windsor in England, vanishing as suddenly as it appeared. It was witnessed by a large proportion of the local population.

On Feb. 23, Prince Charles of England had an experience similar to Premier Wran's. While in an airplane over the Irish Sea, the pilot of his plane radioed air traffic control that a brilliantly luminous glowing red object was hovering near them. Four other planes traveling through that area radioed in similar reports. They all reached their destinations safely. Prince Charles was quoted as saying: "I felt I was in the presence of something outside our knowledge and control."

On March 9, 1986, it was reported that an oval-shaped glowing red UFO about the size of an automobile had flown close to the walls of Windsor Castle in broad daylight, again witnessed by many local residents.

The incidents involving Prince Charles and Windsor Castle were reported only in the tabloids, and were ignored by the 'serious' news media. However, the British royal family made no protest about the publication of these reports, nor did it make any denial that the incidents had in fact taken place.

There have been many occasions when large crowds, sometimes at gatherings such as sports events, at other times a majority of the population of entire towns and cities, have watched aircraft that did not perform like anything made by man. As these witnesses are usually ordinary citizens without any special academic qualifications, govern-ment 'experts' have been able to explain away such incidents without much difficulty, by imputing them to mass psy-chosis or collective delusion.

However, there are other cases on record that are far more difficult to explain away, as the large numbers of wit-nesses were composed of highly trained specialists in air-craft performance and identification.

Approximately 200 British and American military and civilian personnel witnessed a UFO landing near a base which the U.S. Air Force shares with the Royal Air Force at Woodridge in Suffolk, at 3 A.M. on Dec. 27, 1980. Among them was USAF Lieutenant Colonel Charles Halt, the Deputy Commander of the 81st Tactical Fighter Wing, which is stationed beside the RAF at Woodridge. He filed a report on the incident, which was intended to remain confidential. However, a copy of it, bearing his signature, reached the

London weekly *News of the World*, which ran the story on Oct. 2, 1983. The report describes in abundant detail the landing and departure of an unearthly space-craft.

When journalists tried to interview Lt. Col. Halt, he took evasive action, but they finally caught up with him. At first he refused to discuss the matter, on the grounds that it could jeopardize his career, but then tacitly admitted that he had written and signed the report.

Lt. Col. Halt's superior officer at the time of the incident was the Wing Commander, Brigadier General Gordon Williams, who made the following statement when questioned by journalists: "I recall Lt. Col. Halt's report. I don't know exactly what happened. It is all there. He is not a man who would hoax the British Ministry of Defence or the American Air Force Department." Shortly afterwards, the USAF confirmed that the report was genuine.

There are many ramifications of this fascinating case which could be followed up, but other witnesses insist upon remaining anonymous because of the little-known U.S. Service regulation JANAP-146, which provides a penalty of up to ten years imprisonment and $10,000 fine for anyone in government service who makes an unauthorised public statement about UFO phenomena. The British have an equivalent of JANAP-146 in their Official Secrets Act. So rather than delve into statements by anonymous witnesses, which, though very interesting, are not possible to verify, I shall stick to the irrefutable hard evidence. The essentials of the story would, however, be incomplete if I did not at least briefly mention that three small silver-suited occupants of the space-craft were described, as well as the following security procedure.

After the incident all the witnesses were called into the base security office, where they were told that what they had just seen had been classified top secret. These instructions came from two civilians, assumed to be CIA. One presumed CIA agent pointed out that if they ever tried to tell the story, they would not be believed. The other presumed CIA agent added that if any of them should try to talk, then: "bullets are cheap."

The next time that a government "expert" attempts to explain away a multiple-witness UFO sighting as mass hallucination, remember that these objects have left physical landing traces with specific characteristics that are similar in reports from all over the world.

There is now mathematical proof that UFO landing points have been intelligently selected, as the number of isosceles triangles occurring in the pattern of these landing points far exceeds what might be expected from random independent events: the probability for the network of reported landing points in France during the UFO wave of 1954 to be due to chance is less than one in ten thousand billions of billions! Besides the abundance of isosceles triangles in these landing patterns, the number pi (π) and the number of gold turn up in profusion. This has been impeccably demonstrated by Jean-Charles Fumoux in *Preuves Scientifiques OVNI: l'Isocelie,*, published by Editions du Rocher in 1981, and by John F. Gille in "Isoscely-A Scientific Result", published by *Specula* (vol. 5, no. 1) in Huntsville, Alabama, 1982. In a later issue of *Specula* (vol. 5, no. 4) it was reported that approximately half a million people in Argentina, Chile, Peru, and Brazil had witnessed a large UFO on Oct. 31, 1983, whose itinerary formed an enormous isosceles triangle.

Although the relevance of the following fact will not become apparent until the reader has progressed further into this book, in England the ancient sacred sites of Stonehenge, Glastonbury Tor, and Midsummer Hill form a 5: 5: 3 isosceles triangle, which is mathematically accurate to 1 in 1000.

details of a UFO landing case which provides irrefutable hard scientific evidence that UFOs are physically real objects, that they can not be explained away in terms of "earth lights" (piezoelectric phenomena generated by subterranean stress), and that they are not from this planet.

Trans-en-Provence is a little village near Avignon. The incident took place there at 5:10 P.M. on Jan. 8, 1981. Renato Nicolai, aged 55, a retired mason who is now a farmer, saw a strange aircraft land in his garden, where it remained for about one minute. It then took off and disappeared over the horizon.

Mr. Nicolai thought that it was probably some sort of experimental craft being tried out by the French Air Force, as he lives near the Canjuers base. He did not believe in flying saucers. That evening he described what he had seen to his wife Jeanne, aged 52, when she got home from work. The next morning she went with him to look at the markings on the ground, then told a neighbor about the incident. The frightened neighbor informed the police.

A contingent of the Draguignan police came to Mr. Nicolai's farm. He described the craft to them as approximately 6 feet in height and 7½ feet in diameter. The color was a dull gray, like that of lead. The shape was flat and circular, bulging slightly above and below. The craft rested on small telescopic legs. There was no light, and no smoke or flames. There was no sound except for a faint whistling. It first appeared at an altitude of about 150 feet, like a mass of stone falling. However, it came down lightly on the ground. He approached it, and could see the craft clearly. He had advanced about thirty paces toward it, when it took off at very high speed. When he saw the object from beneath, it was round, and had four port-holes.

The police reported that there was a circular outline about half to three-quarters of an inch deep and 7¼ feet in diameter, with skid marks at two places. The site had the appearance of a circular stain, being darker in color than its surroundings. The police collected samples of soil and vegetation along a straight line through the impact site, writing on each sample taken its distance from the impact site. Upon their return to Draguignan, they transmitted their report and the samples to GEPAN (Group for the Study of Unidentified Aerial and Space Phenomena), which is a branch of CNRS (National Center of Space Research, the French equivalent of NASA). GEPAN passed the samples on to INRA (National Institute of Agricultural Research) and several other government research institutes for analysis. GEPAN personnel visited the site to take further samples on two other occasions. On June 17, 1983, after two and a half years of analyses, a bulky preliminary report which assembled data from the different laboratories was turned in. Other examinations have been conducted since then. The results are only now beginning to be made public.

Government scientists attribute the circular outline to a soil fracture caused by the combined action of strong mechanical pressure and a heat of about 600 degrees Centigrade (about 1,100 degrees Fahrenheit).

Dr. Bounias, who is the Director of the Biochemical Laboratory at INRA, personally took charge of the examination of the plant specimens. He carried out the analyses in the most rigorous fashion possible. First he established samples from plants of the same species (alfalfa), taken at different distances from the point of impact. Then he and his assistants meticulously analysed the photosynthetic pigments (such as carotene, chlorophyll, and xantophyle), the glucides, the amino acids, and other constituents. He found differences sufficiently important that the statistical significance of the results is irrefutable. Certain substances which were present in the close-range samples were not present in those taken further away, and vice versa. The biochemical trauma revealed by examination of the leaves diminished as the distance from the UFO impact site increased. Some of the plants had been dehydrated, but were not burned or carbonised. The following year control samples were taken from the site, which confirmed the changes made in the vegetation.

After completing the analyses, Dr. Bounias made this formal statement: "We worked on very young leaves. They all had the anatomic and physiologic characteristics of their age. However, they had the biochemical characteristics of advanced senescence (old age)! This bears no resemblance to anything known to exist on our planet."

Dr. Bounias refused to speculate about the cause for the strange facts he had established, or to propose any explanation at all for them.

Professor Jean-Pierre Petit is a researcher at the National Center for Space Research who specialises in the study of magnetohydrodynamics, and who does not share Dr. Bounias' inhibitions. Professor Petit has been investigating UFO phenomena for twenty years. He declared that he would gladly exchange all research previously carried out during two decades for this one case because of the quality of the evidence involved. He stated categorically: "This is the first UFO case I know of which is scientifically acceptable. It is necessary to give serious consideration to the hypothesis of 'space-ship of unknown origin' because out of all the possible explanations, it is the one which fits best with the INRA laboratory results. This space-ship can not be of terrestrial origin. If such an aircraft existed on this planet, we would know about it. No one on this planet knows how to make a craft capable of performing like a UFO. Therefore all the indications are that they come from elsewhere."

Paris-Match has a position in the French media comparable in prominence to that of *Time* magazine in the United States, and published a long interview with Professor Petit as a feature article in its issue of Oct. 26, 1984. Among the highlights of it was this exchange, which followed the interviewer's suggestion that the Trans-en-Provence case might have been a hoax or a practical joke. Professor Petit replied: "One can always invoke practical jokers. However, in this case, perpetrating a practical joke would have required exceptional resources. Considering the very sophisticated nature of the biological alterations in the samples examined, which would be impossible to reproduce under laboratory conditions with our present scientific knowledge, no ordinary chemical could have produced such results. According to Professor Bounias, in order to act on the nuclei of plant cells, nuclear radiation at the potency of a million rads would be necessary. He conducted such an experiment himself, at the request of the Atomic Energy Commission."

"I suppose that such sources of nuclear energy are not found in nature, nor are they accessible to ordinary citizens?"

"Fortunately not! Besides, Professor Bounias demonstrated that this potency produced much weaker results than those measured from the Trans-en-Provence samples. One must also consider the extent of the area affected, about 300 square meters."

The Italian UFO wave of 1978 began on Sept. 13 of that year. During the next four months, 106 cases were reported. Describing them all would require a book in itself, so I bring into focus only case number 99, as it is of particular interest.

Case No. 99:
Dec. 24, 1978, at 6:50 A.M. in Pietracamela (Teramo).
Mr. Benito Franchi, 45 years old, is an electrical technician employed at the Pietracamela electric plant. He was on duty in a room in which there were two A.C. generators. One of them was working, but the other one *was not plugged in* to the control panel. Mr. Franchi was sitting in front of the control panel, when suddenly he felt sick and very tired. At the very same instant the indicators on the control panel began to oscillate, including the

indicators normally connected to the second generator—which was not connected. This very strange phenomenon lasted approximately one minute, then stopped. Upon discovering that both of the two generators had gone dead, Mr. Franchi tried to pull an alarm signal that would have alerted one of his colleagues, Mr. Di Varano, who was resting in a near-by building, but collapsed on the cement floor "as if paralysed". A few seconds later, he was able to get back on his feet, but his attention was immediately drawn to 3 or 4 violent lightning strokes, which were visible through the large window in the room. They came from a forest about 200 meters from the plant. Mr. Franchi went out of the building and saw a luminous sphere among the branches of the trees. Its outline was not clearly defined. The object was emitting a very bright and intense red light, which did not illuminate its surroundings. Mr. Franchi covered his face with his hands, because the light hurt his eyes. He suffered from conjunctivitis for several days after the experience. A few seconds after he covered his face, the object took off in the direction of the Gran Sasso Mountains, leaving a trail behind it in the sky. Mr. Franchi went back into the building and tried to telephone his colleague. The telephone did not work, so he again left the building and watched the far-away object grow smaller and disappear.

Shortly afterwards a large luminous UFO was reported to be hovering above the summit of Mount Gran Sasso. Meanwhile Mr. Di Varano (51 years old) had been contacted by Mr. Franchi, as the telephone was no longer out of order, and saw the UFO. Quite a few other people in the Prati di Tivo region observed the UFO, and some of them photographed it.

Mr. Rocco Catini was assigned to the task of restoring the two generators to working order. He stated that the plant had been isolated from the electrical network it is part of, and that he did not know what could have damaged the scales of the frequency indicators. A specialist from E.N.E.L. (National Electric Power Generation), Mr. Piero Angelini, declared that there was no way that lightning could have caused such damage. There were other UFO sightings in this same region during the days that followed.

The evidence of UFO involvement in massive electric power failures, widespread animal mutilations, disappearances of ships and planes, and human abductions is now overwhelming. That is, to those who take the trouble to inspect the mountains of existing evidence. What is even more amazing than visitors from elsewhere in the cosmos is how all those government experts and establishment scientists could have the evidence right under their noses for 39 years and still refuse to look at it. None so blind as those who will not see. Those who persist in denying the validity of the evidence without having examined it will go down in history with the colleagues of Galileo who chose to refute his theory by refusing to look through his telescope. It is easy for those in positions of authority to ridicule ordinary citizens who report extraordinary events, casting aspersion on their sanity, intelligence, and integrity. However, in the long run, as reports persist and evidence continues to accumulate, this smear technique becomes less and less credible.

About the time that the Warren Report was foisted on U.S. citizens and the world at large as an adequate explanation for the assassination of President Kennedy, the Condon Report was prepared to explain (a conclusion decided upon before the so-called investigation began) that the study of UFO phenomena had no scientific value and should be discontinued. However, the following incident is one of the cases that the Condon Committee was obliged to admit it was unable to account for.

At Lakenhealth, Suffolk, England, in 1956 a UFO traveling at high speed was tracked on radar from three different Royal Air Force bases. A jet fighter was scrambled, pursued the object, and got a radar lock on it. The UFO literally flew a circle around the plane and came up behind it, so it was now the plane that was being pursued. The jet pilot went through a series of maneuvers to get the UFO off his tail, but was unable to do so. The UFO finally went away without having taken any aggressive action. All this was witnessed by RAF personnel from the ground, also by RAF personnel in an airplane which happened to be above looking down at the time of the incident, and was tracked on three different sets of RAF radar equipment.

On Sept. 14, 1978, a UFO as big as an ocean liner was witnessed by many thousands of people (including police) traveling all the way from the southern end of Sicily up through the entire length of the Italian peninsula to the northern frontier at the French border. The UFO then returned to hover over Rome during the nights of Sept. 15 and 16. Is it no more than an odd coincidence that this was just a fortnight before Pope John-Paul I was found dead under suspicious circumstances, apparently poisoned in the manner of the Borgias while working on a speech he intended to deliver the next day? The text of the speech he had been working on was never made public.

For the first time in the history of the Papacy, an autopsy was demanded by the Pope's family (his brother and sister), as well as by some of the best doctors in Italy. This demand was refused.

Although the Pope supposedly died of a heart attack, he had no previous history of heart trouble. Shortly before he died, his doctor examined him and declared him to be in excellent health. Cardinal Gantin, who was one of the last people to see him alive, said: "Neither his face nor his gestures betrayed any sign of fatigue or weakness."

According to the Vatican, the first person to find him dead was Father Magee, who described his face as peacefully illuminated with his famous smile. However, this detail is in direct contradiction with the official diagnosis of infarctus of the myocardium.

During his brief reign, Pope John Paul I had discovered the existence of corruption on an enormous scale within the Vatican Bank, and had begun to make a whole series of major changes in both the Vatican power structure and Church policies. Some of these changes were so sweeping and of such extreme importance that the appropriate term for them would be 'revolutionary'. On the night of Sept. 28-29, 1978, many highly influential people in key positions had a wide variety of strong motives to poison this Pope with the intention of reforming the Church according to the example set by the usually peaceful and non-violent Jesus, who suddenly seized a whip and, without asking anyone's permission or advice, drove the money-changers from the Temple. Following the signs in the sky over the entire length of Italy, repeated two nights in a row over Rome, it would have been entirely in character for Pope John Paul I to have inaugurated his reform of the Church by revealing to the world the true Fatima message.

The phenomena witnessed by a crowd of over 70,000 people at the Catholic miracle of Fatima in 1917 strongly resemble descriptions of modern UFO sightings. As Jacques Vallee points out in *The Invisible College*, published by E. P. Dutton in 1976: "Not only was a flying disk or globe consistently involved, but its motion, its falling-leaf trajectory, its light effects, the thunderclaps, the buzzing sounds, the strange fragrance, the fall of "angel hair" that dissolves upon reaching the ground, the heat wave associated with the close approach of the disk, *all of these are constant parameters of UFO sightings everywhere.* And so are the paralysis, the amnesia, the conversions, and the healings."

The children around whom the miracle took place entrusted a sealed message to the Church, with instructions that it be opened and transmitted to the world in 1960. However, in 1960 Pope John XXIII chose to suppress this message instead of transmitting it. Instead of being renewed, the ancient covenant between the children of the earth and the children of the stars was broken. Did Pope John-Paul I die on his thirty-third day in office because he was about to transmit to the world the suppressed real Fatima message?

In any confrontation the ability to communicate is essential to avoid misunderstanding and unnecessary hostility. This is particularly true of a historically unprecedented confrontation between human beings and non-human intelligent beings. By failing to face the facts and pretending that our visitors do not exist, it is quite certain that we are giving them an unnecessarily low opinion of humanity. If our reaction to their displaying themselves worldwide in most obvious fashion is to continue to pretend that nothing unusual is going on instead of recognising their existence, what must they think of us? Is it in our interest to give them the idea that we no longer deserve to be the dominant species on this planet?

UFOs have been observed before, during, and after earthquakes. After the earthquake of 1967 in Venezuela, there was a sudden brief abundance of reports concerning the activities of small humanoids. The earthquake that shook the U.S. Air Force base on Shemya Island at the end of the Aleutian chain on Feb. 16th, 1978, struck during the climax of a spectacular UFO display. Five round glowing objects performed complex acrobatics at incredible speeds before and during the earthquake, changing in color as they traveled. When the earth tremors stopped, the UFOs disappeared, and the radar screens became clear of unidentified blips. The usual explanation for luminous phenomena during earthquakes is piezoelectric effects, but piezoelectric effects do not perform complex acrobatics or show up as blips on radar screens. The piezoelectric effect may explain some earthquake lights, but does not explain all of them.

Not all scientists have blindly accepted the preconceived conclusions of the Condon Committee. There are a few rare exceptions who have approached the subject with skepticism but an open mind, and who have, at considerable risk to their personal positions in the social structure, courageously dared to say what they think about this academically taboo subject.

The first scientific study of UFO phenomena in the

field, directly observed at first hand rather than from second-hand reports, was conducted by Dr. Harley D. Rutledge, Chairman of the Physics Department at Southeast Missouri State University. In 1973 residents of southeast Missouri began to persistently report strange lights in the sky, and Dr. Rutledge decided to subject these reported objects to scientific scrutiny. He put together a team of observers with college training or equivalent experience in the physical sciences.

Optical equipment included Celestron, Criterion, and Questar telescopes, high quality cameras and lenses of various focal lengths, and binoculars. These instruments were fitted with devices to detect polarized light and to produce a color spectrum. Color, black and white, and infrared sensitive films were used. A spectrum analyzer to detect electromagnetic frequencies in the radio spectrum was used. Later in the field research, a magnetometer to measure changing magnetic flux and a gravimeter were used.

The following passages have been selected from his history-making landmark of a book entitled *Project Identification: the First Scientific Field Study of UFO Phenomena*, which was published by Prentice-Hall in 1981:

In this research, more was involved than the measurement of physical properties of UFOs by dispassionate observers. A relationship, a cognizance, between us and the UFO intelligence evolved. A game was played. In my opinion, this additional consideration is more important than the measurements or establishing that the phenomenon exists. This facet of the UFO phenomenon perturbed me as much as the advanced technology we observed. It is a facet I cannot really fathom—and I have thought about it every day for more than seven years. . . . In this Project, we dealt with an intelligence equal to or greater than that of man. We interacted with the phenomenon under study. . . . On the second night I was at Piedmont, experiences suggested to me that the UFOs may have purposely attracted our attention, and that they may have reacted to us—although at the time I did not label the sightings as UFOs.... How did the UFOs react to us? They turned lights off, on, moved away, shot away, changed course, changed brightness, and the like.... One type of behavior evident to Project members was the avoidance paths flown by the UFOs. A UFO would approach as if it would pass overhead; then it would go around our position.... Often, we felt that the UFO intelligence knew our moves.... I suspect that UFOs actually dart about in daylight at speeds at which they cannot be seen. I base this on a few cases of reflected sunlight and the circumstances of the disc that hovered within viewing range of my office. Possibly a great deal of UFO activity is subliminal—which, if true, could have serious ramifications.... No, UFOs do not behave according to prevailing technology, and the UFO intelligence does not behave as would a human visiting another planet. Surely the UFO intelligence has gathered all the flora and fauna of the earth, has deciphered all the languages, has determined all of man's technology, and has become cognizant of the world's religions; in short, they must know all there is to know about man. I believe that the UFO intelligence uses this information to mimic man and his technology.

I am reminded of the Air Force jet pilot who was to join with another military jet flying ahead and above. The pilot found a plane ahead and above, all right—a commercial jet airliner. Funny thing, he couldn't catch up with it. Surely, our nation's best and fastest fighter jets can fly faster than a commercial airliner!

Dr. Berthold Eric Schwarz is a psychiatrist with impeccable academic credentials. After receiving his M.D. from New York University, he interned at Mary Hitchcock Memorial Hospital in Hanover, New Hampshire. Dr. Schwarz then became a Fellow in Psychiatry at the Mayo Foundation, where he received an M.S. from the Mayo Graduate School of Medicine. He is a Diplomate of the American Board of Psychiatry and Neurology, a Fellow of the American Psychiatric Association, the Academy of Medicine of New Jersey, and many other medical associations.

Dr. Schwarz has used the methods of his profession to examine highly unusual and extremely elusive, yet persistently recurring, phenomena in a trilogy of masterwork.

The first volume is *Psychic-Nexus: Psychic Phenomena in Psychiatry and Everyday Life*, published by Van Nostrand Reinhold in 1980. This book investigates religious ordeals involving temporary psychosomatic immunity to fire, strychnine, and poisonous snakes. It then explores the subjects of telepathy, telekinesis, precognition, genius, and inter-species (human-animal) telepathic communications. Its final chapter concerns a UFO contactee with the ability to make interdimensional photographs, using equipment that had been thoroughly checked to eliminate any possibility of fraud.

Among the many nuggets of concentrated perception that are scattered through Dr. Schwarz's text is this particularly astute statement: "It cannot be stressed enough that the psychic function blasts the time-space barriers and is seldom the same when it is confined to the laboratory where telepathy, clairvoyance, and precognition are aseptically separated, often stripped of emotional valence, and reduced to ciphers. Psi can be a bucking bronco. You cannot tell which direction it will take and what surprises await you. In life, as seen in a clinical situation, these variegated aspects of psi are often intermingled or occur in rapid-fire volleys that pierce the time-space barrier, shooting back into the past, as well as staying with the present and on occasion leaping into the future. Psi has no boundaries. The definitive laboratory tests for psi have yet to be devised."

The rest of the trilogy has recently been published as a two-book set under the title of *UFO-Dynamics: Psychiatric and Psychic Aspects of the UFO Syndrome* by Rainbow Books, 2299 Riverside Drive, Moore Haven, FL 33471.

As a psychiatrist already known for his investigations of a wide variety of different types of paranormal phenomena, Dr. Schwarz found himself being called in on cases involving UFO contact with ever-increasing frequency. Many of these requests for his services came from reputable research organisations who had already screened the contactees and checked out their stories, and were submitting the cases to multi-disciplinary examinations by academically qualified specialists in different fields. Psychiatric evaluation of these cases showed them to be of high complexity and very difficult to understand. Neat, conventional theories did not fit the facts of what had happened.

Dr. Schwarz describes firsthand field and office interviews with individuals claiming UFO contact. He probes the role of the unconscious mind in such adventures, and considers them from the psychic as well as from the psychiatric point of view. He compares the enormous discrepancy between the wide-spread public interest in UFOs expressed through the popular press and the nearly total absence of serious scientific research in this academically-taboo domain. Although the findings of the Condon Report were negative, that did not put an end to the sightings. As UFOs apparently will not go away, we may as well distill what meaning we can from the substantial bulk of information already on file. Many close encounters are associated with telepathic communications, telekinesis, teleportation, precognition, materialization, dematerialization, the causing or healing of diseases, and entities or humanoids of varying sizes, shapes, and colors.

Dr. Schwarz points out that frequently close encounters are repeater experiences: the individual has had previous UFO experience, or will have a subsequent UFO experience. Sometimes psychic experiences are intermingled with UFO experiences. Many close encounter UFO cases have striking parallels with spontaneous psychic events that are not UFO-related. Whatever the physical parameters of UFOs may be, their psychiatric and psychic aspects are in need of attention.

After describing the Presque Isle, New Jersey, case of

July 31, 1966, Dr. Schwarz asks if it is likely that the group involved had an objective, reality-bound, close encounter with a UFO. Psychiatric evaluation indicated an affirmative answer.

Here are some direct quotations that give a glimpse of the sparkling jewels of insight to be found in *UFO-Dynamics*:

"The Mayo Clinic collaborative investigations of whole families by a team of highly skilled physicians has provided a major breakthrough to the question of trauma, fact versus fantasy. These up-to-date studies seem applicable to the problem of validity for the UFO experiences. For example, one such study of ninety-one patients and the relatives revealed that the majority of schizophrenic patients had actual traumatic assaults by parents or parental surrogates. It was clearly demonstrated how the first schizophrenic delusion represented in a striking, specific manner the essence of a parental assault. By analogy and comparison to the first schizophrenic delusions, the UFO experiences of the healthy subjects—those who did not suffer from gross psychopathological distortions—take on even greater significance for objective reality. Fantasy and delusion versus objective reality is a complicated process, but for the skilled therapist experienced in collaborative psychotherapy dealing with both parent and child, it is entirely possible to separate fact from fantasy. In a healthy person the task is that much easier. Therefore in the absence of psychodynamic motivation for conscious or unconscious fabrication it seems that the four UFO examples are factual and objectively correct. The problem is the interpretation. . . . While it is evident that the physician will undoubtedly come across some crackpot and irresponsible accounts, as a practitioner of an ancient art and science he should scrupulously avoid ridicule and keep an open mind lest he unwittingly discourage significant reports from those who have had valid experiences, and thus inflict damage on them. A condemnatory attitude is as scientifically reprehensible as a gullible one. As Dr. Adelaide Johnson said, in "Psychoanalytic Quarterly", vol. 1, no. 25: "We can now see, that in years past, patients were lost or driven into psychosis by our failure to believe them because of our conviction that much of their account must be fantasy." . . . In thirteen years of private practice in which I have seen 3,391 patients in psychiatric examinations and have participated in thousands of hours of psychotherapy, I have never noted symptoms related to UFOs. A similar finding was confirmed on questioning Theodore A. Anderson, M.D., a senior psychiatrist, and Henry A. Davidson, M.D., then Medical Director of the Essex County Over-brook Hospital. Dr. Davidson recalled no patients with gross UFO symptoms out of three thousand in-patients, nor among all those presented to the staff while he was superintendent; nor of thirty thousand patients who have been hospitalized since the turn of the century. My own check of standard textbooks and journals in psychiatry, psychoanalysis, and neurology also confirmed this absence of UFO-like experiences in various "nerv-ous" and mental diseases. . . . A computerized search of the medical literature in the National Library of Medicine's MEDLARS sys-tem retrieved zero citations covering the years 1964 to 1973. In view of this dearth of data both from practice and the medical literature then, it is indeed interesting that in the past, and even currently, the media and official statements have seen fit to attribute much of UFO phenomena to psychopathology—hallucinations, delusions, religious wish fulfillment, etc. What a specious way to stigmatize and intimidate those who might have had UFO experiences! . . . Why hasn't there been an outcry, if not raucous laughter, over the recent totally unsupported allegations of psy-chiatric pathology for masses of UFO witnesses by those who are not psychiatrists? . . . In many cases and maybe most, the underly-ing force for both psi and the UFO experience could be iden-tical. . . . Is there, and has there always been, another dimension that surrounds us?"

At the other end of the spectrum, among those deter-mined to clamp down the lid of secrecy even more tightly than it is already, we have Dr. Brian T. Clifford of the Pen-tagon, who announced at a press conference (*"The Star"*, New York, Oct. 5, 1982) that contact between U.S. citizens and extra-terrestrials or their vehicles is strictly illegal. According to a law *already on the books* (Title 14, Section 1211 of the Code of Federal Regulations, adopted on July 16, 1969, before the Apollo moon shots), anyone guilty of such contact automatically becomes a wanted criminal to be jailed for one year and fined $5,000. The NASA administrator is empowered to determine *with or without a hearing* that a person or object has been "extraterrestrially exposed" and impose an *indeterminate* quarantine under armed guard, which could not be broken *even by court order*. There is no limit placed on the number of individuals who could thus be arbitrarily quarantined. The definition of "extraterrestrial exposure" is left entirely up to the NASA administrator, who is thus endowed with total dictatorial power to be exercised at his slightest caprice, which is completely contrary to the Constitution. According to Dr. Clifford, whose commanding officers have been assuring the public for the last 39 years that UFOs are nothing more than hoaxes and delusions to be dismissed with a condescending smile: "This is really no joke, it's a very serious matter."

This legislation was buried in the 1,211th sub-section of the 14th. section of a batch of regulations very few members of the government probably bothered to read in its entirety, the proverbial needle in the haystack, and was slipped on to the books without public debate. Thus from one day to the next we learn that, without having informed the public, in its infinite wisdom the government of the United States has created a whole new criminal class: UFO contactees. The lame excuse offered by NASA as a sugar coating for this bitter pill is that extra-terrestrials might have a virus that could wipe out the human race. This is certainly one of the many possibilities inherent in such contact, but just as certainly not the only one, and in itself not a valid reason to make all contact illegal or to declare contactees criminals to be jailed and fined immediately. The primary effect of such a law would not be to prevent contact (which is often involuntary), it would be to silence witnesses. If enforced, the law would prevent publication of contactee reports except under cover of anonymity, and unleash a modern Inquisition in the Land of the Free. However, it is unenforceable, so obviously absurd and unfair that the public will refuse to accept it. The law is an ass. The citizens of the United States will greet it with a resounding Bronx cheer and laugh it out of court, forcing it to be repealed. It should be replaced by clearly worded legislation, not open to interpretation in a multitude of different ways, humanely relevant to the contingency of E.T. contact, debated and passed by Congress openly instead of slipped through 'under the table' without the public being informed.

Shortly after Dr. Clifford of the Pentagon held his press conference, NASA spokesman Fletcher Reel held a press conference, presenting a slightly different version of the same story. According to Mr. Reel: "We have no contingency plans for dealing with an extra-terrestrial landing here." Since it is known that UFO reports during recent years have been averaging about 150 per day worldwide, and that only about one person in ten bothers to report such incidents, I find Mr. Reel's statement extremely hard to believe. According to Mr. Reel, the law as it stands is not immediately applicable, but in case of need could quickly be made applicable. What this means is that it is ambiguously worded, so that it can be interpreted either one way or the other, as the government desires. It looks to me as if this law *is* the contingency plan for dealing with a UFO incident or series of incidents which the government is unable to control, and that Dr. Clifford unveiled it prematurely. If its validity is allowed to stand unchallenged, UFO contactees and researchers may all meet behind barbed wire and armed guards somewhere in Alaska.

As the deluge of questions from concerned citizens continued, Mr. Reel came up with a new twist: the public has no cause to worry about NASA intervention in any extra-terrestrial visitation, because the U.S. Immigration Service would have jurisdictive precedence over NASA in such a case. What this appears to mean is that an extra-terrestrial visitor would be greeted by a customs officer asking for his passport, which seems most unlikely. And what is to prevent the Immigration Service from deciding to yield its precedence to NASA? The explanations offered become less and less convincing.

If there had never before been contact with extra-terrestrials during the course of human history, extreme precautions might be advisable, but contact cases in recent years number in the thousands and tens of thousands. Are all these normally law-abiding citizens to be declared criminals from one minute to the next? What other laws has our government passed surreptitiously without informing the public? What other surprises have our trusted representatives prepared for us? No matter what they may be, one thing is for sure: contact between humans and extra-terrestrials has been occurring at periodic intervals ever since the Sumerians built the ziggurats, and will continue to occur whether the Pentagon likes it or not.

It is certainly not a coincidence that Dr. Clifford held his press conference during the period when the popularity of the film *E.T.* was at its peak. As *E.T.* portrayed a type of extra-terrestrial that was benevolent and lovable, the inference is that the press conference was intended to discourage attempts to communicate or fraternise with UFO occupants. However, instead of having the intended effect, it backfired, causing public furor. There may be some relationship between this fiasco and the next semi-officially endorsed attempt to deal with the subject of extra-terrestrials, the TV film *V*, which has been featured with repeat performances and maximum publicity by major networks worldwide. The aliens portrayed in *V* are the most horrifying and repulsive nightmares imaginable, who are defeated thanks largely to a CIA hit man specialising in covert operations, the tough guy with the heart of gold who with the aid of the handsome hero saves the human race. In my humble opinion, this is obvious and transparent propaganda, designed to do what Dr. Clifford's press conference about the absurd lemon of a law already on the books failed to do: squelch attempts to communicate or fraternise with UFO occupants. There are now literally thousands of case histories on file describing close encounters with different types of aliens, both benevolent and malevolent. However, none of them bear a close resemblance to the made-in-Hollywood aliens depicted in either *E.T.* or *V.*

One way to avoid widespread panic at the announcement of the news that we are under surveillance by nonhuman intelligent beings with a technology far more sophisticated than our own would be to point out that this situation is nothing new, but has literally been going on for millenia.

The *I Ching* or *Book of Changes* is the ancient and fundamental book on which the entire complex edifice of Chinese traditional culture is based. The 64 hexagrams of which it is composed are believed to represent all possible permutations of the dynamic interaction between positive and negative polarities. Its origin can no longer be attributed to primitive Bronze Age tribal leaders, as was the opinion of most Occidental scholars until C. G. Jung pointed out some of its sophisticated subtleties, because its structure has a direct and demonstrable mathematical relationship not only to a lunar year of thirteen lunations, but also to the sunspot cycles, to the zodiacal ages, to the precession of the equinoxes, and to the structure of the DNA helix. These relationships have been impeccably and elegantly demonstrated by Dennis and Terence McKenna in their book *The Invisible Landscape*, published by Seabury Press in 1975. In the *I Ching* each permutation and group of permutations is accompanied by an oracular verse, one of which reads: "Flying dragon in the heavens. It furthers one to see the great man." If the 'flying dragons' intended to attack and destroy us, they could easily have carried out this objective long ago.

Text of the E.T. Law

1211.100 Title 14—Aeronautics and Space
Part 1211—Extra-terrestrial Exposure

1211.100 Scope.
This part establishes: (a) NASA policy, responsibility and authority to guard the Earth against any harmful contamination or adverse changes in its environment resulting from personnel, spacecraft and other property returning to the Earth after landing on or coming within the atmospheric envelope of a celestial body; and (b) security requirements, restrictions and safeguards that are necessary in the interest of national security.

1211.101 Applicability.
The provisions of this part apply to all NASA manned and unmanned space missions which land or come within the atmospheric envelope of a celestial body and return to the Earth.

1211.102 Definitions.
(a) "NASA" and the "Administrator" mean, respectively the National Aeronautics and Space Administration and the Administrator of the National Aeronautics and Space Administration or his authorized representative.
(b) "Extra-terrestrially exposed" means the state or condition of any person, property, animal or other form of life or matter whatever, who or which has:
(1) Touched directly or come within the atmospheric envelope of any other celestial body; or
(2) Touched directly or been in close proximity to (or been exposed indirectly to) any person, property, animal or other form of life or matter who or which has been extra-terrestrially exposed by virtue of paragraph (b) (1) of this section.
For example, if person or thing "A" touches the surface of the Moon, and on "A's" return to Earth, "B" touches "A" and, subsequently, "C" touches "B", all of these—"A" through "C" inclusive—would be extra-terrestrially exposed ("A" and "B" directly; "C"

indirectly).

(c) "Quarantine" means the detention, examination and decontamination of any person, property, animal or other form of life or matter whatever that is extraterrestrially exposed, and includes the apprehension or seizure of such person, property, animal or other form of life or matter whatever.

(d) "Quarantine period" means a period of consecutive calendar days as may be established in accordance with 1211.104(a) . . .

1211.104 Policy.

(a) Administrative actions. The Administrator or his designee . . shall in his discretion:

(1) Determine the beginning and duration of a quarantine period with respect to any space mission; the quarantine period as it applies to various life forms will be announced.

(2) Designate in writing quarantine officers to exercise quarantine authority.

(3) Determine that a particular person, property, animal, or other form of life or matter whatever is extra-terrestrially exposed and quarantine such person, property, animal, or other form of life or matter whatever. The quarantine may be based only on a determination, with or without the benefit of a hearing, that there is probable cause to believe that such person, property, animal or other form of life or matter whatever is extra-terrestrially exposed.

(4) Determine within the United States or within vessels or vehicles of the United States the place, boundaries, and rules of operation of necessary quarantine stations.

(5) Provide for guard services by contract or otherwise, as may be necessary, to maintain security and inviolability of quarantine stations and quarantined persons, property, animals, or other form of life or matter whatever.

(6) Provide for the subsistence, health, and welfare of persons quarantined under the provisions of this part.

(7) Hold such hearings at such times, in such manner and for such purposes as may be desirable or necessary under this part, including hearings for the purpose of creating a record for use in making any determination under this part or for the purpose of reviewing any such determination. . .

(b) (3) During any period of announced quarantine, no person shall enter or depart from the limits of the quarantine station without permission of the cognizant NASA officer. During such period, the posted perimeter of a quarantine station shall be secured by armed guard.

(4) Any person who enters the limits of any quarantine station during the quarantine period shall be deemed to have consented to the quarantine of his person if it is determined that he is or has become extra-terrestrially exposed.

(5) At the earliest practicable time, each person who is quarantined by NASA shall be given a reasonable opportunity to communicate by telephone with legal counsel or other persons of his choice . . .

1211.107 Court or other process.

(a) NASA officers and employees are prohibited from discharging from the limits of a quarantine station any quarantined person, property, animal or other form of life or matter whatever during order or other request, order or demand an announced quarantine period in compliance with a subpoena, show cause or any court or other authority without the prior approval of the General Counsel and the Administrator.

(b) Where approval to discharge a quarantined person, property, animal or other form of life or matter whatever in compliance with such a request, order or demand of any court or other authority is not given, the person to whom it is directed shall, if possible, appear in court or before the other authority and respectfully state his inability to comply, relying for his action on this 1211.107.

1211.108 Violations.

Whoever willfully violates, attempts to violate, or conspires to violate any provision of this part or any regulation or order issued under this part or who enters or departs from the limits of a quarantine station in disregard of the quarantine rules or regulations or without permission of the NASA quarantine officer shall be fined not more than $5,000 or imprisoned not more than 1 year, or both.

There are two points that I wish to make:

1211.101 Applicability. The provisions of this part apply to all NASA manned and unmanned space missions . . .

I could dismiss this whole controversy as a tempest in a teacup if the above passage contained the word "only", so as to read: "The provisions of this part apply only to all NASA manned and unmanned space missions . . . ". However, it does not contain that one little word which would have made such a big difference. If the government was suddenly faced with the accomplished fact of an undeniable overt E.T. visitation, this regulation could therefore be construed as being applicable to all space missions, NASA or non-NASA, whether of terrestrial or extra-terrestrial origin. As it stands, this law is applicable to UFO contact. The meaning would have to be stretched, but the built-in loophole does exist. NASA's general counsel, Neil Hosenball, has admitted that it is applicable to space vehicles not originating from Earth.

1211.102 Definitions. (b) (2): Touched directly or been in close proximity to (or been exposed indirectly to) . . .

Even without including "indirect exposure", anyone involved in a UFO close encounter would become eligible for indefinite quarantine under armed guard according to the above. By including indirect exposure, the NASA administrator is empowered to make the definition mean just about anything he wants it to. An example of indirect exposure is given, but an example is not a definition. Unless indirect exposure is defined precisely, it can mean almost anything. The possibility is not specifically ruled out that other types of indirect exposure than the example given might be considered valid grounds to "quarantine" a citizen or group of citizens.

Chapter Two

FROM DEEP ANTIQUITY TO
MODERN TIMES

It is well known that exceptionally fine paintings were found on the walls and ceilings of caves in the Pyrenees that were used as ceremonial centers by Cro-Magnon man between about 30,000 B.C. and around 10,000 B.C. Among the drawings dating from the Palaeolithic era there are definite UFO shapes, which were collected by Aime Michel. Although not everyone agrees with Mr. Michel's interpretation of the drawings, in the Pech Merle cave there is one for which no other explanation seems possible: that of a UFO shape with a humanoid figure near it, bald and beardless, with an enormous cranium, a pointed chin, no ears, and eyes represented by two lines, very elongated and slanted and running up towards the sides. Similar characteristics have been turning up in encounter-with-occupant reports from all over the world in recent years. It must be noted that the UFO occupant is depicted as having been pierced through by spears.

The Olmec culture is among the earliest known in the Americas. The Olmec preceded the Maya, the Toltecs, and the Aztecs in Mexico. They left behind statues and ceremonial masks (some of them gigantic) of strange baby-faced beings with feline fangs. The giant stone heads left behind by the Olmecs are carved out of black basalt and weigh about 40 tons each. The nearest places where black basalt could be quarried are between forty and seventy miles away. The country which must be crossed consists of swamps and jungle thick with underbrush. How did the Olmecs transport these enormous blocks of basalt?

They also left behind something else. At the San Lorenzo site on the Gulf Coast, they left behind (according to Dr. M. Dobkin de Rios of the University of California): "a monumental earthworks three-quarters of a mile long, reaching out like fingers on its north, west and south sides with long narrow ridges divided by ravines. A pair of ridges on the western side exhibit bilateral symmetry, with every feature on one ridge matched in mirror fashion by its counterpart. The ridges are artificial and consist of fill and debris as deep as 25 feet." As the archaeologist who discovered the site (M.D. Coe of Yale) said: "Such a grandiose plan can only be appreciated from the air." The odds against bilateral symmetry occurring in landscape on a large scale by chance are astronomical. Bilateral symmetry in landscape would be a subtle yet effective way of signaling the location of a terrestrial base to the scanners of ships coming in from deep space.

The San Lorenzo site was dated at between 1400 and 1000 B.C., and another astonishing discovery was made there. One of Mr. Coe's assistants, P. Krotser, excavated an artifact that was designated as M-160. It is a small, precisely shaped, rectangular bar of hematite with a trapezoidal cross-section and a hemicylindrical groove down its central axis. Hematite is hard and brittle and difficult to work. M-160 is a fragment of the original artifact, which was broken off in antiquity. Except for the broken end, all sides are *optically flat* and highly polished. The conclusion of the team of Yale specialists, who examined it with extreme care and at great length, was that it was a piece of a geomagnetic lodestone compass that had functioned by floating in liquid mercury. It had previously been thought that it was the Chinese who invented the compass, but it is now established that the Olmecs had a sophisticated and accurate compass over a thousand years before the earliest known Chinese compass.

"Rings of stone" were discovered recently near Jidda in Saudi Arabia, which strongly resemble the Nazca plateau markings when seen from the air. These rings of stone are located almost precisely on the Tropic of Cancer, as is the Kennedy Space Center at Cape Canaveral. The Tropic of Cancer is as close as one can get on earth to an ideal location for launching space vehicles.

Jidda isn't all that far from Baalbek, in the foundations of which there are three dressed stones weighing between 750 and 1,000 tons each, and where a fourth dressed stone of nearly 2,000 tons was left unfinished in the quarry.

Someone left behind a block of dressed stone weighing approximately 20,000 tons near Sacsahuaman in Peru. Who built Sacsahuaman and Ollantaytambo in Peru, fitting together blocks of roughly quarried stones weighing up to 200 tons without mortar on mountain tops with such extreme precision that a knife blade or a sheet of paper can not be inserted between them?

One of the strangest things about Sacsahuaman is the small tunnels with miniature staircases carved out of solid rock which the fortress is honeycombed with, which could have been used only by midgets. The tunnels are so small that even children can't squeeze through them.

At Raica in Chile, there are extremely ancient ruins of an entire city built exclusively for midgets.

In North America there is a similar complex of small tunnels. It is at Exeter, New Hampshire, which just happens to be famous for the abundance of its UFO sightings.

The monolithic ruins of pyramids and temples at the Monte Alban site in the Oaxaca region of Mexico have been ascribed to the Zapotec culture. During 1932 excavations revealed a now-famous treasure tomb, as well as a puzzling feature that received minimal publicity: an extensive network of stone tunnels in the vicinity of the tomb that were too small for human use, averaging approximately 20 inches high by 25 inches wide, including miniature stone stairways.

Excavation of the ruins of Cuicuilco pyramid near Mexico City was undertaken in 1922. The Cuicuilco site is of particular interest because it was partially submerged by the Pedregal lava flow, which is estimated by geologists to have taken place about 7,000 years ago. Cuicuilco may be the oldest pyramid in the entire world. In spite of this, excavation of the site was never completed, the reason given being the difficulty and expense of digging through the lava. Instead, the site was turned into a tourist attraction, and is now doubly submerged, by both the Pedregal lava flow and the suburbs of Mexico City.

Evidence of a high civilisation in Mexico thousands of years earlier than in Sumer or Egypt would have been even more upsetting to established academic time-tables of human history in 1922 than it would be today. Another aspect of Cuicuilco may turn out to be still more drastically upsetting to Establishment academics: a few days after work started on the excavations, what was described as an "unidentified light" (this was a full quarter of a century before UFOs erupted into public awareness with the Kenneth Arnold sighting of 1947) hovered directly above Cuicuilco, plainly visible to the archaeologist in charge of the project and his entire crew of assistants. The archaeologist in charge, Dr. Byron Cummings of the University of Arizona, refused to speculate on the possible significance of the incident, beyond mentioning that the Mexican laborers thought the apparition to be an indication of buried treasure.

John Haywood wrote *The Natural and Aboriginal History of Tennessee* in 1823. He describes the finding of both giant (8 feet tall) and midget (2 feet 10 inches from ankles to top of skull) human skeletons in mounds near the town of Sparta in White Country. The consensus of the medical faculty at Nashville was that the small skeletons were those of adults.

The following case is taken from Peter Haining's *Ancient Mysteries* (Taplinger, New York, 1977):

The story began in October 1932 when two gold prospectors were working in a gulch at the base of the Pedro Mountains about sixty miles west of Casper in Wyoming. Suddenly they came across what looked like an indication of gold on one of the gulch walls and decided to blast into the stone with dynamite.

Setting their charges, the men withdrew and waited for the explosion. After the smoke and debris had cleared, they returned to find they had exposed a cave about four feet wide by four feet high and fifteen feet deep. Peering inside they were amazed to see the tiny figure of a man sitting cross-armed and cross-legged on a ledge. He was dark bronze in colour, very wrinkled, and no more than fourteen inches high!

The men had never seen anything like the little mummy and decided to take it back to Casper—where not one of the thousands, laymen and scientists alike, who subsequently came to see the creature had either. Some anthropologists thought it was all a hoax—how, after all, could a body be found in solid rock? Yet when an X-ray was taken, a skull, spine, ribcage and bones, almost exactly like those of a normal man, were clearly discernible. Closer study established that the creature weighed about twelve ounces, had a full set of teeth, and was probably about sixty-five years old when he died.

Yet when did he die? And, more important, who was he? These were the questions that baffled everyone. First, it was the turn of the experts to have their say. The Wyoming State Historical Society were in no doubt that the creature was human, and one of their number, Dr. Henry Fairfield, a noted scientist, named it 'Hesperopithicus' after a form of anthropoid that supposedly roamed the North American continent during the middle of the Pliocene period. Anthropologists from Harvard were satisfied that the little man was genuine and shared the opinion of Dr. Henry Shapiro of the American Museum of Natural History, who had x-rayed the tiny body and said it was 'of an extremely great age, historically speaking, and of a type and stature quite unknown to us.' A theory that the creature might be a mummified infant was investigated by the Boston Museum Egyptian Department, which declared emphatically that while the method of its preservation seemed to match that of the Egyptian Pharaohs, there was no question of its having been anything other than fully grown when death had occurred. Although there was a great deal of agreement as to the little man's authenticity, none of the experts seemed to be able to take the matter much further.

Did the Pharaohs and the Incas acquire the tradition of mummification from the Little Men? Was the original purpose of mummification to preserve at least one cell of the body intact for a resurrection through cloning many centuries in the future?

According to American Indian legends, corn and coca were gifts to humanity from the gods, plants brought to earth from elsewhere in the cosmos. On the other side of the world, Sumerian legends ascribe the same origin to wheat, barley, and hemp.

The Sumerians were the first people in recorded history to divide the day into 24 hours of 60 minutes and 60 seconds. They were skilled astronomers who knew the revolution periods of the planets, including Uranus and Neptune—which are invisible to the naked eye. However, that did not save their descendants from being conquered by the Assyrians, who carried the chief treasures of the many tribes and nations that they conquered back to the palace of their cruel king at Nineveh. When the palace of Assurbanipal was excavated in 1875, a library was discovered, among the contents of which was an enormous number, probably of Sumerian origin: 195, 955, 200,000,-000. The significance of this enormous number remained a mystery until recently.

Maurice Chatelain is an engineer whose work for the NASA space program included designing the communications systems used on the Apollo moon missions, which functioned without breakdowns all through the missions. In his *Our Ancestors Came From Outer Space* (Doubleday, 1977), Chatelain tells how he got the shock of his life when he discovered that the huge number from the library of Assurbanipal exactly equals the number of seconds in 240 cycles of the precession of the equinoxes. Each cycle of the precession of the equinoxes lasts 9,450,000 days (approximately 26,000 years). Reduced from seconds to days, the Sumerian number becomes 2,268 million days, a number about which we will have more to say in the Appendix to the next chapter.

The Songs of the South is a collection of the earliest known Chinese poetry, which was brilliantly translated by David Hawkes and published as a Penguin Classic in 1985. The available evidence indicates that the following three poems were written at the Chu court in southern China between 241-223 B.C.

On a lucky day with an auspicious name
Reverently we come to delight the Lord on High.
We grasp the long sword's haft of jade,
And our girdle pendants clash and chime.
From the god's jewelled mat with treasures laden
Take up the rich and fragrant flower-offerings,
The meats cooked in melilotus, served on orchid
mats
And libations of cinnamon wine
    and pepper sauces!
Flourish the drumsticks, beat the drums!
The singing begins softly to a slow,
solemn measure:
Then, as pipes and zithers join in,
    the sound grows shriller.
Now the priestesses come, splendid in
    their gorgeous apparel,
And the hall is filled with a penetrating fragrance.
The five sounds mingle in a rich harmony;
And the god is merry and takes his pleasure.

We have bathed in orchid water and washed
    our hair with perfumes,
And dressed ourselves like flowers
    in embroidered clothing.
The god has halted, swaying above us,
Shining with a persistent radiance.
He is going to rest in the House of Life.
His brightness is like that of the sun and moon.
In his dragon chariot, dressed in
imperial splendour,
Now he flies off to wander round the sky.
The god had just descended in bright majesty,

When off in a whirl he soared again,
far into the clouds.
He looks down on Ji-zhou and the lands
   beyond it;
There is no place in the world that
he does not pass over. . . .

Open wide the door of heaven!
On a black cloud I ride in splendour,
Bidding the whirlwind drive before me,
Causing the rainstorm to lay the dust.
In sweeping circles my lord is descending:
'Let me follow you over the
   K'ung-sang mountain!
See, the teeming peoples of the Nine Lands:
The span of their lives is in your hand!'
Flying aloft, he soars serenely,
Riding the pure vapour, guiding yin and yang.
Speedily, Lord, I will go with you,
Conducting High God to the height of heaven.
My cloud-coat hangs in billowing folds,
My jade girdle-pendants dangle low:
A yin and a yang, a yin and a yang:
None of the common folk know what I am doing.
I have plucked the glistening flower
   of the Holy Hemp
To give to one who lives far away.
Old age has already crept upon me:
I am no longer near him, fast
   growing a stranger.
He drives his dragon chariot
   with thunder of wheels;
High up he rides, careering heavenwards,
But I stand where I am,
   twisting a sprig of cassia:

The longing for him pains my heart. . . .

China was ruled by emperors for over two thousand years. One of the principal traditional titles attributed to an emperor was "Son of Heaven". Here is how David Hawkes elucidates the origin of this title: "When the peoples inhabiting what we now call China were still living in a tribal state, *di* was the name of the god, usually a sky god, from whom the tribe derived its origin. In a typical origin-myth, e.g. that of the Shang people, the *di* ('God') miraculously impregnates a virgin ('Mother of the People') who gives birth to the *zu*, ('First Ancestor') of the tribe. As horizons widened to accommodate a larger world than the tribe, it became evident that there must be more than one *di*. The *Di* were now thought of sometimes as a number of sky gods subordinate to one all-encompassing Top God, or 'Heaven', sometimes as earthly ancestors. Later the word was occasionally somewhat loosely applied to historical or even to living persons. After its arrogation by Qin Shi-huang in the third century B.C. as part of the imperial title, it came to be used exclusively in the sense of 'emperor'."

The resemblance between the Chinese *di* and the Latin *deus* is a reminder that almost without exception, throughout the world in antiquity, the ancestors of the royal families were supposed to have been sky gods. The Babylonian King List is but one of a multitude of such examples that could be cited.

A description of a flying disc and what sounds like prehistoric laser warfare is to be found in the *Vishnu Purana*, which is one of the ancient sacred books of India. This translation is by H. H. Wilson, and was published by Trubner & Co. in London in 1870. Hari, Govinda, and Kesava are different names for Krishna, the hero who was an incarnation of Vishnu.

The environs of Pragjyotisha were defended by nooses, constructed by the demon Muru, the edges of which were as sharp as razors; but Hari, throwing his discus Sudarsana amongst them, cut them to pieces. Then Muru started up; but Kesava slew him, and burned his seven thousand sons like moths with the flame of the edge of his discus. Having slain Muru, Hayagriva, and Panchajana, the wise Hari rapidly reached the city of Pragjyotisha. There a fierce conflict took place with the troops of Naraka, in which Govinda destroyed thousands of demons; and, when Naraka came into the field, showering upon the deity all sorts of weapons, the wielder of the discus and annihilator of the demon-tribe cut him in two with his celestial missile. . . .

Krishna resolved to put Bana to death. The destroyer of the demon-host therefore took up his discus, Sudarsana, blazing with the radiance of a hundred suns . . .

The army of Kasi and the host of demigods attendant upon Shiva, armed with all kinds of weapons, then sallied out to oppose the discus; but, skilled in the use of arms, he consumed the whole of the forces by his radiance, and then set fire to the city in which the magic power of Shiva had concealed herself. Thus was Varanasi burned, with all its princes and their followers, its inhabitants, horses, elephants, and men, treasuries and granaries, houses, palaces, and markets. The whole of a city that was inaccessible to the gods was thus wrapped in flames by the discus of Hari, and was totally destroyed. The discus then, with unmitigated wrath, and blazing fiercely . . . returned to the hand of Vishnu . . .

Then there came to Kesava, when he was private and alone, a messenger from the gods, who addressed him with reverence, and said: "I am sent to you, O Lord, by the deities . . . More than a hundred years have elapsed since thou, in favor of the gods, hast descended upon earth for the purpose of relieving it of its load. The demons have been slain, and the burden of the earth has been removed. Now let the immortals once more behold their monarch in heaven. A period exceeding a century has passed. Now, if it be thy pleasure, return to Swarga. This is the solicitation of the celestials. But should such not be thy will, then remain here as long as may be desirable to thy dependents."

To this Krishna replied: "All that thou hast said to me I am well aware of. The destruction of the Yadavas by me has commenced. The burdens of the earth are not removed until the Yadavas are extirpated. I will effect this also in my descent, and quickly; for it shall come to pass in seven nights. When I have restored the land of Dwaraka to the ocean, and annihilated the race of Yadu, I will proceed to the mansions of the immortals. Apprise the gods that, having abandoned my human body, and accompanied by Sankarshana, I will return to them. The tyrants that oppressed the earth . . . have been killed . . . When, therefore I have taken away this great weight upon the earth, I will return to protect the sphere of the celestials. Say this to them."

The equivalent of Vishnu's disc turns up in Babylon. The original of this text is to be found in *Cuneiform Inscriptions of Western Asia* by Sir Henry Rawlinson, London, 1866. The reference is II, 19. I translated this into English from the French translation which appeared in *La Magie chez les Chaldeens* by Francois Lenormant, Maisonneuve et Cie., Paris, 1874.

In the presence of the immense terror that I spread, like that of Anna, who holds his head high?

I am the master. The steep mountains of the earth are shaken violently from their peaks to their foundations . . .

In my right hand I hold my disc of fire. In my left hand I hold my disc that slays.

I hold the raised weapon of my divinity, the fifty-spoked solar wheel.

I hold the potent breaker of mountains, the solar wheel which cannot be deflected.

I hold the mighty weapon which slays like a sword whole circles of warriors.

I hold the fish with seven fins that makes the mountains bow.

I hold the flaming blade of battle that devastates the rebel country.

I hold the great sword which lays low the ranks of heroes, the sword of my divinity.

I hold the deadly lance which is the hero's joy.

I hold the noose that catches men and the bow that shoots lightning.

I hold the hammer which smashes the houses of the rebel country and the shield.

I hold the lightning in battle, the weapon with fifty points.

I hold the . . . seven-headed like an enormous seven-headed snake.

Like the attack of a great sea-serpent . . . devastating in the shock of battle, I hold the seven-headed weapon whose power extends across the sky as well as across the earth.

I hold the weapon that shines like the sun, like the god burning in the east.

I hold the creator of heaven and earth, the god of fire who has no equal.

I hold in my right hand the potency of the weapon which spreads panic terror through the land, the projectile of marble and gold . . . which works by the power of the life-giving god in his miracles.

I hold the weapon which like . . . destroys the rebel land, the weapon with fifty points.

In some of the close encounters reported with UFO occupants, witnesses have described their speech as "barking" or "dog-like". It may be relevant that in ancient Greece and Rome incantations during magical ceremonies were made in a sort of barking howl, like the cry of a dog or wolf, and were unintelligible to the uninitiated.

The original text of this Greek incantation is in *Papyri Grecae Magicae*, edited by K. Preisendanz, Leipzig, 1928. The translation is by E. M. Butler, who quotes it in his *Ritual Magic*, Cambridge University Press, 1949. It is dated between the first and fourth centuries A.D. The title is:

All-Powerful Might of the
Constellation of the Great Bear

I invoke you, ye holy ones, mighty, majestic, glorious Splendors, holy, and earth-born, mighty arch-daimons; compeers of the great god; denizens of Chaos, of Erebus and of the unfathomable abyss; earth-dwellers, haunters of sky-depths, nook-infesting, murk-enwrapped; scanning the mysteries, guardians of secrets, captains of the hosts of hell; kings of infinite space, terrestrial overlords, globe-shaking, firm-founding, ministering to earth-quakes; terror-strangling, panic-striking, spindle-turning; snow-scatterers, rain-wafters, spirits of air; fire-tongues of summer sun, tempest-tossing lords of fate; dark shapes of Erebus, senders of necessity; flame-fanning fire-darters; snow-compelling, dew-compelling; gale-raising, abyss-plumbing, calm-bestriding air spirits; dauntless in courage, heart-crushing despots; chasm-leaping, overburdening, iron-nerved daimons; wild-raging, unen-slaved; watchers of Tartaros; delusive fate-phantoms; all-seeing, all-hearing, all-conquering, sky-wandering vagrants; life-inspiring, life-destroying, primeval pole-movers; heart-jocund death-dealers; revealers of angels, justicers of mortals, sunless revealers, mas-ters of daimons, air-roving, omnipotent, holy, invincible (magic words), perform my behests.

To what type of beings was this addressed? Could these "watchers" be the same as "the Watchers" described in the Book of Enoch? According to Enoch, some sons of the sky came down from heaven because they saw that the daughters of men were fair. Enoch is quite precise about it: two hundred of them landed on the summit of a specific mountain at a specific time, and immediately began to act like a bunch of randy sailors on a shore-leave spree, or a squadron of hot-blooded space cadets in revolt against Central Command—which reacted by causing the deluge that only Noah's tribe survived. There is a tradition that this incident was the origin of magic, which was considered a special kind of knowledge that had been transmitted to humans by "fallen angels", non-human intelligent beings from elsewhere, earth-bound and in exile from their home star.

According to the Dead Sea Scrolls, the father of Noah was a "Watcher". Perhaps the seemingly meaningless non-sense syllables so frequently encountered in magical texts may have originated as code signals to make contact with "the Watchers".

The earliest known centers of civilisation in Mesopotamia

were characterised by their ziggurats. According to the records left by this culture, the ziggurats were constructed for the purpose of intercourse between a priestess and a god from the sky.

Herodotus described a reconstructed ziggurat which he visited in Babylon: "On the topmost tower there is a spacious temple, and inside the temple stands a great bed covered with fine bed-clothes, with a golden table by its side. There is no statue of any kind set up in the place, nor is the chamber occupied at night by any but a single native woman who—say the Chaldean priests—is chosen by the deity out of all the women of the land. The priests also declare—but I for one do not credit it—that the god comes down in person into this chamber, and sleeps upon the couch."

Nebuchadnezzar was King of Babylon from 604-651 B.C. This is a dream that he recorded before going insane:

Thus were the visions of mine head in my bed: I saw, and behold, a tree in the midst of the earth, and the height thereof was great. The tree grew, and was strong, and the height thereof reached unto heaven, and the sight thereof to the end of all the earth. The leaves thereof were fair, and the fruit thereof much, and in it was meat for all: the beasts of the field had shadow under it, and the fowls of the heaven dwelt in the boughs thereof, and all flesh was fed of it. I saw in the visions of my head upon my bed, and behold a watcher and a holy one came down from heaven. He cried aloud, and said thus: Hew down the tree, and cut off his branches; shake off his leaves; and scatter his fruit; let the beasts get away from under it, and the fowls from his branches. Nevertheless leave the stump of his root in the earth, even with a band of iron and brass, in the tender grass of the field, and let it be wet with the dew of heaven, and let his portion be with the beasts in the grass of the earth. Let his heart be changed from man's, and let a beast's heart be given unto him, and let seven times pass over him. This matter is by the decree of the watchers, and the demand by the word of the holy ones: to the intent that the living may know that the most High ruleth in the kingdom of men, and giveth it to whomsoever he will, and setteth up over it the basest of men. This dream, I King Nebuchadnezzar have seen.

The prophet Enoch described what sounds very much like an abduction experience. The first part of the following quotation is from *The Book of Enoch or 1 Enoch*, translated from the Coptic by R. H. Charles, Clarendon Press, Oxford, 1912. The second part is from *3 Enoch or the Hebrew Book of Enoch*, translated by Hugo Odeberg, Cambridge University Press, 1928.

And lo! the Watchers called me—Enoch the scribe. And the vision was shown to me thus: Behold, in the vision clouds invited me and a mist summoned me, and the course of the stars and the lightnings sped and hastened me, and the winds in the vision caused me to fly and lifted me upward, and bore me into heaven. And I went in till I drew nigh to a wall which is built of crystals and surrounded by tongues of fire, and it began to affright me. And I went into the tongues of fire and drew nigh to a large house which was built of crystals, and its groundwork was of crystal. Its ceiling was like the path of the stars and the lightnings, and between them were fiery cherubim, and their heaven was clear as water. A flaming fire surrounded the walls, and its portals blazed with fire. And I entered into that house, and it was hot as fire and cold as ice: there were no delights of life therein: fear covered me, and trembling got hold upon me. And I looked and saw therein a lofty throne: its appearance was as crystal, and the wheels thereof as the shining sun, and there was the vision of cherubim. And from underneath the throne came streams of flaming fire so that I could not look thereon. And the Great Glory sat thereon, and His raiment shone more brightly than the sun and was whiter than any snow. None of the angels could enter and behold His face by reason of the magnificence and glory, and no flesh could behold Him. The flaming fire was round about Him. And they took me to a place in which those who were there were like flaming fire, and when they wished, they appeared as men.

Three of the ministering angels came forth and brought charges against me in the high heavens, saying before the Holy One, blessed be He: "Said not the Ancient Ones (First Ones) rightly before Thee: "Do not create man!" " The Holy One, blessed be He, answered and said unto them: "I have made and I will bear, yea, I will carry and will deliver." As soon as they saw me, they said before Him: "Lord of the Universe! What is this one that he should ascend to the height of heights? Is not he one from among the sons of the sons of those who perished in the days of the Flood? What doeth he in the Raqia?" As soon as I reached the high heavens, the ministers of the consuming fire, perceiving my smell, said: "What smell of one born of woman and what taste of a white drop is this that ascends on high, and lo, he is merely a gnat among those who divide flames of fire?" After all these things the Holy One, blessed be He, put His hand upon me . . . As soon as the Holy One, blessed be He, took me in His service to attend the Throne of Glory and the Wheels of the Merkaba and the needs of Shekina, forthwith my flesh was changed into flames, my sinews into flaming fire, my bones into coals of burning juniper, the light of my eye-lids into splendours of lightnings, my eye-balls into fire-brands, the hair of my head into hot flames, all my limbs into wings of burning fire and the whole of my body into glowing fire. And on my right were divisions of fiery flames, and on my left fire-brands were burning, round about me storm-wind and tempest were blowing and in front of me and behind me was roaring of thunder with earthquake. And there is a court before the Throne of Glory which no seraph or angel can enter. And there are 24 myriads of wheels of fire. And in the seven Halls are chariots of fire and flame, without reckoning, or end or searching . . .

Metatron, the Angel, the Prince of the Presence, said to me: "Come and behold the letters by which the heaven and earth were created, the letters by which were created the mountains and hills, the letters by which were created the seas and rivers, the letters by which were created the trees and herbs." And I walked by his side and he took me by his hand and raised me upon his wings and showed me those letters, all of them. Said Metatron, the Prince of the Presence: "The God of Israel is my witness in this thing, that when I revealed this secret to Moses, then all the hosts in every heaven on high raged against me and said to me: 'Why dost thou reveal this secret to a son of man, born of woman, tainted and unclean, a man of a putrefying drop, the secret by which were created heaven and earth, the sea and the dry land, the mountains and hills, the rivers and springs, Gehenna of fire and hail, the Garden of Eden and the Tree of Life; and the cattle, and the wild beasts, and the fowl of the air, and the fish of the sea, and Behemoth and Leviathan, and the creeping things, the worms, the dragons of the sea, and the creeping things of the deserts; and the Tora and Wisdom and Knowledge and the Gnosis of things above and the fear of heaven. Why dost thou reveal this to flesh and blood?' "

In the *Old Testament*, verses 8-23 of the sixth chapter of the *Second Book of Kings* describe an incident involving explicit UFO intervention in human affairs, accompanied by extra-sensory perception and mass hypnosis:

Then the king of Syria warred against Israel, and took counsel with his servants, saying, In such and such a place shall be my camp. And the man of God sent unto the king of Israel, saying, Beware that thou pass not such a place; for thither the Syrians are come down. And the king of Israel sent to the place which the man of God had told him and warned him of, and saved himself there, not once nor twice.

Therefore the heart of the king of Syria was sore troubled for this thing; and he called his servants, and said unto them, Will ye not show me which of us is for the king of Israel? And one of his servants said, None, my lord, O king, but Elisha the prophet that is in Israel, telleth the king of Israel the words that thou speakest in thy bedchamber. And he said, Go and spy where he is, that I may send and fetch him. And it was told him, Behold, he is in Dothian. Therefore sent he thither horses, and chariots, and a great host: and they came by night, and compassed the city about.

And when the servant of the man of God was risen early, and gone forth, behold, a host compassed the city both with horses and chariots. And his servant said unto him, Alas, my master! how shall we do? And he answered, Fear not: they that be with us are more than they that be with them. And Elisha prayed, and said, LORD, I pray thee, open his eyes, that he may see. And the LORD opened the eyes of the young man; and he saw: and behold, the mountain was full of horses and chariots of fire round about Elisha. And when they came down to him, Elisha prayed unto the LORD, and said, Smite this people, I pray thee, with blindness. And he smote them with blindness, according to the word of Elisha. And Elisha said unto them, This is not the way, nor is this the city: follow me, and I will bring you to the man ye seek. But he led them to Samaria.

And it came to pass, when they were come into Samaria, that Elisha said, LORD, open the eyes of these men, that they may see. And the LORD opened their eyes, and they saw; and, behold, they were in the midst of Samaria. And the king of Israel said unto Elisha, when he saw them, My father, shall I smite them? Shall I smite them? And he answered, Thou shalt not smite them: wouldst thou smite those whom thou hast taken captive with thy sword and with thy bow? Set bread and water before them, that they may eat and drink, and go to their master. And he prepared great provision for them: and when they had eaten and drunk, he sent them away, and they went to their master. So the bands of Syria came no more into the land of Israel."

Tertullian wrote in 213 A.D. about the Gnostics: "Some of them believe that they came down from the sky, and they are as sure of this as they are convinced that they will go back up there."

This inscription was found on an Orphic-Pythagorean tomb near Rome, dated between the first and fourth centuries A.D.: "I am a son of the earth and the stars of the sky, but I am of the celestial race. May the knowledge be passed on!"

Among the riddles sung by Taliesin, the forefather of all Welsh bards, one finds:

"I know the star-knowledge
of stars before the earth was made
whence I was born."

In the *Mathnawi* by Jalalul-Din Rumi (13th Century A.D.), which is one of the major classics in the traditional literature of Islam, there is a description of the angel Gabriel appearing to the Virgin Mary so that she may conceive

Jesus. As Mary recoils in fear, Gabriel announces who he is and why he has come. During the course of Rumi's version of the Annunciation, the shaft of light from the mouth of Gabriel that shines forth upon Mary and impregnates her is described as being a ray from the star Arcturus.

The Scotch astronomer Duncan Lunan made a study of abnormal echoes in radio transmission that appeared to be intelligent coded messages in *Man and the Stars*, Souvenir Press, London, 1974. He traced their origin to the star Epsilon Bootis in the Bootes constellation. The largest and most visible star in the Bootes constellation is Arcturus.

The Protoevangelion of James is generally acknowledged to be the oldest of the Gnostic gospels that were removed from the Canon and consigned to the Apocrypha at the Council of Nicea in 325 A.D. In this quotation from it, Herod has sent for the Magi, and is examining them, posing the question:

"What sign have you seen in reference to the King that has been born?"

And the Magi said: "We have seen a star of great size shining among these stars, and obscuring their light, so that the stars did not appear; and thus we knew that a king has been born to Israel, and we have come to worship him."

And Herod said: "Go and seek him; and if you find him, let me know, in order that I also may go and worship him."

And the Magi went out. And, behold, the star which they had seen in the east went before them until they came to the cave, and it stood over the top of the cave. And the Magi saw the infant and his mother Mary; and they brought forth from their bag gold, and frankincense, and myrrh. And having been warned by the angel not to go into Judea, they went into their own country by another road.

In the same text there is a description of the birth of Jesus. Joseph goes to look for a midwife. People and animals suddenly go into a state of suspended motion, are frozen in mid-gesture in a temporary paralysis. This type of temporary paralysis turns up frequently and persistently in modern UFO reports. However, Joseph moves among them without being affected. The midwife he finds has also not been affected by the otherwise general temporary paralysis:

> And the midwife went away with him. And they stood in the place of the cave, and behold a luminous cloud overshadowed the cave. And the midwife said: "My soul has been magnified this day, because mine eyes have seen strange things—because salvation has been brought forth to Israel." And immediately the cloud disappeared out of the cave, and a great light shone in the cave, so that the eyes could not bear it. And in a little that light gradually decreased, until the infant appeared, and went and took the breast from his mother Mary.

When an international group of scientists examined the Shroud of Turin, the most plausible explanation they were able to find for the three-dimensional image on it was that it was made by a superficial burn from thermonuclear radiation which lasted only a tiny fraction of a second. If it had lasted any longer, Jerusalem would have been devastated like Hiroshima. The flash of radiation had to be extremely brief and controlled with great precision in order to make no more than a superficial burn that would leave a three-dimensional image on the Shroud.

The next statement is by a Catholic opponent of the Gnostics, attempting to summarise Gnostic doctrine (Epiphanius, Panarion XXXI, from *Gnosis* by R. McL. Wilson, Clarendon Press, Oxford, 1972):

> But they say that His body was brought down from above . . . He had a body from above, as I have already said. But He was not (they maintain) the first Logos, nor the Christ after the Logos, who remained above among the aeons above, but they say that He was brought forth for no other reason than to come and save the spiritual race from above. They deny the resurrection of the

dead, saying something mysterious and ridiculous, that it is not this body which rises, but another one rises from it, which they call spiritual. Only those who are called pneumatics by them, and the others who are called the psychics, will be saved, provided that the psychics behave correctly. The materialists, who are called fleshly and earthy, perish utterly and will not be saved at all.

During the early years of this century G. R. S. Mead made a profound study of the Gnostics, and wrote a brilliant book about them, which opened up this hitherto neglected chapter in the history of religions: *Fragments of a Faith Forgotten*, published by the Theosophical Publishing Society in London in 1906. Having presented the point of view of a Catholic opponent contemporary with them, let's now have the point of view of the late Professor Mead, a highly intelligent and articulate modern proponent of Gnosticism:

If it is difficult to form any precise notion of the evolution of popular religious ideas in Greece, much more difficult is it to trace the various lines of the Mystery-traditions, which were regarded with the greatest possible reverence and guarded with the greatest possible secrecy, the slightest violation of the oath being punishable by death.

The idea that underlay the Mystery-tradition in Greece was similar to that which underlay all similar institutions in antiquity, and it is difficult to find any cult of importance without this inner side. . . .

The institution of the Mysteries is the most interesting phenomenon in the study of religion. The idea of antiquity was that there was something to be *known* in religion. . . .

A persistent tradition in connection with all the great Mystery-institutions was that their several founders were the introducers of all the arts of civilisation; they were either themselves gods or were instructed in them by the gods—in brief, that they were men of far greater knowledge than any who had come after; they were the teachers of infant races. . . .

We find the ancient world honey-combed with these institutions. They were of all sorts and kinds. . . .

It is said that these earliest teachers of humanity who founded the

Mystery-institutions as the most efficient means of giving infant humanity instructions in higher things, were souls belonging to a more highly developed humanity than our own. . . .In the earliest times, according to this view, the Mysteries were conducted by those who had a knowledge of nature-powers which was the acquisition of a prior perfected humanity not necessarily earth-born, and the wonders shown therein such that none of our humanity could of themselves produce. As time went on and our humanity more and more developed the faculty of reason, and were thought strong enough to stand on their own feet, the teachers gradually withdrew, and the Mysteries were committed to the most advanced pupils of this humanity, who had finally to substitute symbols and devices, dramas and scenic representations, for what had previously been revealed by higher means.

The Australian Aborigines of North-Eastern Arnhem Land have preserved the traditions of their people with a tenacity comparable to that of the Hopi Indians in America. Their basic religious myth describes the arrival in Australia of three Ancestral Beings, a brother and two sisters, from whose incestuous relations sprang the different tribes of Aborigines. These three Ancestral Beings were called the Djanggawul. It is interesting that they are closely associated with the planet Venus, as is Quetzalcoatl in America, and are the Kahuna deities of Polynesia. Space probes indicate that the temperature of Venus is now far too high for there to be any chance of life as we know it. However, this does not necessarily mean that it has always been uninhabitable. According to the Roman historian Marcus Varro, in the time of Ogygios (the founder of the Achaean League) Venus went through major changes in color, size, and shape.

In some ways the Djanggawul resemble the Hopi Kachinas. In both cases they are the primordial ancestral beings who laid down the life-pattern followed by that particular culture. The Djanggawul came from far away, having stopped off at a place called Bralgu, the land of the Eternal Beings.

They arrived with certain magical instruments, having left many others behind in Bralgu. They possessed a staff which would produce a spring of water if struck against the ground with the proper incantations (rather like the story of the staff with which Moses struck water from the rock). They also had rods which turned into different types of trees when inserted into the ground. So they traveled over Australia "making the land": making springs and vegetation and animals and people. An important part of their activity was to charge each place they stopped at with their dreams. They left "dreamings" in the form of totemic designs, sacred emblems, body paintings, and rituals. These "dreamings" resemble the Nordic concept of the "runes", universal patterns permeating all nature. While traveling around the country, they were frequently directed from one place to another by the appearance of something in the sky. The following are excerpts from songs which have been handed down from generation to generation since deep antiquity by the Aborigines of North-Eastern Arnhem Land. *The Djanggawul Song Cycle* was translated by Roland M. Berndt in his *Djanggawul*, published by Routledge & Kegan Paul Ltd. in London in 1952.

Star moving along shining! We saw its disc quite close,
skimming the sea's surface, then mounting again above Bralgu.
Close to us it rises above the expanse of the sea; we look back,
    seeing its shine.
Morning Star, sent by the dancing Spirit People, those people of the
    rain, calling out as they dance there with outstretched arms.
They send it for us, that we may travel along its shining path from
    Bralgu.
Close, its feathered ball appears above Dangdangmi! Close is the
Morning Star, on the end of its string and pole!
Close is the Morning Star, stretching from its pole, extending out
    from its string.
Shining from Bralgu, as we paddle through the sea. . . .
As we paddle we see the shine moving.

As we paddle through the glistening water, it follows us.
Going through the great wide sea, through the path of light,
Morning star suspended on end of string from a sapling pole,
Its feathered ball close to us: now skimming the sea's surface,
now rising once more. Shining on us!. . . .
Another star, waridj, a feathered ball held by spirits. Close is the
  Morning Star.
It shines near, as we turn to see it. . . .
See the shine from the disc of the star, close to us, waridj.
The Bralgu spirits are dancing, sending the Star.

The Natchez Indians were totally exterminated in 1731. When they were first contacted by De Soto in 1542, they were more powerful than the other tribes of the region. De Soto, knowing them to be sun worshipers, claimed to be the sun's younger brother. They suggested that he prove this by drying up the Mississippi River. When he failed to make good his boast, they killed him. La Salle made contact with them in 1682. They were the descendants of the Mound Builders, who constructed gigantic earthworks whose shapes can be appreciated only from the air. The resemblance between their chief, whom they called the Great Sun, and the Egyptian Pharaohs (as well as other sun kings of antiquity) is staggering. Their religion was that in the distant past a god from the sky had made them his chosen people, giving them the knowledge that made them more powerful than the other tribes. This god from the sky had left a stone behind him (a transmitter?), which was kept in a pyramidal temple mound. Human and animal idols resembling those of ancient Egypt were also kept in the temple, which the Great Sun consulted to foretell the future. He brought the first fruits of the harvest to the temple, where a perpetual fire was maintained. They believed their spirits to be immortal and were not afraid of death.

The Onondaga and the Mohawk were two tribes of the mighty Iroquois nation, whose social organisation was so intelligently structured that it merits our attention and respect today. J. N. B. Hewitt transcribed and translated this legend in *Iroquoian Cosmology*, published by the Bureau of American Ethnology in Washington, D.C., 1903.

The Onondaga version of the legend begins: "He who was my grandfather was wont to relate that, verily, he had heard the legend as it was customarily told by five generations of grandsires, and this is what he himself was in the habit of telling. He customarily said: "Man-beings dwell in the sky, on the farther side of the visible sky. . . . It is said that they who dwelt there did not know what it is for one to say 'I shall die'.""

Then come a long series of adventures, which result in an Iroquois maiden marrying the chief of the sky people. She then returns to her village, and what happens next is this: "At that time all those who dwelt there undid their lodges by removing the roofs from all severally. Then, verily, when it became night, as soon as the darkness became settled, they heard the sounds made by the raining of the corn, which fell in the lodges. Then they went to sleep. When it became day, they looked and saw that in the lodges corn lay piled up, quite filling them. Now, moreover, their chief said 'Ye must care for it and greatly esteem it; the thing has visited our village.'"

In the Mohawk version, after the maiden has married the chief of the sky people, he gives her these instructions before sending her back to her village: "Thou must tell them that they severally must remove the thatched roofs from their lodges, for, indeed, verily, it will rain corn this very night when thou arrivest there." . . . 'Then, in truth, they removed the roofs from their several lodges, and they retired to sleep. So, when they awakened, in truth, then there was very much corn lying in the lodges. The white corn lay above one's knees in depth. Thus lay the white corn, for so long as they slept it showered white corn. The reason that he gave her people corn was because he had espoused one of their people.'

It seems so obvious that it hardly needs to be pointed out, but the "white corn" dropped to the Iroquois bears a strong resemblance to the "manna" dropped to the Hebrews.

The following passages have been selected from *Comte de Gabalis* by Montfaucon de Villars, which was first published in Paris in 1670. It was translated anonymously into English by "The Brothers" and printed at the Old Bourne Press in London with no date marked. The book looks as if it was printed around 1900.

The Hebrews used to call the beings who are between the angels and men Sadaim, and the Greeks, transposing letters and adding one syllable, called them Daemonas. Among the ancient Philosophers these Daemons were held to be an Aerial Race, ruling over the Elements, mortal, engendering, and unknown in this century to those who rarely seek the Truth in her ancient dwelling place, which is to say, in the Cabala and in the theology of the Hebrews, who possessed the special art of holding communion with that Aerial People and of conversing with all these Inhabitants of the Air. The Teraphim was but the ceremony which had to be observed for that communion. Micah, who complains in the Book of Judges that his gods have been taken from him, only laments the loss of the little images through which the Sylphs used to converse with him. The gods which Rachel stole from her father were also Teraphim. Neither Micah nor Laban are reproved for idolatry, and Jacob would have taken care not to live for fourteen years with an idolater, nor to marry his daughter. It was only a commerce with Sylphs; and tradition tells us that the Synagogue considered such commerce permissible. The image that belonged to David's wife was but the Teraphim by which she conversed with the Elementary Peoples: for you can well imagine that the prophet after God's own heart would not have tolerated idolatry in his household. Among other reasons why Rachel stole her father's images, this is thought to be one: that Laban might not, by consulting with these images, discover what way Jacob took his flight. . . .

In vain does a Philosopher bring to light the falsity of the chimeras people have fabricated, and present manifest proofs to the contrary. No matter what his experience, nor how sound his argument and reasoning, let but a man with a doctor's hood come along and write them down as false—experience and demonstration count for naught, and it is henceforward beyond the power of Truth to re-establish her Empire. People would rather believe in a doctor's hood than in their own eyes. There has been in your native France a memorable proof of this popular mania. The famous Cabalist Zedechias, in the reign of your Pepin, took it into his head to convince the world that the Elements are inhabited by these peoples whose nature I have described. The expedient of which he bethought himself was to advise the Sylphs to show themselves in the air to everybody. They did so sumptuously. These beings were seen in the air in human form. Sometimes on wonderfully constructed aerial ships, whose flying squadrons roved at the will of the Zephyrs. What happened? Do you suppose that ignorant age would so much as reason as to the nature of these marvelous spectacles? The people straightway believed that sorcerers had taken possession of the Air for the purpose of raising tempests and bringing hail upon their crops. The learned theologians and jurists were of the same opinion as the masses. The emperors believed it as well; and this ridiculous chimera went so far that the wise Charlemagne and after him Louis the Debonair imposed grievous penalties upon all these supposed Tyrants of the Air. You may see an account of this in the first chapter of the Capitularies of these two emperors. The Sylphs, seeing the populace, the pedants and even the crowned heads thus alarmed against them, determined to dissipate the bad opinion people had of their innocent fleet by carrying off men from every locality and showing them their beautiful women, their Republic and their manner of government, and then setting them down again in diverse parts of the world. They carried out their plan. The people who saw these men as they were descending came running from every direction, convinced beforehand that they were sorcerers who had separated from their companions in order to come and scatter poisons on the fruit and in the springs. Carried away by the frenzy with which such fancies inspired them, they hurried these innocents off to the torture. The great number of them that was put to death by fire and water throughout the kingdom is incredible. One day, among other instances, it chanced at Lyons that three men and a woman were seen descending from these aerial ships. The entire city gathered about them, crying out that they were magicians, and had been sent by Grimaldus, Duke of Beneventum, Charlemagne's enemy, to destroy the French harvests. In vain the four innocents sought to vindicate themselves by saying that they were their own country-folk, and had been carried away a short time since by miraculous men who had shown them unheard-of marvels, and had desired them to give an account of what they had seen. The frenzied populace paid no heed to their defense, and were on the point of casting them into the fire when the worthy Agobard, Bishop of Lyons, who having been a monk in that city had acquired considerable authority there, came running at the noise, and having heard the accusations of the people and the defense of the accused, gravely pronounced that both one and the other were false. That it was not true that these men had fallen from the sky, and that what they said they had seen there was impossible. The people believed what their good father Agobard said rather than their own eyes, were pacified, set at liberty the four Ambassadors of the Sylphs, and received with wonder the book which Agobard wrote to confirm the judgment which he had pronounced. Thus the testimony of these four witnesses was rendered vain.

The following passage was translated from *Liber de Grandine et Tonitrius* by Agobard, Bishop of Lyons:

We have, however, seen and heard many men plunged in such great stupidity, sunk in such depths of folly, as to believe and say that there is a certain region, which they call Magonia, whence ships sail in the clouds, in order to carry back to that region those fruits of the earth that are destroyed by hail and tempests; the sailors paying rewards to the storm wizards and themselves receiving corn and other produce. Out of the number of those whose blind folly was deep enough to believe such things possible, I saw several exhibiting, in a certain concourse of people, four persons in bonds—three men and a woman who they said had fallen from these same ships. After keeping them for some days in captivity, they had brought them before the assembled multitude, as we have said, in our presence to be stoned. But truth prevailed.

The earliest known UFO sighting in Russia dates from 1663 in the town of Robozero. This is from *UFOs From Behind the Iron Curtain* by Ion Hobana and Julien Weverbergh, published by Souvenir Press, London, 1964:

This document was first published in *Historical files compiled and issued by the archaeological commission*; part IV (St. Petersburg 1842) . . . The authenticity of these files is unquestionable.

'To His Highness the Archimandrite Nikita, to his Eminence Staretz Pavel, to their Highnesses the Starets of the Synod of the Monastery of St. Cyril; Most Venerable Lords, humble greetings from your servant, Ivachko Rjesvkoi. The peasant Levka Fedorov, domiciled in the village of Mys, submitted to me the following first-hand account: On this, the fifteenth day of August in the year 1663, a Sunday, the faithful from the district of Relozero had gone to church in large numbers in the village of Robozero and whilst they were there a great crash sounded from out the heavens and many people left the church of God to assemble outside on the square. Now Levka Fedorov, the farmer already mentioned, was amongst them and saw what happened; to him it was a sign from God. Around the stroke of midday there descended upon Robozero a great ball of fire from the clearest of skies, not from a cloud; moreover it came from the direction from which we get winter and moved across from the church to the lake. The fire was about 45 metres on each side and for the same distance in front of the fire there were two fiery beams. Suddenly it was no longer there but about one hour of the clock later it appeared again, above the lake from which it had disappeared before. It went from the south to the west and was about 500 metres away when it vanished. But once again it returned, filling all who saw it with great dread, travelling westwards and staying over Robozero one hour and a half. Now there were fishermen in their boat on the lake about a mile away and they were sorely burnt by the fire. The lake water was lit up to its greatest depth of nine metres and the fish fled to the banks. The water seemed to be covered with rust under the glow.'

In her superb *Burning Water* (Thames & Hudson, 1957), Laurette Sejourne describes the series of strange phenomena that occurred in Aztec Mexico just before the arrival of the Spanish: "There were inextinguishable fires; comets traversing the sky for hours on end; the enchanted crane bearing the mirror in which the starry sky appeared in the middle of the day; the strange tale of the shepherd borne by an eagle to a shining grotto where he was received by a person compared to whom Moctezuma was as nothing . . . on many nights there appeared a great splendour born in the east, climbing on high, and appearing in the form of a pyramid and with tongues of fire . . . they had news long since, and it was spoken of in their histories, that the times were now approaching in which the things Quetzalcoatl said and foretold would come to pass . . . And as the King of Tezcuco was so skilled in all the sciences they knew and had acquired, especially in astrology, in accord with the prophecies of their past . . . he made little of his kingdom and domain and sent to the captains and leaders of his armies that they should stop the continuous wars they waged against Tlaxcala . . . so that they should enjoy in all peace and tranquility the short time that remained to them of lordship and command."

An epic poem entitled *The Flight of Quetzalcoatl* was translated from the original Nahuatl into Spanish by A. M. Garibay, and from Spanish into English by Jerome Rothenberg, who published it in his *Technicians of the Sacred* (Doubleday, 1968). Its final verse describes the departure of Quetzalcoatl from Mexico in these terms:

It ended with a hulk of serpents formed into a boat
& when he'd made it, sat in it & sailed away
A boat that glided on those burning waters, no
   one knowing when he reached the country of Red Daylight
It ended on the rim of some great sea
It ended with his face reflected in the mirror of its waves

the beauty of his face returned to him
& he was dressed in garments like the sun
It ended on a bonfire on the beach where he would hurl himself
   & burn, his ashes rising & the cries of birds
It ended with the linnet, with the birds of turquoise color, birds
   the color of wild sunflowers, red & blue birds
It ended with the birds of yellow feathers in a riot of bright gold
Circling till the fire had died out
It ended with the morning star with dawn and evening
It ended with his journey to Death's Kingdom with seven days of
   darkness
With his body changed to light
A star that burns forever in the sky

Padma Sambhava was the Root Guru who founded Tibetan Buddhism. The legends concerning his birth indicate that he was not born in the normal human manner. When the time came for him to take his departure from Tibet, he is supposed to have done so by air in a celestial chariot, just as Elijah is supposed to have taken his departure from Israel.

When the master yogi, poet, and saint Milarepa (whose green skin was attributed to his diet of nettles) drank the poison offered to him by a hypocrite and died with a song on his lips, a dispute arose between his human followers and non-human celestials over possession of Milarepa's body, which the celestials carried away in "a sphere of light".

The 84 Siddhas were the principal saints of the early period of Mahayana Buddhism, who founded the different Tibetan religious lineages still in existence today. Their life stories are as essential a part of the Tibetan Buddhist tradition as are the life stories of the saints to the Roman Catholic tradition. In 74 of these 84 life stories, the ending is that the Siddha went to "the realm of the Dakas" in his or her physical body. The Dakas are defined as "sky-traveling beings".

A "dorje" is a double-headed hand-held instrument

which is of great importance in Tibetan Buddhist rituals. One of the titles of the Dalai Lama is that of "the Holder of the Dorje". If made from the proper materials, in the hands of someone who knows how to use it correctly, the dorje is thought to have very special powers. Like the Grail of medieval European legends, the original dorje is believed to have been of celestial origin.

In 1927, just twenty years before the Kenneth Arnold sighting in the United States which first brought UFOs to world-wide attention, the artist Nicholas Roerich was exploring remote regions of the Himalayas. His travel diaries were published under the titles of *Altai-Himalaya* (Jarrolds, London, 1929) and *Heart of Asia* (Roerich Museum Press, New York, 1930). He describes an incident that took place at the dedication of a stupa. A UFO came over the horizon, changed the direction of its flight, and went away. The Tibetan Lamas Roerich was traveling with whispered to each other: "The sign of Shambhala!"

Some Tibetan lamas think that one of the reasons the elusive kingdom of Shambhala is so difficult to find is that its location is extra-terrestrial. There are several different versions of the prophecy associated with the legend of Shambhala, but they are in agreement on this point: the invincible weapon that will be used in his final battle by the King of Shambhala to totally annihilate the armies of evil and transform the Age of Iron into the Age of Gold will be a metallic disc that comes to him from the sky, which has qualities similar to those possessed by the disc of Vishnu in the Hindu legend described earlier in this chapter.

The description of the New Jerusalem descending from the sky in the *Book of Revelations* bears some resemblance to what is now called a 'mother ship'.

One of the possible interpretations of the Sura of the Star and the description of Mohammed's celestial journey in the *Koran* is in terms of UFO phenomena.

Before his death, the Sioux medicine man and prophet, Black Elk, told his friend Joseph Epes Brown: "You will know when I am dying, because there will be a great display of some sort in the sky." Brown was in Europe at the time of Black Elk's death, but upon his return he found that there had indeed been very unusual luminous phenomena in the sky over Pine Ridge Reservation on the night that Black Elk died. The key event in Black Elk's life, which set the course of his career, the Great Vision he had at the age of nine, could be thought of as a close encounter with beings from another dimension during an out-of-the-body experience.

Strange things were also seen in the sky at the birth of the national hero of Wales, Owen Glendower.

Dr. John Dee was the official astrologer of Queen Elizabeth I, and her unofficial secret agent, signing his reports 007. There are definite indications that he was among those responsible for founding the original Rosy Cross, whose Invisible College was supposed to be located 'under the wings of Jehovah'. *A True and Faithful Relation of what passed for many Years Between Dr. John Dee and Some Spirits* by Meric Casaubon was published in London in 1659. This passage was written by Dee in Prague on April 30th, 1586, who recorded it in his diary under the title:

Miraculum, et factum memorandum in perpetuum.
As E.K. stood at the end of the Galery by his Chamber, looking over into the Vineyard he seemed to see the little man the Gardiner, in all manner of behaviour and apparel, who is the chief workman or over-seer of Mr. Carpio his workmen in the same Vine-yard. He seemed very handsomly to prune some of the Trees: at length he approached under the wall by E.K. and holding his face away-ward he said unto him, Quaso dicas Domino Doctori quod veniat ad me. And so went away as it were cutting here and there the Trees very handsomly, and at length over the Cherry-trees by the house on the Rock in the Garden he seemed to mount up in a great piller of fire.

E.K. bade his Wife to go, and see who was in the Garden. She came up, and brought him word, No body.

E.K. then came to me and said, I think there is some wicked
spirit that would allude me, and he told and said to me, as is before
noted. Then said I, I will go into the garden, and bade E.K. come
with me. We went down that way which this Creature did go: but
nothing we saw, went to the Banqueting-house in the Vine-yard,
but that place pleased us not: so, we went along in the way by the
cliffside, and sat down on the bank by the great pyle of Vine-
stakes lying in the very South end of the Vine-yard. And we had
not sat there half a quarter of an hour, but I espyed under the
Almond-tree, and on the South side of it, being the Westerly
almond-tree, that is which is standing on the Westerly side of the
straight path which leadeth from the North toward the South in
the Vineyard. I espyed (I say) like a sheet of faire white paper
lying tossed to and fro in the wind. I rose and went to it, and (to the
prayse of God his truth and power) there I found three of my
Books lying, which were so diligently burnt the tenth day of
April last.

1 The three books were, Enoch his Book,
2 The 48 Claves Angelica.
3 And the third was the Book of my gathering of the thirty
   Aires, and entitled Liber Scientia terrestris auxilii et victoriae.

Thereupon E.K. comming to me, I fell on my knees with great
thanks yielding to the God Almighty, and so did E.K. whose mind
and body were marvailously affected at the sight of the said
Books, having no shew or signs that ever they had been in the fire,
neither by colour or favour, or any thing wanting.

And after we had set half an hour under the fore-said Almond-
trees, praysing God and wondring at the Miracle. Suddenly
appeared by us the self-same Gardiner like person, but with his
face somewhat turned away, and nothing thereof to be adjudged
as of Ave the custome is. He said, Kelly, follow me. E.K. went, and
I sat still, awaiting his return.

This Gardiner went before E.K. and his feet seemed not to
touch the ground by a foot height. And as he went before E.K. so
the doores did seeme to open before him, he led him up the great
stairs on the left hand by the Vineyard door, and so in at his own
Chamber door where E.K. hath his new study, and then the door
going out of that to the stairs opened of itself, and he went up
those stairs, and at length brought him to the Furnace mouth
where all the Books and papers had been burnt the 10 day of this
April. And coming thither, there the spiritual Creature did seem

to set one of his feet on the post on the right hand without the Furnace mouth, and with the other to step to the Furnace mouth, and to reach into the Furnace (the bricks now having been plucked away which stopped the mouth of the Furnace, all saving one brick thick) and as he reached into the Furnace there appeared a great light, as if there had been a window in the back of the Furnace, and also to E.K. the hole which was not greater than the thickness of a brick unstopped, did seeme now more than three or four brick thickness wide, and so over his shoulder backward he did reach to E.K. all the rest of the standing books, excepting the book out of which the last Action was cut, and Fr. Pucci his Recantation, also to E.K. appeared in the Furnace all the rest of the papers which were not as then delivered out.

That being done, he bade E.K. go, and said he should have the rest afterward. He went before in a little fiery cloud, and E.K. followed with the Books under his arm all along the Gallery, and came down the stairs by Fr. Pucci his Chamber door, and then his guide left E.K. and he brought me the books unto my place under the Almond-tree.

The characteristics of the "little man" whose feet "seemed not to touch the ground by a foot height", who moved "in a little fiery cloud", and who suddenly went up into the sky "in a great piller of fire" turn up persistently in modern encounter-with-occupant UFO reports.

John Dee gained acceptance at the court of Emperor Rudolph in Prague by presenting him with an illustrated manuscript written in code, supposed to be the work of the 13th. century Franciscan monk, Roger Bacon. Besides being a monk, Bacon was an alchemist whose heretical ideas got him into trouble with ecclesiastical authorities. Among these ideas were extraordinary precognitive insights concerning the microscope, the telescope, the automobile, the submarine, the airplane, the power latent in gunpowder, and the roundness of the earth. Emperor Rudolph was an ardent collector of alchemical manuscripts. After his death, the collection went to the University of Prague. In 1666 this particular manuscript was sent to the Jesuit scholar Athanasius Kircher, who attempted to break the code it was written in, but was apparently unable to do so. He bestowed the manuscript on the Jesuit College in Rome, which passed it on to Mondragone College, run by the same order, in Frascati. There in 1912 it was bought for an undisclosed sum by Wilfrid Voynich, an American rare book dealer, and was known from then on as *The Voynich Manuscript*.

The first thing Voynich did was to have dozens of copies made and to distribute them among recognised academic experts in various fields, asking for their opinions. It was only then that it was realised how extraordinary the manuscript was. Hundreds of illustrations depicted botanical specimens. However, botanists were unable to identify most of the plants depicted. They are plants, but hardly any of them are of kinds that are known to grow on Earth. There are drawings which resemble cellular tissue under magnification, in particular the epithelial cells and their cilia are portrayed with great precision as if seen through a microscope. There are drawings of star clusters and constellations, and of naked ladies. None of the experts consulted could crack the code the manuscript was written in, including those in charge of the cryptological section of United States Military Intelligence. The director of this top secret elite corps known as MI-8, Herbert Osborne Yardley, and his brilliant assistants finally had to admit defeat, referring to it as "the most mysterious manuscript in the world".

However, in 1921 a professor in medieval history and philosophy at the University of Pennsylvania, William Romaine Newbold, claimed to have decoded the manuscript. This claim was disputed by other experts, and flatly rejected by some, but one particular passage of Dr. Newbold's translation attracted considerable attention: "In a concave mirror, I saw a star in the form of a snail between the navel of Pegasus, the girdle of Andromeda, and the head of Cassiopeia." The great spiral nebula of Andromeda is in that precise position, and it just happens to be snail-shaped. The illustration accompanying this passage depicts the Andromeda nebula, but from an angle from which it cannot be seen on Earth. During World War II, the team of government cryptologists who had broken the Japanese Purple Code tried to break the code of the Voynich Manuscript, but like their predecessors during World War I had to admit defeat. In 1946 Dr. Leonell C. Strong claimed to have decoded a portion of the manuscript, which gave a formula for a contraceptive that actually worked. This claim was also disputed, and the mystery of the manuscript remains complete. Is it of extraterrestrial origin, copied by a 13th. century English monk?

Besides the Voynich Manuscript, Dr. John Dee also delivered another mind-blowing out-of-this-world enigma to posterity. In the passage previously quoted from his diary, concerning the incident that occurred in Prague in 1586, three books that had been burned were restored to him in paranormal fashion: *The Book of Enoch, The 48 Claves Angelica,* and *The Book of the Thirty Aires.* All three of those books were essential factors in the transmission of the "Alphabet of the Angels" and the Enochian language formed from it, which Dee described in considerable detail in both his published and his unpublished diaries, and to which he attributed the greatest importance.

We have no way of knowing how Dee originally received or acquired this "Alphabet of the Angels". However, it is possible to reconstruct from the diaries the method he used to develop words, sentences, and meaningful messages from it. In a room which had been prepared according to the rules of ritual magic, Dee sat at a table with the letters of the alphabet spread out before him, arranged in a specific order. Dee's assistant, Edward Kelly, sat at another table, on which was placed a crystal. Within this crystal, Kelly would see what he described as an angel with a wand. The angel would not transmit a letter directly, but would indicate with the wand this or that location in the arranged order, thereby indirectly designating letters and forming words. Dee, Kelly, and the hypothetical occupant of the crystal all believed the letters to be such potent symbols that it would be dangerous to make use of them directly. As an extra precaution, some of the messages were transmitted backwards. After having received them, Dee would then reverse them to obtain their meanings. *The 48 Claves Angelica* and *The Book of the Thirty Aires* consisted of material which had been transmitted in this fashion, and though only a fraction of the total, were nevertheless an important part of it.

At this point, the scientifically minded will be tempted to explain the Enochian language in terms of delusion, hoax, or mere nonsense syllables. However, they should first pause to consider the fact that the Enochian language has not only an alphabet and a vocabulary, but also a grammar and a syntax. It is obvious from both the published and the unpublished diaries that when Dee recorded the indications that Kelly transmitted, he was interested only in the information content of the messages, and demonstrated a nearly total lack of concern about such matters as the language's grammar and syntax.

Edward Kelly was a semi-illiterate thief who had suffered the punishment of having his ears cut off, a professional criminal Dr. Dee had rescued from the gutter because of his psychic abilities, in particular his ability to visualise in crystals. Kelly was a devious person who was accustomed to living by his wits, with a lifetime of practice in the arts of deception. It would have been entirely in character for him to have imposed nonsense syllables on Dr. Dee, claiming an angelic origin and fanciful meanings for them. However, there is no way that someone with Kelly's background could have invented an entirely new and previously unknown language with not only an alphabet and a vocabulary, but also a grammar and a syntax.

The incident in Prague is usually explained as a deception by the rogue, Kelly, of his credulous benefactor, Dr. Dee. But if so, how come the characteristics of the "little man" Dee described surface so persistently in modern UFO reports?

In England toward the end of the 19th century an esoteric group that included such people as W. B. Yeats and Aleister Crowley became intensely interested in the obscure language described in Dr. Dee's almost-forgotten diaries, which had fortunately been preserved in the British Museum. The group was known as the Golden Dawn, and will be discussed at length in a later chapter of this book. Israel Regardie belonged to it, and compiled the definitive compendium of its ceremonies and procedures (*The Golden Dawn*, published by Llewellyn in 1971).

Regardie concurs with the hypothesis expressed by G. R. S. Mead earlier in this chapter, that during deep antiquity a higher type of intelligence came into close contact with primitive terrestrial humanity, thereby stimulating the psyche of our race. Among the stated objectives of the Golden Dawn was this: "that the Grace and Sanctification of the Holy and Glorious Zion may be communicated to the Zion which is on Earth." Regardie indicates the importance to the Golden Dawn of Dr. Dee's diary notes in the following terms: "the Enochian system . . . is the most complicated of the Order sub-systems, and really is used as the basis for synthesizing all the previously given knowledge of the Order. Qabalah, Tarot, Geomancy, skrying, ritual magic, etc. are all drawn together and worked up into a single majestic system." It is clear that in this system the Enochian angelic intelligences are Watchers over the Earth, and are key elements in a complex web of correspondences on many levels permeating all known phenomena. By visualising a pyramid with a missing capstone from above, and then visualising the appropriate Enochian symbol in the square formed where the capstone was missing, the initiated Adept was supposed to be able to project his consciousness out of his body to whatever region corresponded to that symbol.

Regardie's book gives an idea of the complexity of the Enochian correspondences, but does not delve as deeply into the precise details of the system as does *Enochian Magic* by Gerald J. Schueler, published by Llewellyn in 1985. In Schueler's book we learn that the Enochian words inscribed around the circumference of the table on which Kelly did his crystal-gazing had the following meaning: "This is the place of the outpouring of forgotten treasure in the form of ecstasy. Only Fire is substantial here. This is the way of Babalon and of the Beast who is the First Form.* The eyes only need rest upon the name of any guardian and its representative will speedily be encountered."

Schueler warns would-be magicians that "large shaggy sharp-toothed monsters are not the prime danger in magic of this type. The danger is a psychological one, and it is very real indeed. Things will happen to anyone who uses this magic, even if no angels or deities are encountered at all. Just because a magician doesn't see a demon, doesn't mean that the demon isn't there. In the psychic world, thoughts are things. There is no such thing as *only* a thought or *merely* an impulse. If one enters (the square with the Enochian symbol) unprepared and then has terrible nightmares later, or comes down with the flu, or has an unfortunate accident, we are perfectly free to say "coincidence"; but we could also correctly say that this magic brought to fruition certain karmic seeds that lay unconscious until the experience (in the square) germinated them into manifestation."

---

* An alternative translation of this sentence: "This is the way to Kabarel-Tor, where you can contact the Ancient One who keeps his original shape."

For those who wish to investigate this subject more thoroughly, the Llewellyn "Starwares" computer programs make the complex correspondences of the Enochian system much more manageable.

John Clare was an English farm laborer who became famous as "the Peasant Poet" This is from *The Journals, Essays, and the Journey from Essex*, which he wrote about 1830:

The Will O Whisp or Jack Lanthorn

I have often seen those vapours or whatever philosophy may call them but I never witnessed so remarkable an instance of them as I did last night which has robbed me of the little philosophic reasoning which I had about them I now believe them spirits but I will leave the facts to speak for themselves—there had been a great upstir in the town (Helpstone) about the appearance of the ghost of an old woman who had been recently drowned in a well it was said to appear at the bottom of neighbour Billings close in a large white winding sheet dress and the noise exited the curosity of myself & my neighbour to go out several nights together to see if the ghost would be kind enough to appear to us & mend our broken faith in its existence but nothing came on our return we saw a light in the north east over eastwell green & I thought at first it was a bright meoter it presently became larger & seemed like a light in a window it then moved & danced up & down & then glided onward as if a man was riding on horseback at full speed with a lanthorn light soon after this we discovered another rising in the south east on 'deadmoor' they was about a furlong asunder at first & as if the other saw it it danced away as if to join it which it soon did & after dancing together a sort of reel as it were it chased away to its former station & the other followed it like things at play & after suddenly overtaking it they mingled into one in a moment or else one disappeared & sunk in the ground we stood wondering & gazing for a while at the odd phenomenon & then left the willowisp dancing by itself to hunt for a fresh companion as it chose—the night was dusky but not pitch dark & what was rather odd for their appearance the wind blew very briskly it was full west—now these things are generally believed to be vapours rising from the foul air from bogs & wet places where they are generally seen & being as is said lighter than the common air they float about at will—Now this is all very well for Mrs Philosophy who is very knowing but how is it if a vapour lighter than air that it could face the wind which was blowing high & always floated sideways from north to south & back—the wind affected it nothing but I leave all as I find it I have explained the fact as well as I can.

I heard the old alewife at the Exeters arms behind the church (Mrs Nottingham) often say that she has seen from one of her chamber windows as many as fifteen together dancing in & out in a company as if dancing reels & dances on eastwell moor there is a great many there—I have seen several there myself one night when returning home from Ashton on a courting excursion I saw one as if meeting me I felt very terrified & on getting on a stile I determined to wait & see if it was a person with a lanthorn or a will o wisp it came on steadily as if on the pathway & when it got near me within a poles reach perhaps as I thought it made a sudden stop as if to listen to me I then believed it was someone but it blazed out like a whisp of straw and made a crackling noise like straw burning which soon convinced me of its visit the luminous haloo that spread from it was of a mysterious terrific hue & the enlarged size & whiteness of my own hands frit me the rushes appeared to have grown up as large & tall as walebone whips & the bushes seemed to be climbing the sky every thing was extorted out of its own figure & magnified the darkness all round seemed to form a circular black wall & I fancied that if I took a step foreward I should fall into a bottomless gulph which seemed yawing all round me so I held fast by the stilepost till it darted away when I took to my heels & got home as fast as I could so much for will o wisps.

Between 1819 and 1842 the *Journal de Savoie*, a regional newspaper covering south-eastern France, printed a series of articles that strongly resemble modern UFO reports.

Four of the incidents occurred at the town of Chambery.

August 20, 1819, at 2 A.M.: "A luminous meteor, which looked like a globe of fire, crossed the sky. It shone so brightly that it turned night into day, and terrified those who saw it. Some people thought it was the beginning of the end of the world."

Jan. 6, 1829, at 5:30 P.M.: "A luminous meteor passed overhead at low altitude, traveling from north to south. It was quite large, oblong in shape, and left a trail of sparks in its wake like those that come from rockets."

Dec. 12, 1841, between 6 and 7 P.M.: "A fiery meteor was seen by many people. It shone very brightly. It was a fiery globe which left a luminous trail behind it. It made a sort of whistling noise, and then disappeared in mid-air. This meteor was also seen in the Jura region, at Gex, at Rousses, and at Morez."

July 7, 1842, at 6 P.M.: "Men were stacking hay on the slope of Charmettes hill, when they saw very clearly to the east a swiftly traveling fiery meteor, which left a luminous trail behind it. What is remarkable is that it was so clearly visible in broad daylight before sunset."

The *Journal de Savoie* also covered three incidents from across the frontier in Italy.

In October, 1828: "A fiery globe of considerable size was seen over Parma. It traveled from east to west at great speed, and left behind a long trail of all the colors of the rainbow. The phenomenon lasted four seconds."

Again over Parma, in November, 1837: "A very beautiful luminous globe was seen, about three times the size of Venus, emitting a very bright deep blue light as it passed over. It disappeared over the horizon without any explosion or whistling. There was no odor. The sky was clear. There was no wind either before or afterwards."

At Yvree on Oct. 26, 1840: "At 2:20 A.M. the sentinels on guard duty were dazzled by the brilliance of a fiery globe traveling from north to south. The corporal of the guard and the sentinel walking beside him both saw this globe, which seemed to be about three meters in diameter and at an altitude of between 300 and 350 meters. The light emitted by this meteor was extremely bright, and it left a long trail behind it. At 4:05 A.M. another globe, smaller and not as bright, passed over the city. It arrived from the same direction as the first one, but when above the city it was seen to change its direction and go to the east."

The *Journal de Savoie* also printed this report from Switzerland:

Near Basle on Feb. 19, 1842, at 4 A.M. "a remarkable meteor was seen, having the shape of a fiery globe, larger than the moon, traveling from the north-west to the south-east. The next day a similar phenomenon, deep red and in the shape of an ellipse, was seen west of Wurtenberg at 11:15 P.M. It was traveling east almost horizontally, leaving a luminous blue trail behind it."

We now shift the focus of our attention to the American Wild West. Betty Loudon of the Nebraska State Historical Society wrote an article about UFO sightings in Nebraska, which appeared in the Nov. 13, 1985 *Daily Sun* of Beatrice, Nebraska. After discussing some recent sightings, Mrs. Loudon went on to say:

"Reports of similar sightings in almost every section of Nebraska have circulated for many years. In fact, Ralph Umland writing in the 1930's said that "phantom airship parties" were held in many Nebraska communities, as early as the 1890's, so that people might watch the strange phenomenon.

But probably the most unusual tale of all surfaced on June 8, 1884 when the *Daily State Journal* at Lincoln printed the following:

Benkelman, June 7. A most remarkable phenomenon occurred about 1 o'clock yesterday afternoon at a point thirty-five miles northwest of this place. John W. Ellis, a well-known ranchman, was going out to his herd in company with three of his herders and several other cowboys engaged in the annual roundup. While riding along a draw they heard a terrific rushing, roaring noise overhead, and looking up, saw what appeared to be a blazing meteor of immense size falling at an angle to the earth. A moment later it struck the ground out of sight over the bank. Scrambling up the steep hill they saw the object bounding along half a mile away and disappear into another draw. Galloping toward it with all their speed, they were astounded to see several fragments of cogwheels and other pieces of machinery lying on the ground, scattered in the path made by the aerial visitor, glowing with heat so intense as to scorch the grass for a long distance around each fragment and make it impossible for one to approach it. Coming to the edge of the deep ravine into which the strange object had fallen, they undertook to see what it was. But the heat was so great that the air about it was fairly ablaze and it emitted a light so dazzling that the eye could not rest upon it more than a moment. An idea of the heat may be gained from the fact that one of the party, a cowboy named Alf Williamson, stood with his head incautiously exposed over the bank, and in less than half a minute he fell senseless. His face was desperately blistered and his hair singed to a crisp. His condition is said to be dangerous. The distance from the aerolite, or whatever it is, was nearly 200 feet. The burned man was taken to Mr. Ellis' house, cared for as well as circumstances would allow and a doctor sent for. His brother, who lives in Denver, has just been telegraphed for.

Finding it impossible to approach the mysterious visitor, the party turned back on its trail. Where it first touched the earth the ground was sandy and bare of grass. The sand was fused to an unknown depth over a space about twenty feet wide by eighty feet long, and the melted stuff was still bubbling and hissing. Between this and the final resting place there were several other like spots where it had come in contact with the ground, but none so well marked.

This morning another visit was made to the spot. In the party were E. W. Rawlings, brand inspector for this district, who came into Benkelman tonight, and from whom a full verification of particulars is obtained. The smaller portions of the scattered machinery had cooled so that they could be approached, but not handled. One piece that looked like the blade of a propellor screw, of a metal in appearance like brass, about sixteen inches wide, three inches thick and three and a half feet long, was picked up on a spade. It would not weigh more than five pounds, but appeared as strong and compact as any known metal. A fragment of a wheel with a milled rim, apparently having had a diameter of seven or eight feet, was also picked up. It seeed to be of the same material and had the same remarkable lightness.

The aerolite, or whatever it is, seems to be about fifty or sixty feet long, cylindrical, and about ten or twelve feet in diameter. Great excitement exists in the vicinity and the round-up is suspended while the cowboys wait for the wonderful find to cool off so they can examine it.

Mr. Ellis is here and will take the first train to the land office with the intention of securing the land on which the strange thing lies, so that his claim to it cannot be disputed.

A party left here for the scene an hour ago, and will travel all night. The country in the vicinity is rather wild and rough, and the roads are hardly more than trails. Will telegraph all particulars as fast as obtained.

The *Daily State Journal* printed its final report on the incident on June 10, 1884, with these headlines:

The Magical Meteor
It Dissolves Like a Drop of Dew Before the Morning Sun
The Most Mysterious Element of the Strange Phenomenon

Special to the State Journal. Benkelman, June 9, 1884. Your correspondent has just returned from the spot where the aerial visitor fell last Friday. It is gone, dissolved into air. A tremendous rain storm fell yesterday afternoon, beginning about 2 o'clock. As it approached, in regular blizzard style, most of those assembled to watch the mysterious visitor fled to shelter. A dozen or more, among whom was your correspondent, waited to see the effect of the rain upon the glowing metal. The storm came down from the north, on its crest a sheet of flying spray and a torrent of rain. It was impossible to see more than a rod through the driving, blinding mass. It lasted for half an hour, and when it slackened so that the aerolite should have been visible it was no longer there. The draw was running three feet deep in water, and supposing it had floated off the strange vessel the party crossed over at the risk of their lives.

They were astounded to find that the queer object had melted, dissolved by the water like a spoonful of salt. Scarcely a vestige of it remained. Small, jelly-like pools stood here and there on the ground, but under the eyes of the observers these grew thinner and thinner till they were but muddy water joining the rills that led to the current a few feet away. The air was filled with a faint sweetish smell.

The whole affair is bewildering to the highest degree, and will no doubt forever remain a mystery.

Alf Williamson, the injured cowboy, left today for Denver, accompanied by his brother. It is feared he will never recover his eyesight, but otherwise he does not appear to be seriously injured.

In my opinion, the storm was artificially created so that a UFO concealed within the clouds could retrieve the wreckage of the crashed UFO.

It is well-known that there was an epidemic of strange objects being sighted in the sky during the spring of 1897 all across the United States. Many of the bizarre stories that emerged from this brief but wide-spread intense outburst of unidentified aerial activity have been refused serious consideration on the grounds that they were exaggerated or fictitious accounts, dreamed up by unscrupulous journalists trying to outdo each other with sensational headlines. However, as the following quotation from an editorial run by *The Kansas City Star* on March 28, 1897, shows, some journalists were more concerned with playing down the story than with exploiting it:

"The planet Venus, which is now 26 million miles from the earth . . . has been taken by credulous correspondents in various parts of Kansas for a fully equipped airship cruising about among the clouds within a mile of the earth's surface. These correspondents, with more imagination than astronomy, have telegraphed stories to various Kansas City and St. Louis newspapers describing the monster. . . . Some of the correspondents say that it is supposed that this harmless planet, which is the nearest neighbor of earth, is an airship of the British War Department, spying through the country for fortifications. Friday night members of one family in Kansas City, Kan., declared that they saw the strange craft of the air with the blazing beacon of light. The story was passed from mouth to mouth and last evening hundreds of people of the city viewed the planet with awe, and the question on every lip was: "Have you seen the airship?" It disappeared from view about 9:30 o'clock."

Among these stories was one which was long dismissed as a hoax: that a cigar-shaped UFO had crashed near Aurora, Texas, on April 19, 1897, leaving the badly-mangled body of a "small man" among debris at the site of the explosion. According to surviving witnesses of the incident, the object had struck the windlass over the water well on Judge Proctor's farm, exploding with a chain reaction that had caused a flash vivid enough to have been visible over three miles away. On the same day that the crash took place, the body of the small pilot had been buried in the local cemetery.

Bill Case is the Texas director for the Mutual UFO Network. Instead of dismissing this as a fictitious account dreamed up by an unscrupulous journalist, Mr. Case decided to thoroughly check it out, using sophisticated scientific equipment and a team of academically qualified experts in diverse fields. These methods promptly located the crash site at about 100 feet from the well on what had been Judge Proctor's property. The team began to collect a variety of metal scraps. Bill Case made the following statement in the New York *News World* of Jan. 8, 1983: "From all indications there was definitely an explosion. The pattern established by metals recovered indicate the craft exploded on the lower right side first, blowing bits and pieces over a two or three acre area east and northeast of the well site on top of a rocky limestone hill. Immediately the rest of the craft exploded, throwing other samples to the north and west."

Although it is possible that some of these fragments may have been left behind by the generations of farmers who had lived at this location, some of them were scientifically demonstrated to have very unusual properties.

The team of scientists checked out one fragment with an electron dispersion x-ray analyzer, reporting it to be pure aluminum with a small trace of iron, which had been in a molten state when it impacted against the limestone rock. They also tried x-ray fluorescence analysis, and found that the sample did not contain any zinc or copper at all, not even in trace amounts. Copper is normally included with iron as an alloy in standard operating procedures to manufacture aluminum in industry as we know it. The sample was a crystalline structure of high purity that was stress-free, conforming to the shape of the rock it had been found embedded in, and must have been molten on impact.

Bill Case and his team went to the local cemetery and found the headstone. Instrument readings taken at the grave strongly indicated the presence of something unusual; the readings were similar to the strong unmistakable readings recorded at the site of the explosion. Mr. Case requested permission from the local authorities to dig up the grave. This permission was refused, and the headstone was removed, leaving the grave unmarked.

As we go to press, that is the actual situation. Anyone with ideas about how to persuade the local authorities to change their minds should contact Bill Case at the Mutual UFO Network, 103 Oldtowne Road, Seguin, Texas 78155.

Antonio Ribera was in charge of the first Spanish archaeological and submarine exploration expedition to investigate Easter Island, during March and April of 1975. An unexpected result of his investigation was an abundance of local UFO reports. I translated the following passages from his article, which appeared in the April 1976 issue of *Vues Nouvelles*:

Let us pass on the actual UFO sightings. It is an odd fact that they are all situated within a triangle whose sides are included in the zone between Rano Ravaku and the "ditch of the Hanau eepe", which divides the main body of the island from the Poike peninsula and continues to Hano oonu. All the sightings that I studied took place within this small area.

It is necessary to bear in mind a remarkable peculiarity which Easter Island has: "a major magnetic disturbance", which is situated on the northern coast, in the grandiose and desolate

Maungo Terevaka territory, which is still largely unexplored, next to Ranoi Oro volcano. Ranoi Oro, which was responsible for the 4th century catastrophe, has an altitude of 600 meters and is the highest point on the island. This magnetic disturbance is indicated on several maps. For example, the nautical map made by the Hydrographic Institute of the Chilean Army (which we were using on a scale of 1:50,000) indicates the zone in question with "strong magnetic disturbances on this coast".

These disturbance may be so strong that they completely alter the functioning of gyropilots and compasses in the Lan-Chile airplanes which make weekly flights to Mataveri Airport.

We know of other regions of the world where similar magnetic disturbances occur. One of them is none other than the Nazca plateau, where the mysterious and famous figures visible only from the sky are located, on the Peruvian coast. Another is on Canigou mountain in the French Pyrenees. Yet another is at Tindouff, in the Algerian Sahara, near the Moroccan frontier. There are other such points in the world, but it is difficult to explain such an anomaly on Easter Island, which is entirely volcanic. Is it possible that there might be a gigantic ferro-nickel meteorite buried in the region of Maunga Terevaka? It is a mystery.

Perhaps a ferro-nickel meteorite, or perhaps some unusual equipment not made by human hands? This is an excerpt from one of the contemporary UFO reports that Antonio Ribera found himself collecting along with the data from antiquity his expedition was designed to investigate:

Between 9 and 10 at night a luminous object appeared about 100 meters above the summit of Rano Ravaku volcano. It was rather large, between ten and twenty meters in diameter. It emitted multicolored rainbow flashes frequently. I saw objects enter it and leave it; from far away they looked like birds, but they were probably small machines or bodies.

Why is UFO activity so clandestine? Why do they conceal their bases in volcanic areas, on the ocean floor, and under the polar ice caps? When the existing data was fed into computers, one of the significant patterns to emerge was that there were more sightings between midnight and dawn than during the rest of the day, and most landings took place in sparsely populated areas. But as the Cro-Magnon drawings in the caves of the Pyrenees demonstrate, they have been sharing this planet with us at least since Palaeolithic times.

The boat of Ra, the boat of the sun, the boat of millions of years may not be confined to Egyptian mythology. It may still be very much with us, and have a decisive part to play in our present-day reality.

Chapter Three

THE BOAT OF MILLIONS OF YEARS

The puzzling relics left behind by certain civilisations that came into being, flourished, and disappeared in deep antiquity have inspired much fantastic speculation. Modern science has been quite properly skeptical about wild theories impossible to verify, but has also displayed a tendency to be most improperly cynical about them, dismissing them almost automatically as unworthy of consideration after only superficial examination, which is not a valid scientific attitude.

So many extravagant theories have been proposed concerning the Great Pyramid in Egypt that they tend to obscure the remarkable and scientifically demonstrable facts that are known about it. Peter Tompkins has performed a public service by sorting out the facts actually known about this extraordinary structure from the tangle of conflicting theories. The following is from his *Secrets of the Great Pyramid*, published by Allen Lane (Penguin) in 1973:

Recent studies of ancient Egyptian hieroglyphs and the cuneiform mathematical tablets of the Babylonians and Sumerians have established that an advanced science did flourish in the

Middle East at least three thousand years before Christ, and that Pythagoras, Eratosthenes, Hipparchus and other Greeks reputed to have originated mathematics on this planet merely picked up fragments of an ancient science evolved by remote and unknown predecessors.

The Great Pyramid, like most of the great temples of antiquity, was designed on the basis of a hermetic geometry known only to a restricted group of initiates, mere traces of which percolated to the Classical and Alexandrian Greeks.

These and other recent discoveries have made it possible to reanalyze the entire history of the Great Pyramid with a whole new set of references: the results are explosive. The common—and indeed authoritative—assumption that the Pyramid was just another tomb built to memorialize some vainglorious Pharaoh is proved to be false.

For a thousand years men from many occupations and many stations have labored to establish the true purpose of the Pyramid. Each in his own way has discovered some facet, each in its own way valid. Like Stonehenge and other megalithic calendars, the Pyramid has been shown to be an almanac by means of which the length of the year, including its awkward .2422 fraction of a day, could be measured as accurately as with a modern telescope. It has been shown to be a theodolite, or instrument for the surveyor, of great precision and simplicity, virtually indestructible. It is still a compass so finely oriented that modern compasses are adjusted to it, not vice versa.

It has also been established that the Great Pyramid is a carefully located geodetic marker, or fixed landmark, on which the geography of the ancient world was brilliantly constructed; that it served as a celestial observatory from which maps and tables of the stellar hemisphere could be accurately drawn; and that it incorporates in its sides and angles the means for creating a highly sophisticated map projection of the northern hemisphere. It is, in fact, a scale model of the hemisphere, correctly incorporating the geographical degrees of latitude and longitude.

The Pyramid may well be the repository of an ancient and possibly universal system of weights and measures, the model for the most sensible system of linear and temporal measurements available on earth, based on the polar axis of rotation, a system first postulated in modern times a century ago by the British astronomer Sir John Herschel, whose accuracy is now confirmed by the mensuration of orbiting satellites.

Whoever built the Great Pyramid, it is now quite clear, knew the precise circumference of the planet, and the length of the year to several decimals—data which were not rediscovered till the seventeenth century. Its architects may well have known the mean length of the earth's orbit around the sun, the specific gravity of the planet, the 26,000 year cycle of the equinoxes, the acceleration of gravity and the speed of light.

But to disentangle the authentic from the phony in what has been attributed to the builders of the Great Pyramid has required the technique of a Sherlock Holmes.

Two British researchers, M. W. Saunders and Duncan Lunan, have investigated the puzzle of the Great Pyramid in the tradition of Sherlock Holmes, and have come up with some extraordinary results in their *Destiny Mars* (Downs Books, Caterham, Surrey, 1975).

Using a computer to compare known pyramid data with known astronomical data, they discovered that the alignment of the Cheops Pyramid with the Pyramid of the Sun in Teotihuacan, Mexico, defines an orbital period which locks with the rotation of Mars. They are of the opinion that these two pyramids are geodetic markers indicating the location of information banks, and have found a multiplicity of correlations between astronomical measurements concerning Mars (as generally accepted among astronomers) and measurements concerning the Cheops Pyramid (as generally accepted among Egyptologists). Saunders and Lunan found subtle complex methematical games in the relationship between the Cheops Pyramid and Mars that had been played according to the rules of sophisticated science, an elegantly interwoven network of cross-correspondences which dates from deep antiquity. For further details, see the Appendix.

When the Viking spacecraft orbited Mars in 1977, among the pictures that came back was one that included a gigantic Sphinx-like stone face, staring straight upward, as if designed to be seen from above. About ten miles away was a rectangular pyramid, approximately 1 mile wide and 1.6 miles long, dwarfing our Great Pyramid, with precisely defined sides and corners, one of which points due Martian north. The stone face is about 1 mile long. Pyramids were discovered at another location on Mars by the Mariner 9 space shot. NASA dismissed the stone face as a trick of lighting, a freak reflection, and still sticks to that explanation, in spite of the fact that a second photo of it turned up on a different pass, and in spite of the developments about to be described. The pyramids are explained away as having been produced by "wind faceting" or "shifting of subterranean plates", about as convincing as explaining away UFOs as weather balloons or flocks of geese.

An electrical engineer and a computer scientist, Vincent Di Pietro and Gregory Molenaar, made history by submitting the "trick of light" to digital computer analysis, enlarging the facial features, which they found to exhibit *bilateral symmetry*. Hairline, mouth, eye cavity, and eyeball are clearly visible. The odds against that occurring by chance are close to infinite. It is a full frontal view of a face. Di Pietro and Molenaar have told the story of this extremely important discovery in their book *Unusual Martian Surface Features*, published by Mars Research, P.O. Box 284, Glenn Dale, Maryland 20769, in 1982. The way NASA kept misplacing, and misfiling and losing track of the photos required for their research seems extraordinary to say the least, but enough material did come through to enable Di Pietro and Milenaar to prove that the great stone face is not a trick of light: it is real.

Richard Hoagland is a former NASA consultant to the Goddard Space Center, who in collaboration with Eric Burgess created the plaque carried into outer space by Pioneer 10, which was intended to make contact with extra-terrestrial intelligent beings, indicating the basic characteristics of our species and our location in the galaxy. He has become involved in the research pioneered by Di Pietro and Molenaar. His book, entitled *The Monuments of Mars*, is about to be released by Prentice-Hall. When interviewed by Jeff Greenwald in the San Francisco *Examiner & Chronicle* of July 14, 1985, Hoagland made the statements that are summarised here:

While inspecting the NASA photos depicting the controversial Great Stone Face, he noticed that a few miles southwest of the Face there was a collection of very organised pyramidal objects. The more he looked at them, the more their form and organisation became apparent. Furthermore, they were not just approximately to the left, they were in perfect alignment with the eyes and mouth of the Face. These objects that related geometrically implied a conscious design. The archipelago of features southwest of the Face contains an almost perfect pentagon of mountains shaped like pyramids, and a triangular object in the vicinity of two nearly perpendicular walls. The pentagon and the triangle form the base of a triangle whose apex is the Face. Half a million years ago, sunrise at the summer solstice would have been in alignment with the Face. Although Mars no longer has an atmosphere or surface water, there are indications that it once did.

If a line through the Earth from the Great Pyramid at Giza to the Pyramid of the Sun at Teotihuacan does in fact define an orbital period which locks with the rotation of Mars, that in itself constitutes irrefutable evidence that we had visitors from the cosmos during deep antiquity who left their mark on this planet, who sealed it with their seal.

Besides its permanent markings, Mars has a history of persistent but transient anomalous phenomena. There is the blue haze that at irregular intervals suddenly comes or goes. Astronomical observers for over a century have repeatedly reported both extraordinary bright spots and intensely dark spots, temporary in nature. One series of observations was made by a highly respected Japanese astronomer, at first on Jan. 15, 1950. Tsuneo Saheki had specialised in the observation of Mars since 1933, so his statement was made against a background of seventeen years of professional study. What Saheki saw on Jan. 15, 1950, was a brilliant glow, as of an explosion, that lasted for several minutes, and was followed by a luminous yellow-gray cloud, estimated to be from 60 to 120 miles high and 465 miles in diameter. Then on Dec. 1, 1951, Saheki saw a brilliant flare that attained the brightness of a sixth-magnitude star and lasted for five minutes. As V.A. Firsoff points out in *Life Beyond Earth*, Basic Books, 1963: "No terrestrial volcano could produce a light of such brilliance; a megaton hydrogen bomb could." Saheki cautiously raised the possibility that he might have witnessed nuclear explosions.

Clearly defined, brilliant but temporary, bright spots that sometimes moved or changed color were reported by astronomers in 1890, 1892, 1894, 1900, 1911, 1924, 1937, 1952, 1954, 1967 and 1971. When approximate locations were marked on a map of Mars, their distribution was obviously non-random. Intensely dark spots, transient in nature, were observed in 1925, 1952 and 1954.

Another puzzle is the grooves on Phobos, which turns out to be much older than Mars, and from a different region of the cosmos. Among the possibilities to be considered is the possibility that the grooves might have been made by cables during the transport process, when Phobos was being steered into its very special orbit. The types of entities who did that steering may still be around.

High priority should be given to finding out whether the information satellites hypothesized by Saunders and Lunan actually exist and are retrievable.

Are there information banks from a previous high civilisation hidden here on earth? Could this be the meaning of the legends that recur in different traditions about sleeping heroes with invincible weapons, or magic treasures concealed by the lotus-born guru for the hour of greatest need during the crisis of world renewal at the end of the era?

The Norwegian version of this quasi-universal myth was put in a nutshell by A. Nutt in his *Upon the Irish Vision of the Happy Otherworld*, published in 1895:

The Volospa summarizes the history of the universe in terms of Norse mythology. It describes the creation of the material universe, the creation of man, the strife among the god clans with its consequent train of moral and physical ills, culminating in the final disappearance of the present order, divine as well as human, to make way for a brighter and better world. But where were the inhabitants of this world to come from? The survival of part of the kin of the gods is expressly provided for. How about man? The existing race is *ex hypothesi* corrupt and unfit to inhabit the new universe. Provision is therefore made for the seclusion of a human pair, Lif and Leifthraser, before the human race has suffered corruption, in a land into which death cannot enter, a land free from all ills, from which, after the final catastrophe which is to overwhelm both Asgard and Midgard, i. e. the existing politics both of gods and men, they are to issue and repeople the Universe. This land is Odainsakr, the acre of the not dead, *jord lifanda manna*, the earth of living men. It is guarded by the seven sons of Mimer, the giant smiths who fashioned the primeval weapons and ornaments; these, sunk in deep sleep, which shall last until the Dusk of the gods, when they awake to take their part in the final conflict between the powers of good and evil, and to ensure the existence of Odainsakr, rest in a hall wherein are preserved a number of products of their skill as smiths, as also Heimdall's horn, the blast of which is to summon the gods and their allies against the impious kin of Loki. The mortals who have penetrated thither and sought to carry off these objects, necessary in the final conflict, or to waken the sleepers before the destined time when, Asgard and its inmates having disappeared, upon them alone rests the hope of a rejuvenated world, these mortals are punished by death or dire disease.

One of the possible interpretations of the above text is that the sleeping giants refer to our latent long-dormant ESP abilities being galvanised into action by a very particular set of circumstances, a specific emergency situation which has been foreseen and prepared for. An end-of-the-world type of situation such as is at present staring humanity right in the face. The same government leaders who suppress information concerning UFOs are deliberately making the nightmare of nuclear war impossible to avoid. The politicians in charge of our destinies are setting us up for the ultimate disaster. Us, and all other forms of life on this planet, for nuclear war will destroy the biosphere of Earth if it is allowed to happen. In this nightmare situation, extra-terrestrials are the wild card in the game, the joker in the pack, the hidden variable which can change the whole picture. Symbols of the boat of Ra, the boat of the sun, the boat of millions of years may be gathering dust in our museums, but the real thing is hovering above our heads. Sooner or later, whether we like it or not, we are going to have to come to terms with it. The politicans in charge of our nations are no longer all-powerful. They can ignore the wishes of the masses of humanity almost completely, but there is no way they can continue to pretend that the alien humanoids who have this planet under surveillance do not exist. Too many people from all over the world have now had first-hand experience with UFO phenomena, having seen it with their own eyes, and the numbers grow each day.

Abductions which involve physical examinations occur with ever-increasing frequency. On Nov. 28, 1980 a British policeman in Todmorden, Yorkshire, was abducted while on duty, given a physical examination by aliens, and then retuned to his patrol car. There is ample documentation available demonstrating the widespread abundance of human abduction cases.

Missing Time by Budd Hopkins (Marek, 1981) is the

best book out on the subject so far. Hopkins collaborates with professional psychiatrists and psychologists in researching the cases, and his integrity is above reproach. In his opinion, the abductions that have been investigated represent only the tip of the iceberg. They are far more widespread than is generally believed. He suspects that the human abductions which have not been reported may number in the hundreds of thousands. After the publication of his first book, he was deluged with so many reports that he has only been able to investigate a small proportion of them. Approximately 90% of the entities described by the people he has investigated are of the short large-headed type. In his second book, now in preparation, Hopkins explores the possibility that these abductions are part of a genetic experiment on an enormous scale, being carried out on terrestrial humanity by extra-terrestrial humanoids. I am in agreement with his hypothesis, but point out that this experiment is also on an enormous scale in time, definitely going back at least as far as the Sumerians, and probably going back to the sudden appearance of Cro-Magnon man, if not before.

David Webb is another reputable and scrupulously careful researcher into the activities of extra-terrestrial humanoids. His analysis of the 1973 UFO/humanoid wave (*1973: Year of the Humanoids*, published by the Center for UFO Studies in 1976) is meticulously documented and free of the sensationalism which distorts most accounts of such activities in the popular press. At the 1985 MUFON Symposium in St. Louis, Webb reported his findings concerning abduction cases, based on his investigation of 129 cases:

About a third of the people who have been abducted are able to remember the experience without being regressed under hypnosis. Slightly more than half of them are unable to remember the experience at all until they are regressed under hypnois. The reported appearance, behavior, and number of entities, as well as the duration of the abductions, appear to be independent of the use of hypnosis. Basic details of the physical environment (the inside of the UFO) during the abduction experience are remarkably similar in the different accounts. In about two-thirds of the cases, the person was alone when abducted. In about one-third, others were also abducted. Men are abducted slightly more often than women, but both sexes are almost equally represented.

Returning now to my own discussion of the subject, it looks as if UFO occupants are helping themselves to generous samples of our population. In many of the abduction cases, the people have been returned to the region from which they were picked up, sometimes under shock after the deep probing of a physical examination, which may include the taking of tissue samples and the insertion of implants, such as we insert in wild animals we wish to study. Not all abductions involve physical examinations, but many of them do. There are sharp contrasts in the attitudes of different types of UFO occupants towards the humans they examine. Some types conduct the examination procedure in a considerate fashion, demonstrating concern for human well-being and attempting to minimise the trauma. Other types make the examination a nightmare, treating humans like our scientists treat laboratory animals.

There have been some cases, only a few in comparison to the total number but undeniably existing, in which abducted humans did not return but disappeared permanently, or were found dead after a UFO encounter. There have been cases in which people suffered severe physical injuries of various kinds from exposure to UFO phenomena. Some of these may be due more to the nature of the force-field the UFO operates in than to hostile intent on the part of the occupants. Many of the injuries are of a type that would be caused by over-exposure to microwave radiation. Sensations of physical heat, sometimes described as unbearable, are frequently reported by close-encounter UFO witnesses. An area of grass over which a UFO had hovered was found to have this peculiarity: the blades of grass above the surface of the ground appeared to be undamaged, yet the roots beneath the ground were burnt to ashes. After a landing took place in New Zealand, bushes which had been affected were examined by a horticulturist, who reported: "The shrub is radioactive and has been cooked instantaneously from the inside outward. I know of no earthly source of energy which could produce this effect . . . Some kind of high-frequency radiation cooked the material from the inside outward. The energy received reduced the pith to black carbon, without the outside showing any kind of burning . . . A meteorite or lightning would not do this, and it was too sudden for combustion." (*Flying Saucer Review*, Jan/Feb. 1969). What happened to the bushes in New Zealand may be what happened to the human beings in the category of case histories known as "spontaneous human combustion", a rare but persistently recurring phenomenon for which it is difficult to find a plausible explanation. Typically, a person's body or portions thereof is burnt to ashes without burning the clothes the person happens to be wearing.

In 687 B.C. Sennacherib, King of Assyria, led his enormous army against the Hebrews and laid siege to Jerusalem. A "blast from heaven" reduced the bodies of 185,000 Assyrian soldiers to ashes but left their clothes intact.

In modern times targets for microwave radiation at an intensity which reduces flesh to ashes while leaving clothes intact appear to be selected at random. Frequently, but not always, the victims are elderly people who live alone. One woman who had committed suicide was struck after she was dead, her corpse half-consumed by fire although it was in a closed coffin at the time.

Witchcraft in the sense of projection of the etheric body for destructive purposes may be a valid explanation for those cases in which UFO activity seems unlikely. Perhaps under certain circumstances concentrated hatred or anger may manifest as extreme heat.

Emission of microwave energy at lower levels of intensity paralyses humans or animals temporarily without doing permanent damage. UFO-related cases of temporary paralysis are reported far more frequently than "spontaneous human combustion" or severe burns. UFO occupants have been described as possessing an instrument about the size of a ball-point pen which can be adjusted to either temporarily paralyse or "spontaneously combust" the target indicated.

It should not be forgotten that there are a few well-authenticated cases of UFO activity being responsible for healing the sick and even rejuvenating the aged. A Wyoming rancher who followed alien instructions after a series of close encounters and dug a well at the spot indicated tapped an abundant water source which transformed his barren land into a fertile farm. Angels and demons may turn out to be far more real than almost anyone in recent years imagined.

One puzzling feature in some of the cases of spontaneous human combustion is the lack of outcry, as if the victim had been hypnotised or anesthetised. This is a detail that was first mentioned by Charles Fort, who pioneered research into unexplained phenomena ignored by dogmatic scientists long before it became fashionable to do so, during the 1920s. He devoted serious study to the subject of UFOs decades before this became a popular pastime, and his point of view remains of fundamental relevance to the present situation.

APPENDIX TO CHAPTER THREE

From *Destiny Mars* by M. W. Saunders and Duncan Lunan (Downs Books, Caterham, Surrey, England, 1975):

It has in recent years been proposed that civilisations (wherever they might emerge in the universe) might very likely destroy themselves when they reach the stage where nuclear, germ, or chemical wars become possible. It may be reasoned that if new civilisations could make contact with advanced civilisations in distant planetary systems, then they might possibly learn how to overcome the self-destruction phenomenon. But maybe this kind of contact is technically likely only at a stage of civilisation considerably later than the time when self-destruction is likely. . . .

When a civilisation with nuclear explosives has reached the point where satellites can be accurately placed and retrieved, then it has reached a stage where self-destruction with nuclear (multi-headed) orbital craft is possible.

If information is placed such that it can be retrieved only by a civilisation which can reach and recover satellites, then it follows that this information can be retrieved by civilisations which (assuming they possess nuclear weapons) have the power to destroy themselves by using orbiting nuclear weapons. . . .

A straight line extended from the Pyramid of Cheops in Egypt, through the Pyramid of the Sun in Mexico and continued into space, intersects the equatorial plane at a height of about 20,884.2 kilometers.

A straight line started from a point on the ground at unit length from the middle of the north side of the Pyramid of Cheops, and extended through the summit of the pyramid, intersects the equatorial plane at a height of about 20,888.2 kilometers. This height, when expressed in the builders' unit of length, is only about 0.17% shorter than forty million such units of length.

The Pyramid of Cheops, the greatest pyramid in the Old

World, is reckoned to be more than 4,000 years old; and it was constructed with very considerable precision. It has been estimated to contain about 2.3 million stone blocks, each averaging 2.5 tons.

The Pyramid of the Sun, the greatest pyramid in the New World, is reckoned to be less than 2,000 years old; and an investigation tunnel has indicated that, unlike most Mexican pyramids, it was probably built in one operation. This pyramid is a brick construction faced with dressed stone, and its baselength is about 9% less than that of the Pyramid of Cheops. It is situated in Teotihuacan, which was then an important city with, it appears, none of the human sacrifices practised in other parts of Mexico . . .

The ancient main street of Teotihuacan is wide, and runs parallel to the western side of the Pyramid of the Sun. It is about 2 km. in length; the pyramid being about three-quarters of the way along from the south, and conveniently to one side. The street could make an ideal aircraft runway for visiting this pyramid. If Teotihuacan had visitors who for most of the time wished to minimise their influence on mankind, they would probably have kept out of the way by using, for example, a remote island base. The orientation of the main street of Teotihuacan is about 15 degrees west of south, and consequently points to within about two degrees of a suitable island—Easter Island. . . .

There is a possibility that ancient civilisations were caused to temporarily excel their pyramid-building abilities, in such a way as to produce long-lasting markers.

These markers could indicate the orbiting height of a large number of very small satellites, each one of which could contain the same advice about the location of information depositories.

Guidance provided in this way would become available on discovering how to retrieve satellites; this being at the very stage of development when there would be a threat of self-destruction by orbital weapons—a threat which might arise even in civilisations which, in the main, were progressing on good lines.

This system would reduce the possibility of a civilisation receiving guidance if it had little interest in conservation, since the markers might then get destroyed before their meaning could be understood. . . .

There seem to be relationships between the Great Pyramid, the Martian moons, and the largest volcanoes on Earth and Mars. These appear to pin-point exact sites on Mars, Phobos and Jupiter

V. . . .

Duncan Lunan was the first to discover the connection between the pyramids and Mars; by observing that the alignment of the Great Pyramid with the Pyramid of the Sun in Mexico defined an orbital period which locked with the rotation of Mars. . . .

If a data bank was set up, it could have been arranged that the manner of indication would not be understood until nuclear war in space (again) became possible. Things could also have been such that unless mankind "made the grade" the indication system would not be preserved. As it turns out, the Great Pyramid has been almost stripped of its outward precision, and has survived more by luck than by concern. And society as a whole seems unwilling to accept that there is, or has ever been, any advanced civilisation other than the present one. . . .

Great Pyramid:

1. The Great Pyramid at Giza is a 2π pyramid. It weighs about 6 million tons; and was constructed . . . very early in the known period of civilisation.

2. The north slope of the Great Pyramid points to a height above the equator equal to 2π times the equatorial radius of Mars. (Error: 0.5%).

Volcanoes:

3. The latitude of the largest volcano on Earth (Hawaii) is about 0.6° above 19° N; and its longitude is, in effect, almost opposite that of the Great Pyramid.

4. The latitude of the largest volcano on Mars is about 0.6° below 19° N.

Satellite Heights:

5. Deimos orbits Mars at a mean height equal to π times the Earth's equatorial radius (Error: 0.32%).

6. Phobos orbits Mars at the same height as the π satellite (hypothetical information satellite orbiting the Earth).

Satellite Revolutions:

7. Phobos orbits Mars π times for every rotation of Earth. (Error: about 0.5%).

8. If a satellite orbited Earth at the same height as Phobos, it would revolve 2π times for every rotation of Earth. (Error: about 0.5%).

9. Deimos orbits Mars $\pi/4$ times for every rotation of Earth. (Error: about 0.5%).

10. If a satellite orbited Earth at the same height as Deimos, it would revolve twice for every rotation of Earth. (Error: about 0.5%).

Planet Distances:

11. The mean Earth-Sun distance equals 1000 million times the height of the Great Pyramid. (Error: 2%).

12. The mean Mars-Sun Distance equals 1000 million times the baselength of the Great Pyramid. (Error: 1%).

13. The maximum Mars-Earth distance equals 1000 million times the Great Pyramid's baselength plus height. (Error: 0.14%).

14. The Cubit equals the Mars-Earth Indicated Baselength divided by 440, which equals 0.524279 m. (Errors: (a) 0.14% longer than Pyramid baselength divided by 440. (b) 0.04% longer than Petrie's "King's Chamber" cubit. (c) 0.01% longer than a cubit determined by the north baselength of the King's Chamber).

Internal Dimensions:

15. The orbital eccentricity of Mars equals the displacement of the centre of the King's Chamber from the east-west centre-line, divided by the mean semibase. (Error: 0.0023%).

16. The ratio of the equatorial diameter of Mars to that of Earth equals the distance separating the access corridor from the west side, expressed as a ratio of the mean baselength. (Error: 0.16%).

17. The slope of the Great Pyramid equals the Earth's equatorial radius plus the Moon's equatorial radius divided by the Earth's equatorial radius. (Error: 0.06%).

18. The perimeter of the Great Pyramid equals the length of half a minute of a degree of longitude at the equator. (Error: 0.67%).

19. The Earth's polar radius divided by ten million equals the baselength of the Great Pyramid divided by the number of days in a year. (Error: 0.77%).

If the organisers intended that knowledge should be obtained only if the pyramids on Earth had been preserved, then it follows that information might be located such that it would be found, not by accident, but only as a result of its being deliberately sought in an area indicated.

NOTE: A recent article by Maurice Chatelain ("Our Mexican Ancestors" in *Pursuit*, vol. 18, no. 2, whole no. 70, pp. 78-84) gives Saunders and Lunan long-overdue credit for their discoveries. Chatelain also states that the enormous Sumerian number found in the library of Assurbanipal, when translated from seconds into days, becomes 2268 million days. He then points out that the Grand Avenue at Teotihuacan had a length of 2268 ancient Mexican yards, and that the dimensions in ancient Mexican yards of all the city's buildings (as well as of all the intervals between the buildings) were exact fractions of 2268. He goes on to say that: "The archeological complex of Teotihuacan was an important center of religious observance, but it was also a remarkable astronomical observatory and a fantastic cosmic computer. Recent discoveries show that every dimension of the sacred city had an astronomical or mathematical meaning; and several of these dimensions were so interrelated as to replicate some of the constants of nuclear physics used by contemporary scientists. . . . Obviously Teotihuacan was not built by the Mayas; moreover, the number 2268 is also found in the Nineveh Constant of the Sumerians, which indicates that the Mexican and Sumerian civilisations were related or shared a common origin." I would like to add to this the significant fact that Laurette Sejourne, in her brilliant *Burning Water* (Thames & Hudson, 1957), reaches the conclusion, after carefully surveying the available evidence, that human sacrifice was not practised by the Quetzalcoatl cult in Teotihuacan, and was considered abhorrent to Quetzalcoatl until after the barbarous Aztec tribes conquered the highly cultured Toltecs, changing the religion into a diabolical travesty of what it had been previously.

—George Andrews

Chapter Four

CHARLES FORT BREAKS THE ICE

Speculations concerning extra-terrestrial activities on Earth are scattered through the works of Charles Fort. Most of his references to this subject are quite brief. His typical manner is to bring the subject up, to propose a hypothesis which may or may not be tongue-in-cheek, then after a few comments to change the subject. Almost every time he touches on the idea, he discusses it only in passing rather than going into it at length. Yet he brings it up again and again and again. It is definitely a recurrent theme that runs all through his work. I wondered whether this oblique hit-and-run treatment of the subject could have been motivated by fear of ridicule, or whether his persistent interest in it could have been based on a personal contactee experience, and decided to gather together what seemed the most significant of these scattered references. The result is a bouquet with a potent aroma from somewhere else. The quotations are separated from each other by ellipses (triple periods): . . . I have appended a list of the relevant page numbers in the Dover edition of *The Complete Books of Charles Fort* in case anyone wishes to look up the quotations.

Charles Fort on Extra-Terrestrials

A procession of the damned. By the damned, I mean the excluded. We shall have a procession of data that Science has excluded. . . . The power that has said to all these things that they are damned, is Dogmatic Science. . . . This book is an assemblage of data of external relations of this earth. We take the position that our data have been damned, upon no consideration for individual merits or demerits, but in conformity with a general attempt to hold out for isolation of this earth. . . . The fall of animal-matter from the sky. I'd suggest, to start with, that we'd put ourselves in the place of deep-sea fishes: How would they account for the fall of animal-matter from above?. . . . Or an aerial battle that occurred in inter-planetary space several hundred years ago—effect of time in making diverse remains uniform in appearance. . . . suppose there should be vast celestial super-oceanic, or inter-planetary vessels that come near this earth and discharge volumes of smoke at times. . . . the irritations that occur to those cloistered minds that must repose in the concept of a snug, isolated little world, free from contact with cosmic wickednesses, safe from stellar guile, undisturbed by inter-planetary prowlings and invasions. . . . there have been red rains that very strongly suggest blood or finely divided animal matter—Debris from inter-planetary disasters. Aerial battles. Food-supplies from cargoes of super-vessels, wrecked in inter-planetary traffic. . . . It is not so much that they are inimical to all data of externally derived substances that fall upon this earth, as that they are inimical to all data discordant with a system that does not include such phenomena. . . . If there be not an overhead traffic in commodities similar to our own commodities carried over this earth's oceans—I'm not the deep-sea fish I think I am. . . . .

Some day I shall look over old stories of demons that have appeared sulphurously upon this earth, with the idea of expressing that we have often had undesirable visitors from other worlds. . . . every living thing upon this earth may, ancestrally, have come from—somewhere else. . . . that evolution upon this earth has been. . . . induced by external influences; that evolution, as a whole, upon this earth, has been a process of population by immigration or by bombardment. . . . Bombardments of this earth—Attempts to communicate. . . . I begin to suspect something else: something more subtle and esoteric than graven characters upon stones that have fallen from the sky, in attempts to communicate. The notion that other worlds are attempting to communicate with this world is widespread: my own notion is that it is not attempt at all—that it was achievement centuries ago. I should like to send out a report that a "thunderstone" had fallen, say, somewhere in New Hampshire—And keep track of every person who came to examine that stone—trace down his affiliations—keep track of him—Then send out a report that a "thunderstone" had fallen at Stockholm, say—Would one of the persons who had gone to New Hampshire, be met again in Stockholm? But—what if he had no anthropological, lapidarian, or meteorological affiliations—but did belong to a secret society. . . . I began with a notion of some other world, from which objects and substances have fallen to this earth. . . modifying, because of data which will pile up later, into acceptance that some other world is not attempting but has been, for centuries, in communication with a sect, perhaps, or a secret society, or certain esoteric ones of this earth's inhabitants. . .

If I say I conceive of another world that is now in secret communication with certain esoteric inhabitants of this earth, I say I conceive of still other worlds that are trying to establish communication with all the inhabitants of this earth. . . . Then I think I conceive of other worlds and vast structures that pass us by, within a few miles, without the slightest desire to communicate, quite as tramp vessels pass many islands without particularizing one from another. Then I think I have data of a vast construction that has often come to this earth, dipped into an ocean, submerged there for a while, then going away—Why? . . . . I accept that, though we're usually avoided, probably for moral reasons, sometimes this earth has been visited by explorers. . . . I accept that some of the other worlds are of conditions very similar to our own. I think of others that are very different—so that visitors from them could not live here—without artificial adaptations . . . a stone bearing inscriptions unassimilable with any known language upon this earth is said to have fallen from the sky . . . we are interested in many things that have been found, especially in the United States, which speak of a civilisation, or of many civilisations not indigenous to this earth. . . . It is difficult to accept that the remarkable, the very extensive, copper mines in the region of Lake Superior were ever the works of American aborigines. . . . The Indians have no traditions relating to the mines. I think that we've had visitors: that they have come here for copper, for instance. . . . Our data are of things that have been cached, and of things that seem to have been dropped—Or a Lost Expedition from—Somewhere. Explorers from somewhere, and their inability to return—then a long, sentimental, persistent attempt, in the spirit of our own Arctic relief-expeditions—at least to establish communication—What if it may have succeeded?

We think of India—the millions of natives who are ruled by a small band of esoterics—only because they receive support and direction from—somewhere else . . . the queer-shaped mounds upon this earth were built by explorers from Somewhere, unable to get back, designed to attract attention from some other world. . . . The greatest of mysteries: Why don't they ever come here, or send here, openly? . . . Would we, if we could, educate and sophisticate pigs, geese, cattle? Would it be wise to establish diplomatic relations with the hen that now functions, satisfied with mere sense of achievement by way of compensation? I think we're property. I should say we belong to something: That once upon a time, this earth was No-Man's land, that other worlds explored and colonized here, and fought among themselves for possession, but that now it's owned by something: That something owns this earth—all others warned off . . surreptitious visits . . . voyagers who have shown every indication of intent to evade and avoid . . . Pigs, geese, and cattle. First find out that they are owned. Then find out the whyness of it. I suspect that, after all, we're useful—that among contesting claimants, adjustment has occurred, or that something now has a legal right to us, by force, or by having paid out analogues of beads for us to former, more primitive, owners of us—all others warned off—that all this has been known, perhaps for ages, to certain ones upon this earth, a cult or order, members of which function like bellwethers to the rest of us, or as superior slaves or overseers, directing us in accordance with instructions received—from Somewhere else—in our mysterious usefulness.

But I accept that in the past, before proprietorship was established, inhabitants of a host of other worlds have—dropped here, hopped here, wafted, sailed, flown, motored—walked here, for all I know—been pulled here, been pushed; have come singly, have come in enormous numbers; have visited occasionally, have visited periodically for hunting, trading, replenishing harems, mining: have been unable to stay here, have established colonies here, have been lost here; far-advanced peoples, or things, and primitive peoples or whatever they were. . . . Or parent-worlds and their colonies here. . . . Or that, despite modern reasoning upon this subject, there was once something that was super-parental or tutelary to early orientals. . . . Worlds that were once tutelarian worlds—before this earth became sole property of one of them. . . . That upon the wings of a super-bat, he broods over this earth and over other worlds, perhaps deriving something from them: hovers on wings, or wing-like appendages, or planes that are hundreds of miles from tip to tip—a super-evil thing that is exploiting us. By Evil I mean that which makes us useful. He obscures a star. He shoves a comet. I think he's a vast, black, brooding vampire. . . .

I have been very much struck with phenomena of "cup marks". They look to me like symbols of communication. But they do not look to me like means of communication between some of the inhabitants of this earth and other inhabitants of this earth. My own impression is that some external force has marked, with symbols, rocks of this earth, from far away. I do not think that cup marks are inscribed communications among different inhabitants of this earth, because it seems too unacceptable that inhabitants of China, Scotland, and America should all have conceived of the same system. Cup marks are strings of cup-like impressions in rocks. Sometimes there are rings around them, and sometimes they have only semi-circles. Great Britain, America, France, Algeria, Circassia, Palestine: they're virtually everywhere—except in the far north, I think. In China, cliffs are dotted with them. Upon a cliff near Lake Como, there is a maze of these markings. In Italy and Spain and India they occur in enormous numbers. Given that a force, say, like electric force, could, from a distance, mark such a substance as rocks, as, from a distance of hundreds of miles, selenium can be marked by telephotographers—but I am of two minds—the Lost Explorers from Somewhere, and an attempt, from Somewhere, to communicate with them: so a frenzy of showering of messages toward this earth, in the hope that some of them would mark rocks near the lost explorers-That perhaps forces behind the history of this earth have left upon the rocks of Palestine and England and India and China records that may someday be deciphered, of their misdirected instructions to certain esoteric ones—Order of the Freemasons—the Jesuits—I emphasize the row-formation of cup marks: Prof. Douglas (*Saturday Review*, Nov. 24, 1883): "Whatever may have been their motive, the cup-markers showed a decided liking for arranging their sculpturings in regularly spaced rows." That cup marks are an archaic form of inscription was first suggested by Canon Greenwell many years ago. But more specifically adumbratory to our own expression are the observations of Rivett-Carnac (*Jour. Roy. Asiatic Soc.*, 1903-515): That the Braille system of raised dots is an inverted arrangement of cup marks: also that there are strong resemblances to the Morse code. But no tame and systematized archaeologist can do more than casually point out resemblances, and merely suggest that strings of cup marks look like messages, because—China, Switzerland, Algeria, America—if messages they be, there seems to be no escape from attributing one origin to them—then, if messages they be, I accept one external origin, to which the whole surface of this earth was accessible, for them. Something else that we emphasize: That rows of cup marks have often been likened to footprints. But, in this similitude, their unilinear arrangement must be disregarded—of course often they're mixed up in every way, but arrangement in single lines is very common. It is odd that they should so often be likened to footprints: I suppose there are exceptional cases, but unless it's something that hops on one foot, or a cat going along a narrow fence-top, I don't think of anything that makes footprints one directly ahead of another. Cop in a station house, walking a chalk line, perhaps. Upon the Witch's Stone, near Ratho, Scotland, there are twenty-four cups, varying in size from one and a half to three inches in diameter, arranged in approximately straight lines. Locally it is explained that these are tracks of dog's feet (*Proc. Soc. Antiq. Scotland*, 2-4-79). Similar marks are scattered bewilderingly all around the Witch's Stone—like a frenzy of telegraphing, or like messages repeating and repeating, trying to localize differently. In Inverness-shire, cup marks are called "fairies' footmarks". At Valna's church, Norway, and St. Peter's Ambleteuse, there are such marks, said to be horses' hoofprints. The rocks of Clare, Ireland, are marked with prints supposed to have been made by a mythical cow (*Folklore*, 21-184).We now have such a ghost of a thing that I'd not like to be interpreted as offering it as a datum: it simply illustrates what I mean by the notion of symbols, like cups, or like footprints, which, if like those of horses or cows, are the reverse of, or the negatives of, cups—of symbols that are regularly received somewhere upon this earth—steep, conical hill, somewhere, I think—but that have often alighted in wrong places—considerably to the mystification of persons waking up some morning to find them upon formerly blank spaces. An ancient record—still worse, an ancient Chinese record—of a courtyard of a palace—dwellers of the palace waking up one morning, finding the courtyard marked with tracks like the foot-prints of an ox—supposed that the devil did it. . . .

I think that there are, out in inter-planetary space, Super Tamerlanes at the head of hosts of celestial ravagers—which have come here and pounced upon civilisations of the past, cleaning them up all but their bones, or temples and monuments—for which later historians have invented exclusionist histories. But if something now has a legal right to us, and can enforce its pro-prietorship, they've been warned off. It's the way of all exploita-tion. I should say that we're now under cultivation: that we're conscious of it, but have the impertinence to attribute it all to our own nobler and higher instincts . . . there are modes and modes and modes of inter-planetary existence . . . the super-mercantile, the super-piratic, the super-evangelical. . . . In the *Canadian Institute Proceedings*, 2-7-198, there is an account, by the Deputy Com-missioner at Dhurmsalla, of the extraordinary Dhurmsalla meteorite—coated with ice. But the combination of events related by him is still more extraordinary: That within a few months of the fall of this meteorite there had been a fall of live fishes at Benares, a shower of red substance at Furruckabad, a dark spot observed on the disk of the sun, an earthquake, "an unnatural darkness of some duration," and a luminous appearance in the sky that looked like an aurora borealis—But there's more to this climax: We are introduced to a new order of phenomena: Visitors. The Deputy Commissioner writes that, in the evening, after the fall of the Dhurmsalla meteorite, or mass of stone covered with ice, he saw lights. Some of them were not very high. They appeared and went out and reappeared. I have read many accounts of the Dhurmsalla meteorite—July 28, 1860—but never in any other of them a mention of this new correlate—something as out of place in the nineteenth century as would have been an air-plane. . . . This writer says that the lights moved like fire balloons, but: "I am sure that they were neither fire balloons, lanterns, nor bonfires, or any other thing of that sort, but bona fide lights in the heavens." It's a subject for which we shall have to have a separate expression—trespassers upon territory to which something else has a legal right—perhaps someone lost a rock, and he and his friends came down looking for it, in the evening—or secret agents, or emissaries, who had an appointment with certain esoteric ones near Dhurmsalla—things or beings coming down to explore, and unable to stay down long. . . . The quay of Lisbon. We are told that it went down. A vast throng or persons ran to the quay for refuge. The quay and all the people on it disappeared. If it and they went down—not a single corpse, not a shred of clothing, not a plank of the quay, nor so much as a splinter of it ever floated to the surface . . . whether there are inter-planetary trade routes and vast areas devastated by Super-Tamerlanes—whether sometimes there are visitors to this earth—who might be pursued and captured and questioned. . . . Our greasy, shiny brains. That they may be of some use after all: that other modes of existence place a high value on them as lubricants; that we're hunted for them; a hunting expedition to this earth—the newspapers report a tornado . . . or that Elijah did go up in the sky in something like a chariot, and may not be Vega, after all, and that there may be a wheel or so left of whatever he went up in. . . .

I think of as many different kinds of visitors to this earth as there are visitors to New York, to a jail, to a church—some persons go to church to pick pockets, for instance. My own acceptance is that either a world or a vast super-construction—or a world, if red substances and fishes fell from it—hovered over India in the summer of 1860. Something then fell from somewhere, July 17, 1860, at Dhurmsalla. Whatever "it" was, "it" is so persistently alluded to as "a meteorite" that I look back and see that I adopted this convention myself. But in the *London Times* Dec. 26, 1860, Syed Abdoolah, Professor of Hindustani, University College, London, writes that he had sent to a friend in Dhurmsalla, for an account of the stones that had fallen at that place. The answer: " . . . diverse forms and sizes, many of which bore great resemblance to ordinary cannon balls just discharged from engines of war." It's an addition to our data of spherical objects that have arrived upon this earth. Note that they are spherical stone objects. And, in the evening of this same day that something—took a shot at Dhurmsalla—or sent objects upon which there may be decipherable markings— lights were seen in the air. . . . However, as to most of our data, I think of super-things that have passed close to this earth with no more interest in this earth than have passengers upon a steamship in the bottom of the sea—or passengers may have a keen interest, but circumstances of schedules and commercial requirements forbid investigation of the bottom of the sea. Then, on the other hand, we may have data of super-scientific attempts to investigate phenomena of this earth from above—perhaps by beings from so far away that they had never even heard that something, somewhere, asserts a legal right to this earth . . . if super-vessels, or super-vehicles have traversed this earth's atmosphere, there must be mergers between them and terrestrial phenomena: observations upon them must merge away into observations upon clouds and balloons and meteors. . .

I think that we're fished for. It may be that we're highly esteemed by super-epicures somewhere. It makes me more cheerful when I think that we may be of some use after all. I think that dragnets have often come down and have been mistaken for whirlwinds and waterspouts. Some accounts of seeming structure in whirlwinds and waterspouts are astonishing. And I have data that, in this book, I can't take up at all—mysterious disappearances. I think we're fished for. But this is a little expression on the side: relates to trespassers; has nothing to do with the subject that I shall take up at some other time—or our use to some other mode of seeming that has a legal right to us. . . . Vast, black thing poised like a crow over the moon . . . Vast wheel-like super-constructions—they enter this earth's atmosphere, and, threatened with disintegration, plunge for relief into an ocean, or into a denser medium. Of course the requirements now facing us are: Not only data of vast wheel-like super-constructions that have relieved their distresses in the ocean, but data of enormous wheels that have been seen in the air, or entering the ocean, or rising from the ocean and continuing their voyages. . . . Text-books tell us that the Dhurmsalla meteorites were picked up "soon", or "within half an hour". Given a little time the conventionalists may argue that these stones were hot when they fell, but that their great interior coldness had overcome the molten state of their surfaces. According to the Deputy Commissioner of Dhurmsalla, these stones had been picked up "immediately" by passing coolies. These stones were so cold that they benumbed the fingers. But they had fallen with a great light. It is described as "a flame of fire about two feet in depth and nine feet in length." Acceptably this light was not the light of molten matter . . . my own acceptance is that super-geographical trade routes are traversed by torpedo-shaped super-constructions that have occasionally visited, or that have occasionally been driven into this earth's atmosphere. . . . That devils have visited this earth: foreign devils: human-like beings, with pointed beards: good singers; one shoe ill-fitting—but with sulphurous exhalations, at any rate. I have been impressed with the frequent occurrence of sulphurousness with things that come from the sky. . . . London *Times*, Feb. 16, 1855: "Considerable sensation has been caused in the towns of Topsham, Lymphstone, Exmouth, Teignmouth, and Dawlish, in Devonshire, in consequence of the discovery of a vast number of foot tracks of a most strange and mysterious description." The story is of an incredible multiplicity of marks discovered in the morning of Feb. 8, 1855, in the snow, by inhabitants of many towns and regions between towns. . . . The tracks were in all kinds of unaccountable places: in gardens enclosed by high walls, and up on the tops of houses, as well as in the open fields. There was in Lymphstone scarcely one unmarked garden. . . . And, because they occurred in single lines, the marks are said to have been "more like those of a biped than of a quadruped"—as if a biped would place one foot precisely ahead of another—unless it hopped—but then we have to think of a thousand, or of thousands. It is said that the marks were "generally 8 inches in advance of each other." "The impression of the foot closely resembles that of a donkey's shoe, and measured from an inch and a half, in some instances, to two and a half inches across." Or the impressions were cones in incomplete, or crescentic basins. The diameters equaled diameters of very young colts' hoofs: too small to be compared with marks of donkey's hoofs. . . . But they're in a single line. It is said that the marks from which the sketch was made were 8 inches apart, and that this spacing was regular and invariable "in every parish". Also other towns besides those named in the *Times* were mentioned. The writer, who had spent a winter in Canada, and was familiar with tracks in snow, says that he had never seen "a more clearly defined track." Also he brings out the point that was so persistently disregarded by Prof. Owen and the other correlators—that "no known animal walks in a line of single footsteps, not even man." With these wider inclusions, this writer concludes with us that the marks were not footprints. It may be that his following observation hits upon the crux of the whole occurrence: That whatever it may have been that made the marks, it had removed, rather than pressed, the snow. According to his observations the snow looked "as if branded with a hot iron." . . .

Some day I shall publish data that lead me to suspect that

many appearances upon this earth that were once upon a time interpreted by theologians and demonologists, but are now supposed to be the subject-matter of psychic research, were beings and objects that visited this earth, not from a spiritual existence, but from outer space. . . . I now conceive of successful and flourishing Exclusionism as an organization that has been in harmony with higher forces. Suppose we accept that all general delusions function sociologically. Then, if Exclusionism be general delusion; if we shall accept that conceivably the isolation of this earth has been a necessary factor in the development of the whole geosystem, we see that exclusionistic science has faithfully, though falsely, functioned. It would be world-wide crime to spread worldwide too soon the idea that there are other existences nearby and that they have been seen and that sounds from them have been heard: the peoples of this earth must organize themselves before conceiving of, and trying to establish, foreign relations. . . .

Lost tribes and the nations that have disappeared from the face of this earth. . . . The Mayans—and what became of them? Bones of the Mayans, picked white as frost by space-scavengers, regioned to this day in a sterile luxuriance somewhere, spread upon existence like the pseudo-breath of Death, crystallized on a sky-pane. Three times gaps wide and dark in the history of Egypt—and that these abysses were gulfed by disappearances—that some of the eliminations from this earth may have been upward translations in functional suctions. We conceive of Supervision upon this earth's development, but for it the names of Jehovah and Allah seem old-fashioned—that the equivalence of wrath, but like the storms of cells that, in an embryonic thing, invade and destroy cartilage-cells, when they have outlived their usefulness, have devastated this earth's undesirables . . . extramundane vandals may often have swooped down upon this earth, and they may swoop again. . . . It is our expression that temporary isolations characterize embryonic growth and superembryonic growth quite as distinctly as do expansions and co-ordinations. Local centers of development in an egg—and they are isolated before they sketch out attempting relations. Or in wider being—hemisphere isolated from hemisphere, and nation from nation—then the breaking down of barriers—the appearance of Japan out of obscurity—threads of a military plasm are cast across an ocean by the United States. Shafts of light that have pierced the obscurity surrounding planets—and something like a star shines in Aristarchus of the moon. Embryonic heavens that have dreamed—and that their mirages will be realized some day. Sounds and an interval; sounds and the same interval; sounds again—that there is one integrating organism and that we have heard its pulse. . . . If lights that have been seen in the sky were upon the vessels of explorers from other worlds—then living in New York City, perhaps, or in Washington, D.C., perhaps, there are inhabitants of Mars, who are secretly sending reports upon the ways of this world to their goverenments? . . .

Maybe it was only coincidence—or what may there be to Napoleon's own belief that something was supervising him? Suppose it is that, in November, 1812, Napoleon's work, as a factor in European readjustments, was done. There was no military power upon this earth that could remove this one, whose work was done. There came coldness so intense that it destroyed the Grand Army. . . . It is as if with intelligence, or with the equivalence of intelligence, something has specialized upon transporting, or distributing, immature and larval forms of life. . . . If, in other worlds, or in other parts of one relatively little existence, there be people who are far ahead of terrestrians, perhaps, teleportatively, beings from other places have come to this earth. And have seen nothing to detain them. Or perhaps some of the more degraded ones have felt at home here, and have hung around, or have stayed here. I'd think of these fellows as throwbacks: concealing their origin, of course; having perhaps only a slightly foreign appearance; having affinity with our barbarisms, which their own races had cast off. I'd think of a feeling for this earth, in other worlds, as corresponding to the desire of most of us, now and then, to go to a South Sea Island and be degraded. Throw-backs translated to this earth, would not, unless intensely atavistic, take to what we regard as vices, but to what their own far-advanced people regard as perhaps unmentionable, or anyway, unprintable degradations. They would join our churches, and wallow in pews. They'd lose all sense of decency and become college professors. Let a fall start, and the decline is swift. They'd end up as members of Congress. . . .

Melbourne Argus, Feb. 28, and March 1, 1890—a wandering monster. A list of names and addresses of persons who said that they had seen it, was published. It was a creature about thirty feet long, and was terrorizing the people of Euroa. "The existence of some altogether unheard-of monster is vouched for by a crowd of credible witnesses." I am tired of the sensible explanations that are holding back new delusions. So I suggest that this thing, thirty feet long, was not a creature, but was a construction, in which explorers from somewhere else, were traveling back and forth, near one of this earth's cities, having their own reasons for not wanting to investigate too closely. . . . There was a volley of monsters from some other world, about the time of the Charleston earthquake, or some one thing skipped around with marvelous agility, or it is that, just before the quake, there were dull times for the newspapers. So many observations in places far apart can be reconciled by thinking that not a creature but explorers in a construction, had visited this earth. They may have settled down in various places. . . . Someone else who bothered the conventionalists was the Captain of the Royal Yacht, the *Osborne*, who, in an official report to the Admiralty, told of having seen a monster—not serpent-like—off the coast of Sicily, May 2, 1877. The creature was turtle-like, visible part of the body about fifty feet long-. . . . There was another story told, about the same time. *New Zealand Times*, Dec. 12, 1883—report by a sea captain, who had seen something like a turtle, 60 feet long, and 40 feet wide. Perhaps stories of turtle-backed objects of large size relate to submersible vessels. If there were no submersible vessels of this earth, in the year 1883, we think of submersibles from somewhere else. Why they should be so secretive, we can't much inquire into now, because we are so much concerned with other concealments and suppressions.

I suspect that, in other worlds, or in other parts of one existence, there is esoteric knowledge of the human beings of this earth, kept back from common knowledge. This is easily thinkable, because even upon this earth there is little knowledge of human beings. There have been suggestions of an occult control upon the minds of the inhabitants of this earth. Let anybody who does not like the idea that his mind may be most subtly controlled, think back to what propagandists did with his beliefs in the years 1914-1918. . . . I accept that, if explorers from somewhere else should visit this earth, and if their vessels, or the lights of their vessels, should be seen by millions of the inhabitants of this earth, the data would soon be conventionalized. If beings, like human beings, from somewhere else, should land upon this earth, near New York, and parade up Broadway, and then sail away, somebody, a year or so later, would "confess" that it had been a hoax by him and some companions, who had dressed up for their parts, and had jabbered, as they thought extra-mundanians should jabber. New Yorkers would say that from the first they had suspected something wrong. Who ever heard of distinguished foreigners coming to New York, and not trying to borrow something? . . . If there is a selective force, which transports stones exclusively, or larvae, and nothing but larvae, or transports living things of various sizes, but nothing but living things, such a selective force might affect a number of human beings, leaving no trace, because unaffective to everything else. . . . Crews of vessels have disappeared, and vessels have disappeared. It may be that something of which the inhabitants of this earth know nothing, is concerned in these disappearances, or seizures. . . . *New York Times*, June 22, 1921—"More ships added to the mystery list— almost simultaneous disappearances, without a trace, regarded as significant." *Times*, June 24—about a dozen vessels in the list. And yet such a swipe by an unknown force, of the vessels of a nation, along its own coast, was soon thought of no more. Anything could occur, and if not openly visible, or if observed by millions, would soon be engulfed in forgetfulness. Or soon it would be conventionalized. In the year 1921, it was customary to accuse the Russians. I think that the climax was reached, in the year 1927, when unruliness of natives in the jungles of Peru was attributed to Russian agents. Still, I suppose that, for years, whenever there is revolt against misrule and oppression, propagandists will tell us the same old yarn of otherwise contented natives, misled by those Russians. In June, 1921, the way of explaining the disappearance of a dozen vessels was by saying it was thought that the Soviet Government was stealing them. It may be that constructions from somewhere else have appeared upon this earth, and have seized crews of this earth's ships. . . . It may be that if beings from somewhere else would seize inhabitants of this earth, wantonly, or out of curiosity, or as a matter of scientific research, the preference would be for an operation at sea, remote from observations by other humans of this earth. If such beings exist, they may in some respects be very wise, but—supposing secrecy to be desirable—they must have neglected psychology in their studies, or unconcernedly they'd drop right into Central Park, New York, and pick up all the specimens they wanted, and leave it to the wisemen of our tribes to explain that there had been a whirlwind, and that the Weather Bureau, with its usual efficiency, had published warnings of it. . . . The standardized explanation of mysterious human strangers, who have appeared at points upon this earth, acting as one supposes inhabitants of some other world would act, if arriving here, or acting as inhabitants of other parts of this earth, transported in a state of profound hypnosis, would probably act, is that of imposture. . . . If there ever have been instances of teleportations of human beings from somewhere else to this earth, an examination of inmates of infirmaries and workhouses and asylums might lead to some marvelous astronomical disclosures. I suppose that I shall be blamed for a new nuisance, if after the publication of these notions, mysterious strangers start cropping up, and when asked about themselves, point up to Orion or Andromeda.

Suppose any human being ever should be translated from somewhere else to this earth, and should tell about it. Just what chance would he have for some publicity? I neglected to note the date, but early in the year 1928, a man did appear in a town in New Jersey, and did tell them he had come from the planet Mars. Wherever he came from, everybody knows where he went, after telling that. . . . Whatever the significance may be, I have noted a number of "mysterious strangers", or "wild men", who were naked. . . . "Naked in the street—strange conduct by a strange man." See the *Chatham (Kent, England) News*, Jan. 10, 1914. Early in the evening of January 6th.—"weather bitterly cold"—a naked man appeared, from nowhere that could be found out, in High Street, Chatham. The man ran up and down the street, until a policeman caught him. He could tell nothing about himself. "Insanity", said the doctors, with their customary appearance of really saying something. I accept that, relatively, there is insanity, though no definite line can be drawn as to persons in asylums, persons not in asylums, and persons not yet in asylums. If by insanity is meant processes of thought that may be logical enough, but that are built upon false premises, what am I showing but the insanity of all of us? I accept that as extremes of the state that is common to us all, some persons may be considered insane: but, according to my experience with false classifications, or the impossibility of making anything but false classifications, I suspect that many persons have been put away, as insane, simply because they were gifted with uncommon insights, or had been through uncommon experiences. It may be that, hidden under this cloakery, are the subject-matters of astonishing, new inquiries. There may be stories that have been told by alleged lunatics that some day will be listened to, and investigated, leading to extraordinary disclosures. . . . The naked man of Chatham appeared suddenly. Nobody had seen him on his way to his appearing-point. His clothes were searched for, but could not be found. Nowhere near Chatham was anyone reported missing. . . . Five "wild men" and a "wild girl" appeared in Connecticut, about the first of January, 1888. . . . I have records of six persons, who, between Jan. 14, 1920, and Dec. 9, 1923, were found wandering in or near the small town of Romford, Essex, England, unable to tell how they got there, or anything else about themselves. . . . If human beings ever have been teleported, and, if some mysterious appearances of human beings be considered otherwise unaccountable, an effect of the experience is effacement of memory. . . .

It was said that Kaspar Hauser was murdered to suppress political disclosures. If it be thinkable that Kaspar was murdered to suppress a mystery, whether political, or not so easily defined, there are statements that support the idea that also some of the inhabitants of Nuremberg, who were prominent in Kaspar's affairs, were murdered. One can read that von Feuerbach was murdered, or one can read that von Feuerbach died of a paralytic stroke . . . soon after the death of Kaspar Hauser, several persons, who had shown much interest in his case, died, and . . . it was told in Nuremberg that they had been poisoned. They were Mayor Binder, Dr. Osterhauser, Dr. Preu, and Dr. Albert. "Kaspar Hauser showed such an utter deficiency of words and ideas, such perfect ignorance of the commonest things and appearances of Nature, and such horror of all customs, conveniences, and necessities of civilized life, and, withal, such extraordinary peculiarities in his social, mental, and physical disposition, that one might feel oneself driven to the alternative of believing him to be a citizen of another planet, transferred by some miracle to our own" (von Feuerbach).

NOTE: Page numbers from the Dover edition of *The Complete Books of Charles Fort*: 3, 17, 26-28, 32, 39, 45, 55, 67, 83, 98, 123-124, 136, 143-144, 146-148, 152, 157, 162-164, 172, 210, 213-217, 245-248, 250, 252, 254, 259-261, 264-265, 268, 272, 280-281, 291, 301, 307-309, 419, 424-425, 480-482, 532, 542-543, 548, 573-574, 613, 615-618, 629, 634-637, 641, 672, 678, 686-689, 709-710.

Charles Fort devoted special attention to unusual events

that took place in England during the winter of 1904-1905, as there were more strange things going on in that particular time and space frame than during any other period anywhere that he had investigated. Certain aspects of this outbreak of paranormal activity are very much with us today, such as UFO sightings and animal mutilations. This was before the invention of the airplane, so UFO phenomena during this period can't be explained away in terms of lights from airplanes.

It may be worth noting that Neptune and Uranus were in opposition during the winter of 1904-1905. According to astrology, this means that extraordinary events were to be expected.

The most spectacular UFO sightings centered around Mrs. Mary Jones, a poor woman who lived with her husband on an almost barren farm near the small town of Egryn in northern Wales. After having a vision of Jesus, she felt inspired to preach at the Egryn chapel. At first attendance at her prayer meetings was sparse, but strange lights began to appear over the chapel when she was speaking, and to follow her home. As attendance increased to large crowds and she was invited to preach in churches in other parts of Wales, the strange lights accompanied her, sometimes manifesting inside of buildings. The lights were witnessed not only by pious country folk, but also by cynical sharp-witted London reporters who had been sent out to cover the story of the "Egryn Lights". Here is a section of the article that appeared in the *Daily News* on Sept. 2nd., 1905:

When after several hours' friendly chat with Mrs. Jones in her own house, I rose to leave, she stopped me with the remark:

"You had better wait that you may see the Light for yourself. It would be a pity for you to go back without seeing it."

I waited and saw.

After tea, having two miles to walk to the chapel where the service was to be held, it behoved us to be early on the move.

Besides myself, there were present the Rev. Llewellyn Morgan, Harlech, the Rev. Roger Williams, Dyffryn, and one other. Mrs. Jones came in dressed for her journey. Going outside, she immediately returned, remarking:

"We cannot start yet, the Light has not come."

Five minutes later she again went out, returning promptly to say:

"Now we can go. The Light has come"—just as though she said the cab was at the door.

The announcement was received with a perceptible tremor by one—the only unbelieving member of our company.

We had just passed the level-crossing of the Cambrian railway in the fields when Mrs. Jones directed our attention to the southern sky. While she yet spoke, between us and the hills, and apparently two miles away, there suddenly flashed forth an intensely brilliant white light, and emitting from its whole circumference dazzling sparklets like flashing rays from a diamond.

"It may be the head light of the train?" faintly suggested our doubting Thomas.

"No", was Mrs. Jones quiet reply; "it is too high for that."

Even as she spoke, and as though in corroboration, the star made a sudden huge jump towards the mountains, returning almost immediately to its old position, and then rushing at an immense speed straight for us. Then came the unmistakeable rumbling roar of the train approaching from the direction of Barmouth.

"I thought it was the train," came with a sigh of relief from our unbeliever.

False hope!

"No", was Mrs. Jone's confident contradiction. "That is not the train light, which has yet to come."

And a second light, very different in character from the first, became as she spoke perceptible at some distance below the star, both obviously rushing towards us. As the train drew near the "star" disappeared. With a rush and a roar the train was past. But before our Thomas's sigh of thankfulness at the disappearance of the star was well out the mysterious star reappeared nearer, and if possible more brilliant than ever. Then it vanished as suddenly as it had first appeared.

"Wait!" was Mrs. Jones' quiet injunction. In a moment, high up on the hillside, quite two miles away from where the "Star" had been a moment previously, a "Light" again flashed out, illuminating the heather as though bathed in brilliant sunshine. Again it vanished—only again to reappear a mile further north evidently circling the valley, and in the direction for which we were bound.

But our experience was to be stranger still before we got to the meeting.

So far the "Light" and "Star" had been equally visible to and seen alike by the five who formed our company. Now it made a distinction.

Having left the fields and proceeded some distance along the main road, all five walking abreast, I suddenly saw three brilliant rays of dazzling white light stride across the road from mountain to sea, throwing the stone wall into bold relief, every stone and interstice, every little fern and bit of moss, as clearly visible as at noonday, or as though a searchlight had been turned on that particular spot. There was not a living soul near, nor a house from which the light could have come.

Another short half-mile, and a blood-red light, apparently within a foot of the ground, appeared to me in the centre of the village street just before us. I said nothing until we had reached the spot. The red light had disappeared as suddenly and mysteriously as it had come—and there was absolutely nothing which could conceivably account for its having been there a moment before.

"Mrs. Jones," I said—and this was the first intimation the three other members of the party had of what I had seen—"unless I am mistaken, your Light still accompanies us."

"Yes," she calmly replied. "I kept silent on both occasions to see whether any of you had perceived it for yourselves. The first time you know it was white; but I have seen it sometimes blood-red, as you saw it now!"

I had not told Mrs. Jones what the nature of the Lights I had seen was; but no sooner had I intimated that I had seen the Light than she described the two appearances precisely as I have described them above, thus establishing beyond question the fact that we had both seen the self-same manifestation.

Those are the simple facts. I offer no comment on them. I only state what I saw.

Another London reporter who witnessed similar

phenomena while in the company of Mrs. Jones described "an oval mass of grey" as the source of the brilliant celestial nocturnal light he saw. He was from the *Daily Mirror*.

There is an abundance of other eyewitness reports. The phenomena were often witnessed by large crowds. Then an establishment scientist explained it all away as "balls of luminous insects", and newspaper coverage ceased.

Here is what Charles Fort had to say about the strange events which were taking place in England during that period of time when there was an unprecedented climax of paranormal activity:

There was a marauding animal in England, toward the end of the year 1905. *London Daily Mail*, Nov. 1, 1905—"the sheep-slaying mystery of Badminton." It is said that, in the neighborhood of Badminton, on the border between Gloucestershire and Wiltshire, sheep had been killed. Sergeant Carter, of the Gloucestershire Police, is quoted—"I have seen two of the carcasses myself, and can say definitely that it is impossible for it to be the work of a dog. Dogs are not vampires, and do not suck the blood of a sheep, and leave the flesh almost untouched." . . .

In October, 1904, a wolf, belonging to Captain Bains of Shotley Bridge, twelve miles from Newcastle, England, escaped, and soon afterward, killing of sheep was reported from the region of Hexham, about twenty miles from Newcastle.

There seems to be an obvious conclusion.

We have had some experience with conclusions that were said to be obvious.

A story of a wolf in England is worth space, and the London newspapers rejoiced in this wolf story. Most of them did, but there are several that would not pay much attention to a dinosaur-hunt in Hyde Park. Special correspondents were sent to Hexham, Northumberland. Some of them, because of circumstances that we shall note, wrote that there was no wolf, but probably a large dog that had turned evil. Most of them wrote that undoubtedly a wolf was ravaging, and was known to have escaped from Shotley Bridge. Something was slaughtering sheep, killing for food, and killing wantonly, sometimes multilating four or five sheep, and devouring one. An appetite was ravaging, in Northumberland.

We have impressions of the capacity of a large and hungry dog but, upon reading these accounts, one has to think that they were exaggerations, or that the killer must have been more than a wolf. But, according to developments, I'd not say that there was much exaggeration. The killings were so serious that the farmers organized into the Hexham Wolf Committee, offering a reward, and hunting systematically. Every hunt was fruitless, except as material for the special correspondents, who told of continuing depredations, and reveled in special announcements. It was especially announced that, upon December 15th., the Haydon foxhounds, one of the most especial packs in England, would be sent out. These English dogs, of degree so high as to be incredible in all other parts of the world, went forth. It is better for something of high degree not to go forth. Mostly in times of peace arise great military reputations. So long as something is not tested it may be of high renown. But the Hayden foxhounds went forth. They returned with their renown damaged.

This takes us to another of our problems:
Who can blame a celebrity for not
smelling an absence?

There are not only wisemen: there are wisedogs, we learn. The Wolf Committee heard of Monarch, "the celebrated blood-hound." This celebrity was sent for, and when he arrived, it was with such a look of sagacity that the sheepfarmers' troubles were supposed to be over. The wisedog was put on what was supposed to be the trail of the wolf. But, if there weren't any wolf, who can blame a celebrated bloodhound for not smelling something that wasn't? The wisedog sniffed. Then he sat down. It was impossible to set this dog on the trail of a wolf, though each morning he was taken to a place of fresh slaughter.

Well, then, what else is there in all this? If, locally, one of the most celebrated intellects in England could not solve the problem, it may be that the fault was in taking it up locally.

Throughout my time of gathering material for this book, it was my way to note something, and not to regard it as isolated; and to search wisely for other occurrences that might associate with it. So, then, I noted this wolf story, and I settled upon this period, of the winter of 1904-1905, with the idea of collecting records of seemingly most incongruous occurrences, which, however, might be germs of correlations.

Such as this, for instance—but what could one of these occurrences have to do with the other?

That in this winter of 1904-5, there were two excitements in Northumberland. One was the wolf-hunt, and the other was a revival-craze, which had spread from Wales to England. At the time of the wolf-hunt, there was religious mania in Northumberland. Men and women staggered, as they wept and shouted, bearing reeling lights, in delirious torchlight processions.

If Monarch, the celebrated bloodhound sniffed and then sat down, I feel, myself, that the trail cannot be picked up in Hexham.

It was a time of widespread, uncanny occurrences in Great Britain. But in no account of any one uncanny occurrence have I read of any writer's awareness that there were other uncanny occurrences, or more than one or two other uncanny occurrences. There were many, special scares, at this time, in Great Britain. There was no general scare. The contagions of popular delusions cannot be lugged in, as a general explanation.

Strange, luminous things, or beings, were appearing in Wales.

In Wales had started one of the most widely hysterical religious revivals of modern times.

A light in the sky—and a pious screech—I sniff, but I don't sit down.

A wolf and a light and a screech.

There are elaborate accounts of the luminous things, or beings, in the *Proc. S. P. R.*, vol. 19, and in the first volume of the *Occult Review*. We are told that, over the piously palpitating principality of Wales, shining things traveled, stopping and descending when they came to a revival meeting, associating in some unknown way with those centers of excitement, especially where Mrs. Mary Jones was the leader. There is a story of one shining thing that persistently followed Mrs. Jones' car, and was not shaken off, when the car turned abruptly from one road to another.

So far as acceptability is concerned, I prefer the accounts by newspaper men. It took considerable to convince them. Writers, sent to Wales by London newspapers, set out with blithe incredulity. Almost everybody has a hankering for mysteries, but it is likely to be an abstract hankering, and when a mystery comes up in one's own experience, one is likely to treat it in a way that warns everybody else that one is not easily imposed upon. The first reports that were sent back by the Londoners were flippant: but, in the *London Daily Mail*, Feb. 13, 1905, one of these correspondents describes something like a ball of fire, which he saw in the sky, a brilliant object that was motionless for a while, then disappearing. Later he came upon such an appearance, near the ground, not 500 feet away. He ran toward it, but the thing disappeared. Then Bernard Redwood was sent, by the *Daily Mail*, to investigate. In the *Mail*, February 13, he writes that there were probably will-o'-the-wisps, helped out by practical jokers. As we very well know, there are no more helpful creatures than practical jokers, but, as inquiry-stoppers, Will-o'-the-wisps have played out. A conventionalist, telling the story, today, would say that they were luminous bats from a chapel belfry, and that a sexton had shot one. Almost every writer who accepted that these things were, thought that in some unknown, or unknowable, way, they were associated with the revival. It is said that they were seen hovering over chapels.

According to my methods, I have often settled upon special periods, gathering data, with the idea of correlating, but I have never come upon any other time in which were reported so many uncanny occurrences.

There were teleportations in a butcher shop, or things were mysteriouly flying about, in a butcher shop, in Portmadoc, Wales. The police were called in, and they accused a girl who was employed in the butcher shop. "She made a full confession" (*News of the World*, February 26). A ghost in Barmouth: no details (*Barmouth Advertiser*, January 12). Most of the records are mere paragraphs, but the newspapers gave considerable space to reported phenomena in the home of Mr. Howell, at Lampeter, Wales. As told in the *London Daily News*, February 11 and 13, "mysterious knockings" were heard in this house, and crowds gathered outside. The Bishop of Swansea and Prof. Harris investigated, but could not explain. Crowds in the street became so great that extra police had to be called out to regulate traffic, but nothing was learned. There were youngsters in the house, but they did not confess. Mr. Howell had what is known as "standing", in his community. It's the housemaid, or the girl in a butcher shop, with parents who presumably haven't much "standing", who is knocked about, or more gently slugged, or perhaps only slapped in the face, who confesses, or is said to have confessed. Also, as told in the *Liverpool Echo*, February 15, there was excitement at Rhymney, Wales, and investigations that came to nothing. Tapping sounds had been heard, and strange lights had been seen, in one of the revival-centers, the Salvation Army Barracks. Whether these lights were like the other lights that were appearing in Wales, I cannot say. It was the assertion of the Rev. J. Evans and other investigators, who had spent the night in the Barracks, that they had seen "very bright lights".

In the *Southern Daily Echo*, February 23, is an account of "mysterious rappings" on a door of a house in Crewe, and of a young woman, in the house who was said to have dropped dead. A physician "pronounced" her dead. But there was an inquest, and the coroner said: "There is not a single sign of death." Nevertheless, she was officially dead, and she was buried, anyway. I am too dim in my notions of possible correlations, to go into details, but along with my supposition that ordinarily catalepsy is of rare occurrence, I note that I have records of three persons, who, in this period, were aroused from trances, in time to save them from being buried alive. There were data of "strange suicides", that I shall pass over. I have several dozen records of "mysterious fires", in this period.

Slaughter in Northumberland—farmers who could, housing their sheep, at night—others setting up lanterns in their fields. Monarch, the celebrated bloodhound, who could not smell something that perhaps was not, got no more space in the newspapers, and, to a woman, the inhabitants of Hexham stopped sending him chrysanthemums. But faith in celebrities kept up, as it always will keep up, and when the Hungarian Wolf Hunter appeared, the only reason that a brass band did not escort him, in showers of torn-up telephone books, is that, away back in this winter, Hexham, like most of the other parts of England, was not yet Americanized. It was before the English were educated. The moving pictures were not of much influence then. The Hungarian Wolf Hunter, mounted on a shaggy Hungarian pony, galloped over hills and dales, and, with strange, Hungarian hunting cries, made what I think is called the *welkin* ring. He might as well have sat down and sniffed. He might as well have been a distinguished General, or Admiral, at the outbreak of a war.

Four sheep were killed at Low Eschelles, and one at Sedham, in one night. Then came the big hunt, of December 20th., which, according to expectations, would be final. The big hunt set out from Hexham: gamekeepers, woodmen, farmers, local sportsmen and sportsmen from far away. There were men on horseback, and two men in "traps", a man on a bicycle, and a mounted policeman: two women with guns, one of them in a blue walking dress, if that detail's any good to us.

They came wandering back, at the end of the day, not having seen anything to shoot at. Some said that it was because there wasn't anything. Everybody else had something to say about Capt. Bains. The most unpopular person, in the north of England, at this time, was Capt. Bains, of Shotley Bridge. Almost every night, something, presumably Capt. Bains' wolf, even though there was no findable statement that a wolf had been seen, was killing and devouring sheep.

In Brighton, an unknown force, or thing, struck notes on a musical instrument (*Daily Mail*, December 24). Later, there were stories of "a phantom bicyclist" near Brighton (*London Daily Mirror*, February 6). In the *Jour. S. P. R.*, 13-259, is published some-body's statement that, near the village of Hoe Benham, he had seen something that looked like a large dog turn into a seeming donkey. Strange sounds heard near Bolton, Lancashire—"nothing but the beating of a rope against a flagstaff." Then it was said that a figure had been seen (*Lloyd's Weekly News*, January 15). A door-bell was mysteriously ringing, at Blackheath, London: police watching the house, but unable to find out anything (*Daily Mirror*, February 13). But in not one of these accounts is shown knowl-edge that, about the same time, other accounts were being published. Look in the publications of the S. P. R. and wonder what the Society was doing. It did investigate two of the cases told of in this chapter, but no awareness is shown of a period of widespread occurrences. Other phenomena, or alleged phenomena—a ghost, at Exeter Dearnery: no details (*Daily Mail*, December 24). Strange sounds and lights, in a house in Epworth (*Liverpool Echo*, January 25). People in Bradford thought that they saw a figure enter a club house-police notified—fruitless search (*Weekly Dispatch*, January 15). At Edinburgh, Mr. J. E. Newlands, who held the Fulton chair, at the United Free College, saw a "figure" moving beside him (*Weekly Dispatch*, April 16).

But the outstanding phenomenon of this period was the revival.

Liverpool Echo, January 18—"Wales in the grip of Super-natural Forces!"

This was in allusion to the developing frenzies of the revival, and the accompanying luminous things, or beings, that had been reported. "Supernatural" is a word that has no place in my vocabulary. In my view, it has no meaning, or distinguishment. If there never has been, finally, a natural explanation of anything, everything is, naturally enough, the supernatural.

The grip was a grab by a craze. The excitement was combustion, or psycho-electricity, or almost anything except what it was supposed to be, and perhaps when flowing from human batteries there was a force that was of use to the luminous things that hung around. Maybe they fed upon it, and grew, and glowed, brilliant with nourishing ecstasies. See data upon astonishing growths of plants, when receiving other kinds of radio-active nourishment, or stimulation. If a man can go drunk on God, he may usefully pass along his exhilarations to other manifestations of godness.

There were flares where they'd least be expected. In the big stores, in the midst of waiting on customers, shop girls would suddenly, or electrically, start clapping hands and singing. Very likely some of them cut up such capers for the sport of it, and enjoyed keeping hard customers waiting. I notice that, though playing upon widely different motives, popular excitements are recruited and kept going, as if they were homogenous. There's no understanding huge emotional revolts against sin, without considering all the fun there is in them. They are monotony-breakers. Drab, little personalities have a chance to scream themselves vivid. There were confession-addicts who, past possibility of being believed, proclaimed their own wickedness, and then turned to public confessions for their neighbors, until sinful neighbors appealed to the law for protection. In one town, a man went from store to store, "returning" things that he had not stolen. Bands of girls roved the streets, rushing earnestly and mischievously into the more sedate churches, where the excitation was not encouraged, singing and clapping their hands—all of them shouting, and some of them blubbering, and then some of the most sportive ones blubbering, compelled into a temporary uniformity. This clapping of hands, in time with the singing, was almost irresistible: some vibrational reason: power of the rhythm to harmonize diverse units; primitive power of the drum-beat. Special trains set out from Liverpool to Welsh meeting-places, with sightseers, who hadn't a concern for the good of their souls; vendors of things that might have a sale; some earnest ones. Handclapping started up, and emotional furies shot through Wales.

There were ghost-scares in the towns of Blyth and Dover. *Blyth News*, March 14—crowds gathered around a school house— something of a ghostly nature inside—nothing but the creaking of a partition.

I pick up something else. We wonder how far our neo-medievalism is going to take us. Perhaps—though our inter-pretations will not be the same—only medievalism will be the limit. *Blyth News*, February 28—smoke that was seen coming from the windows of a house, in Blyth. Neighbors broke in, and found the body of the occupant, Barbara Bell, aged 77, on a sofa. Her body was burned, as if for a long time it had been in the midst of intense flames. It was thought that the victim had fallen into the fireplace. "The body was fearfully charred."

Something was slaughtering sheep—and things in the sky of Wales—and it may be that there were things, or beings, that acted like fire, consuming the bodies of women. *London Daily News*, Dec. 17, 1904—"Yesterday morning, Mrs. Thomas Cochrane, of Rosehall, Falkirk, widow of a well-known, local gentleman, was found burned to death in her bedroom." No fire in the grate— "burned almost beyond recognition"—no outcry—little, if any-thing else burned—body found, "sitting in a chair, surrounded by pillows and cushions." *London Daily Mail*, December 24—inquest on the body of a woman, who had died of the effects of "mysterious burns". "She could give no account of her injuries." An almshouse, late at night—and something burned a woman. Trinity Almshouse, Hull—story told, in the *Hull Daily Mail*, January 6. Body covered with burns—woman still living, when found in the morning— strange that there had been no outcry—bed unscorched. The woman, Elizabeth Clark, could tell nothing of her injuries, and she died without giving a clew to the mystery. "There was no fire nor light in the room."

On both sides of the River Tyne, something kept on slaughter-ing. It crossed the Tyne, having killed on one side, then killing on the other side. At East Dipton, two sheep were devoured, all but the fleece and the bones, and the same night two sheep were killed on the other side of the river.

"The Big Game Hunter from India!"

Another celebrity came forth. The Wolf Committee met him at the station. There was a plaid shawl strapped to his back, and the flaps of his hunting cap were considered unprecedented.

Almost everybody had confidence in the shawl, or felt that the flaps were authoritative. The devices by which he covered his ears made beholders feel that they were in the presence of Science.

Hexham Herald—"The right man, at last!"

So finally the wolf hunt was taken up scientifically. The ordinary hunts were going on, but the wiseman from India would have nothing to do with them. In his cap, with flaps such as had never before been seen in Northumberland, and with his plaid shawl strapped to his back, he was going from farm to farm, sifting and dating and classifying observations: drawing maps, card-indexing his data. For some situations, this is the best of methods: but something that the methodist-wiseman cannot learn is that a still better method is that of not being so tied to any particular method. It was a serious matter in Hexham. The ravaging thing was an alarming pest. There were some common hunters who were unmannerly over all this delay, but the *Hexham Herald* came out strong for Science—"The right man in the right place, at last!"

There was in this period, another series of killings. Upon a farm, near Newcastle, late in this year 1904, something was killing poultry. The depredations were so insistent, and the marauder was so evasive that persons who are said to be superstitious began to talk in a way that is said to be unenlightened.

Then the body of an otter was found.

The killing of poultry stopped.

For a discussion of the conclusion that to any normal logician looks obvious, see the *Field*, Dec. 3, 1904. Here we learn that otters, though ordinarily living upon fish, do sometimes vary their diet. But no data upon persistent killing of poultry, by otters, came out.

This body of an otter was found, lying on a railroad line.

France in the grip of military forces, August, 1914—France was invaded, and the people of France knew that France was invaded. It is my expression that they so knew, only because it was a conventional recognition. There were no wisemen to say that reported bodies of men moving along roads had nothing to do with mutilated persons appearing in hospitals, and that only by coincidence was there devastation. The wiseman of France did not give only a local explanation to every local occurrence, but of course correlated all, as the manifestations of one invasion. Human eyes have been made to see human invaders.

Wales in the grip of "supernatural forces". People in England paid little attention, at first, but then hysterias mobbed across the border. To those of us who have some failings, and now and then give a thought to correcting them, if possible, but are mostly too busy to bother much, cyclones of emotions relating to states that are vaguely known as *good* and *evil*, are most mysterious. In the Barmouth Advertiser (April 20) it is said that, in the first three months of this year 1905, there had been admitted to the Denbigh Insane Asylum, 16 patients, whose dementias were attributed to the revival. It is probable that many cases were not reported. In the *Liverpool Echo*, November 25, are accounts of four insane revivalists, who were under restraint in their own homes. Three cases in one town are told of in this newspaper, of January 10th. The craze spread in England, and in some parts of England it was as intense as anywhere in Wales. At Bromley, a woman wrote a confession of her sins, some of which, it is said, she could not have committed, and threw herself under a railroad train. In town after town, police stations were invaded by exhorters. In both England and Wales, bands stood outside theaters, calling upon people not to enter. In the same way they tried to prevent attendance at football games.

December 29—"Wolf killed on a railroad line!"

It was at Cumwinton, which is near Carlisle, about thirty miles from Hexham. The body was found on a railroad line— "Magnificent specimen of male gray wolf—total length five feet— measurement from foot to top of shoulder, thirty inches."

Captain Bains, of Shotley Bridge, went immediately to Cumwinton. He looked at the body of the wolf. He said that it was not his wolf.

There was doubt in the newspapers. Everybody is supposed to know his own wolf, but when one's wolf has been made material for a host of damage suits, one's recognitions may be dimmed.

This body of a wolf was found, and the killings of sheep stopped.

But Capt. Bains' denial that the wolf was his wolf was accepted by the Hexham Wolf Committee. Data were with him. He had reported the escape of his wolf, and the description was on record in the Shotley Bridge police station. Capt. Bains' wolf was, in October, no "magnificent" full-grown specimen, but a cub, four and a half months old. Though nobody had paid any attention to this circumstance, it had been pointed out, in the *Hexham Herald*, October 15.

The wolf of Cumwinton was not identified, according to my reading of the data. Nobody told of an escape of a grown wolf, though the news of this wolf's death was published throughout England. The animal may have come from somewhere far from England. . . .

But what became of the Shotley Bridge wolf?

All that can be said is that it disappeared.

The mystery begins with this statement:

That, in October 1904, a wolf, belonging to Capt. Bains, of Shotley Bridge, escaped, and that about the same time began a slaughtering of sheep, but that Capt. Bains' wolf had nothing to do with the slaughter.

Or the statement is that there was killing of sheep, in Northumberland, and that then came news of the escape of a wolf, by which the killing of a few sheep might be explained.

But that then there were devourings, which could not be attributed to a wolf-cub.

The wolf-cub disappeared, and there appeared another wolf, this one of a size and strength to which the devourings could be attributed.

Somewhere there was science.

If it had not been for Capt. Bains' prompt investigation, the reported differences between these two animals would have been overlooked, or disbelieved, and the story would be simply that a wolf had escaped from Shotley Bridge, had ravaged, and had been killed at Cumwinton. But Capt. Bains did investigate, and his statement that the wolf of Cumwinton was not his wolf was accepted. So then, instead of a satisfactory explanation, there was a new mystery. Where did the wolf of Cumwinton come from?

There is something that is acting to kill off mysteries. . . .

Killing of poultry, and the body of the otter on the railroad line—and the killing of poultry stopped.

Or that there may be occult things, beings and events, and that also there may be something of the nature of an occult police force, which operates to divert human suspicions, and to supply explanations that are good enough for whatever, somewhat of the nature of minds, human beings have—or that, if there be occult mischief-makers and occult ravagers, they may be of a world also of other beings that are acting to check them, and to explain them, not benevolently, but to divert suspicion from themselves, because they, too, may be exploiting life upon this earth, but in ways more subtle, and in orderly, or organized fashion.

We have noticed, in investigating obscure, or occult, phenomena, or alleged phenomena, that sometimes in matters that are now widely supposed to be rank superstitions, orthodox scientists are not so uncompromising in their oppositions, as are those who have not investigated. In the *New Orleans Medical and Surgical Journal*, April, 1894, is an account of a case of "spontaneous combustion of human bodies". The account is by Dr. Adrian Hava, not as observed by him, but as reported by his father. In *Science*, 10-100, is quoted a paper that was read by Dr. B. H. Hartwell, of Ayer, Mass., before the Massachusetts Medico-Legal Society. It was Dr. Hartwell's statement that, upon May 12, 1890, while driving through a forest, near Ayer, he had been called, and, going into the woods, saw, in a clearing the crouched form of a woman. Fire which was not from clothing, was consuming the shoulders, both sides of the abdomen, and both legs. See Dr. Dixon Mann's *Forensic Medicine* (edition of 1922), p. 216. Here, cases are told of and are accepted as veritable—such as the case of a woman, consumed so by fire that on the floor of her room there was only a pile of calcined bones left of her. The fire, if in an ordinary sense it was fire, must have been of the immensity of a furnace: but a table cloth, only three feet from the pile of cinders, was unscorched. There are other such records.

I think that our data relate, not to "spontaneous combustion of human bodies", but to things, or beings that, with a flaming process, consume men and women, but, like werewolves, or alleged werewolves, mostly pick out women. Occurrences of this winter of 1904-5 again. Early in February, in London, a woman, who was sitting asleep, before a fire in a grate, awoke, finding herself flaming. A commonplace explanation would seem to be sufficient: nevertheless it is a story of "mysterious burns", as worded in *Lloyd's Weekly News*, February 5. A coroner had expressed an inability to understand. In commenting upon the case, the coroner had said that a cinder might have shot from the grate, igniting this woman's clothes, but that she had been sitting, facing the fire, and that the burns were on her back.

Upon the morning of February 26th. (*Hampshire Advertiser*, March 4) at Butlock Heath, near Southampton, neighbors of an old couple, named Kiley, heard a scratching sound. They entered the house, and found it in flames, inside. Kiley was found, burned to death, on the floor. Mrs. Kiley, burned to death, was sitting in a chair, in the same room, "badly charred, but recognizable."

A table was overturned, and a broken lamp was on the floor.

So there seems to be an obvious explanation. But, at the inquest, it was said that an examination of this lamp showed that it could not have caused the fire. The verdict was: "Accidental death, but by what means, they (the jury) were unable to determine."

Both bodies had been fully dressed, "judging by fragments of clothes." This indicates that the Kileys had been burned before their time for going to bed. Hours later, the house was in flames. At the inquest, the mystery was that two persons, neither of whom had cried for help, presumably not asleep in an ordinary sense, should have been burned to death in a fire that did not manifest as a general fire, until hours later.

Something had overturned a table. A lamp was broken.

Again the phenomenon of scene-shifting.

Soon after the killing of poultry ceased, near Newcastle, there were uncanny occurrences upon Binbrook Farm, near Great Grimsby. There is an account, in the *Jour. S. P. R.*, 12-138, by the Rev. A. C. Custance, of Binbrook Rectory. There was no confession, this time, but this time the girl in the case—the young housemaid again—was in no condition to be dragged to a police station. It will not be easy to think that it was trickery by the girl in this case. The story is that objects were thrown about rooms: that three times, near "a not very good, or big, fire," things burst into flames, and that finally a servant girl was burned, or was attacked by something that burned her. In the *Liverpool Echo*, January 25, is published a letter from a school teacher of Binbrook, in which it is said that a blanket had been found burning in a room in which there was no fireplace. According to the report by Col. Taylor, to the S.P.R., the first manifestations occurred upon the 31st of December.

Something was killing chickens, in the farm yard, and in the henhouse. All were killed in the same way. A vampirish way? Their throats were torn.

I go to a newspaper for an account of phenomena, at Binbrook. The writer was so far from prejudice in favor of occult phenomena, that he began by saying: "Superstition dies hard." In the *Louth and North Lincolnshire News*, January 28, he tells of objects that unaccountably fell from shelves in the farmhouse, and of mysterious transportations of objects, "according to allegations." "A story that greatly dismays the unsophisticated is that of the servant girl, who, while sweeping the floor, was badly burned on the back. This is how the farmer relates it: 'Our servant girl, whom we had taken from the workhouse, and who had neither kin nor friend in the world that she knows of, was sweeping the kitchen. There was a very small fire in the grate: there was a guard there, so that no one can come within two feet or more of the fire, and she was at the other end of the room, and had not been near. I suddenly came into the kitchen, and there she was, sweeping away, while the back of her dress was afire. She looked around, as I shouted, and I smothered the fire out with wet sacks. But she was terribly burned, and she is at the Louth Hospital, now, in terrible pain.'

"This last sentence is very true. Yesterday our representative called at the hospital, and was informed that the girl was burnt extensively on the back, and lies in a critical condition. She adheres to the belief that she was in the middle of the room, when her clothes ignited."

A great deal, in trying to understand this occurrence, depends upon what will be thought of the unseen killing of chickens.

"Out of 250 fowls, Mr. White says that he has only 24 left. They have all been killed in the same weird way. The skin around the neck, from the head to the breast, has been pulled off, and the windpipe drawn from its place and snapped. The fowl house has been watched night and day, and, whenever examined, four or five birds would be found dead."

In London, a woman sat asleep, near a grate, and something, as if taking advantage of this means of commonplace explanation, burned her, behind her. Perhaps a being, of incendiary appetite, had crept up behind her, but I had no data upon which so to speculate. But, if we accept that, at Binbrook Farm, something was savagely killing chickens, we accept that whatever we mean by a *being* was there. It seems that, in the little time taken by the farmer to put out the fire of the burning girl, she could not have been badly scorched. Then the suggestion is that, unknown to her, something behind her was burning her, and that she was unconscious of her own scorching flesh. All the stories are notable for absence of outcry, or seeming unconsciousness of victims that something was consuming them.

The town of Market Rasen is near Binbrook Farm. The address of the clergyman who reported, to the S. P. R., the fires and the slaughterings of chickens, upon the farm, is "Binbrook Rectory, Market Rasen." Upon January 16th, as told in the *Louth and North Lincolnshire News,* January 21, there was, in a chicken house, at Market Rasen, a fire in which 57 chickens were consumed. Perhaps a fire in a chicken house is not much of a circumstance to record, but I note that it is said that how this fire started could not be found out.

The girl of Binbrook Farm was taken to the Louth Hospital. In *Lloyd's Weekly News,* February 5, there is an account of "mysterious burns". It is the case of Ashton Clodd, a man aged 75, who, the week before, had died in the Louth Hospital. It is said that he had fallen into a grate, while putting coals in it, and that, for some reason, probably because of his rheumatism, had been unable to rise, and had been fatally burned. But a witness at the inquest is quoted: "If there was a fire in the fireplace, it was very little."

All around every place that we have noted, the revival was simmering, seething, or raging. In Leeds, women, who said that they were directed by visions, stood in the streets, stopping cars, trying to compel passengers to join them. A man in Tunbridge Wells, taking an exhortation literally, chopped his right hand off. "Holy dancers" appeared in London. At Driffield, someone led a procession every night, trundling his coffin ahead of him. And all this in England. And, in England, it is very much the custom to call attention to freaks and extravagances in other parts of the world, or more particularly in one other part of the world, as if only there occurred all the freaks and extravagances. Riots broke out in Liverpool, where the revivalists, with a medieval enthusiasm, attacked Catholics. The Liverpool City Council censured "certain so-called religious meetings, which create danger to life and property." Also at South-end, there were processions of shouters, from which rushed missionaries to slug Catholics, and to sling bricks at houses in which lived Catholics. In the *Liverpool Echo,* February 6, is quoted a magistrate, who said to a complainant, who, because of differences in a general doctrine of loving one's neighbors, had been assaulted: "When you see one of these processions, you should run away, as you would from a mad bull."

Upon all the occurrences that we have noted was the one enveloping phenomenon of the revival. There is scarcely a place that I have mentioned, in any of the accounts, that was unagitated.

Why is it that youngsters have so much to do with psychic phenomena? I have gone into that subject, according to my notions. Well, then, when a whole nation, or hosts of its people, goes primitive, or gives in to atavism, or reverts religiously, it may be that conditions arise that are susceptible to phenomena that are repelled by matured mentality. A hard-headed materialist says, dogmatically: "There are no occult phenomena." Perhaps he is right about this, relatively to himself. But what he says may not apply to children. When, at least to considerable degree, a nation goes childish with medievalism, it may bring upon itself an invasion of phenomena that in the middle ages were common, but that were discouraged, or alarmed, and were driven more to concealment, when minds grew up somewhat.

If we accept that there is Teleportation, and that there are occult beings, that is going so far that we may as well consider the notion that, to stop inquiry, a marauding thing, to divert suspicion, teleported from somewhere in Central Europe, a wolf to England: or that there may be something of the nature of an occult police force, which checks mischief and slaughter by the criminals of its kind, and takes teleportative means to remove suspicion—often solving one problem, only by making another, but relying upon conventionalizations of human thought to supply cloakery.

The killing of poultry—the body on the railroad line— stoppage—scene-shifting.

The killing of sheep—the body on the railroad line— stoppage.

Farm and Home, March 16—that hardly had the wolf been killed, at Cumwinton, in the north of England, when farmers, in the south of England, especially in the districts between Tunbridge and Seven Oaks, Kent, began to tell of mysterious attacks upon their flocks. . . .

Early in the year 1905, there were many mysterious disappearances in England. . . .Here we have an account of one of them, which was equally a mysterious appearance. I take it from the *Liverpool Echo*, February 8. Upon the 4th. of February, a woman was found, lying unconscious, upon the shore, near Douglas, Isle of Man. No one had seen her before, but it was supposed that she had arrived by the boat from England, upon the 3rd of February. There were many residents of the island, who had, in their various callings, awaited the arrival of this boat, and had, in their various interests, looked more than casually at the passengers: but 200 Manxmen visited the mortuary, and not one of them could say that he had seen this woman arrive. The news was published, and then came an inquiry from Wigan, Lancashire. A woman had "mysteriously disappeared" in Wigan, and by her description the body found near Douglas was identified as that of Mrs. Alice Hilton, aged 66 of Wigan. As told, in the *Wigan Observer*, somebody said that Mrs. Hilton had last been seen, upon February 2nd, on her way to Ince, near Wigan, to visit a cousin. But nobody saw her leave Wigan, and she had no known troubles. According to the verdict, at the inquest, Mrs. Hilton had not been drowned, but had died of the effects of cold and exposure upon her heart. . . .

Upon Sept. 4, 1905, London newspapers reported the disappearance, at Ballycastle, Co. Antrim, Ireland, of Prof. George A. Simcox, Senior Fellow of Queen's College, Oxford. Upon August 28th, Prof. Simcox had gone for a walk, and had not returned. There was a search, but nothing was learned.

Several times before, Prof. Simcox had attracted attention by disappearing. The disappearance at Ballycastle was final. . . .

I have notes upon an outbreak of ten "wild men", who appeared in different parts of England, in that period of extraordinary phenomena, the winter of 1904-5. One of them, of origin that could not be found out, appeared in a street in Cheadle. He was naked. An indignant policeman, trying to hang his overcoat about the man, tried to reason with him, but had the same old trouble that Euclid and Newton and Darwin had, and that everybody else has, when trying to be rational, or when trying, in the inorganic, or scientific way, to find a base to argue upon. I suppose the argument was something like this.

Wasn't he ashamed of himself?

Not at all. Some persons might have reasons for being ashamed of themselves, but he had no reason for being ashamed of himself. What's wrong with nakedness? Don't cats and horses and dogs go around without clothes on?

But they are clothed with natural, furry protections.

Well, Mexican dogs, then.

Let somebody else try—somebody who thinks that, as products of logic, the teachings of astronomy, biology, geology, or anything else are pretty nearly final, though with debatable minor points, to be sure. Try this simple, little problem to start with. Why shouldn't the man walk around naked? One is driven to argue upon the base of conventionality. But we are living in an existence, which itself may be base, but in which there are not bases. Argue upon the basis of conventionality, and one is open to well-known counter-arguments. What is all progress but defiance of conventionality?

The policeman, in Euclid's state of desperation, took it as self-evident disgracefulness. Euclid put theorems in bags. He solved problems by encasing some circumstances in an exclusion of whatever interfered with a solution. The policeman of Cheadle adopted the classical method. He dumped the "wild man" into a sack, which he dragged to the station house.

Another of these ten "wild men" spoke in a language that nobody had ever heard of before, and carried a book, in which were writings that could not be identified, at Scotland Yard. Like a traveler from far away, he had made sketches of things that he had seen along the roads. At Scotland Yard, it was said of the writings: "They are not French, German, Dutch, Italian, Spanish, Hungarian, Turkish. Neither are they Bohemian, Greek, Portuguese, Arabic, Persian, Hebrew nor Russian." See London newspapers, and the *East Anglian Daily Times*, Jan. 12, 1905.

NOTE: Page numbers from the Dover edition of *The Complete Books of Charles Fort*: 645, 649-666, 684-685, 690-691.

At the time of the winter of weirdness in England, 1904-1905, no one thought of trying regressive hypnosis on these amnesia-stricken "wild men". The police simply handed them over for confinement in lunatic asylums. Their stories never surfaced.

Fort's suggestion that the luminous apparitions were in some way nourished by the collective ecstasies of the large crowds at the revival meetings they were frequently seen hovering in the vicinity of, particularly if Mrs. Jones happened to be preaching, brings to mind the ecstatic crowds of young people high on LSD gathered at the early rock concerts during the Flower Power period, at which UFOs were frequently witnessed. It also brings to mind the late T. C. Lethbridge's theory that the stone circles of antiquity were used for tribal ecstatic round dancing, which builds up a cone of energy that was tapped by UFOs hovering overhead. The rituals which took place at specific times of the year, such as the solstices, were a form of rendezvous between children of the Earth and children of the stars.

Researcher Salvador Freixedo, whose books are only available in Spanish, has suggested that besides deriving nourishment from the collective ecstasies of large crowds in churches, sports arenas, and political mass-meetings, UFO occupants may also feed upon the collective agonies of armies inflicting pain, terror, and death upon each other in battle. The human propensity for selecting paranoid leaders, eager to send their followers into war over nebulous affronts to pride or honor, would thus be encouraged by non-human entities in order to manipulate us into self-destructive situations. Does the same type of UFO occupant derive nourishment from both human ecstasy and agony, or are different types involved? The history of religion and the tradition of ritual magic indicate that the non-human beings who feed on human misery and set us up for mutual slaughter are not of the same type as those who try to raise our levels of awareness.

At the time that Fort was writing his book *Lo!*, not much was known about the group of magicians known as the Golden Dawn. Since then, several versions of the history of the Golden Dawn have been written.

What was the Golden Dawn up to during the winter of 1904-1905?

It had just broken up into a number of warring factions, those on the right-hand path separating from those on the left-hand path. These groups then fragmented into extremists and moderates and other assorted tendencies. As long as the Golden Dawn was functioning as a single group, the extremists on the left-hand path were held in check and had their activities restrained. When the Golden Dawn broke up in 1903, they went their own way, no longer under any restraint whatsoever. By the winter of 1904 they were ripe for action. A spirit named Aiwass dictated *The Book of the Law* to Aleister Crowley. The following verses from it give some idea of this extremist splinter group's philosophy:

We have nothing with the outcast and the unfit: let them die in their misery. For they feel not. Compassion is the vice of kings: stamp down the wretched and the weak: this is the law of the strong: this is our law and the joy of the world. . . .

Love one another with burning hearts; on the low men trample in the fierce lust of your pride, in the day of your wrath. . . .

Pity not the fallen! I never knew them. I am not for them. I console not: I hate the consoled & the consoler. . . .

I am unique & conqueror. I am not of the slaves that perish. Be they damned & dead! Amen. . . .

Therefore strike hard & low, and to hell with them, master! . . .

Lurk! Withdraw! Upon them! This is the law of the Battle of Conquest: thus shall my worship be about my secret house. . . .

Worship me with fire & blood; worship me with swords and with spears. Let the woman be girt with a sword before me: let blood flow to my name. Trample down the Heathen; be upon them, O warrior, I will give you of their flesh to eat! . . .

Sacrifice cattle, little and big: after a child. . . .

Kill and torture; spare not; be upon them! . . .

Crowley spent the winter of 1904-1905 at his property near Loch Ness in Scotland (the "secret house"?). He was engaged in magical warfare with the man who had taught him magic, MacGregor Mathers. They were each invoking all the demons they knew the names of to destroy the other. Mathers emerged from the confrontation a broken man.

According to the Abra-Melin system of magic, which Crowley learned from Mathers, the magician makes contact either with his Holy Guardian Angel or his Malevolent

Demon. In Egyptian mythology, these two opposing principles are personified as Horus and Set. The word Satan is derived from Set, whose hieroglyphic symbol is the donkey.

One of the puzzling incidents reported during 1904-1905 was a man who saw a large dog in an area where mysterious killing of sheep had been persistently occurring. As he watched it, the large dog turned into a donkey.

Members of the Golden Dawn gave considerable attention to the study of materialising thought forms, and had access to Tibetan "tulpa" techniques. Could the large dog that turned into a donkey have been Crowley astrally projecting on a werewolf trip? Although scientists scoff at explaining werewolf phenomena in terms of astral projection, stories from all over the world and different periods of history indicate that the sorcerer goes into trance and projects his consciousness out of his body into the body of an animal of a species with which he has previously established alliance. He may temporarily take over the body of an existing animal, or he may materialise a thought-form of an animal and use that as a vehicle. The risk the sorcerer takes on such an expedition is that if the animal is wounded or killed while he is using it as a vehicle, his human body in cataleptic trance is wounded in corresponding fashion or killed. What the sorcerer apparently gains from werewolf activity is that the astral body is brought back to the physical body charged with the energy of his victims. If Crowley was using a Tibetan "tulpa" technique and found himself under observation while in the form of a large dog, which would be shot on sight in a region where sheep were being killed, it would be entirely logical for him to shift shape to that of a donkey, which no sane Englishman would shoot.

Among the paranormal experiences reported concerning Mrs. Mary Jones, who was followed by UFOs, is one where she was dropped off at night from a carriage on a lane near her house. In the faint light she saw a man approaching she at first thought was her brother. When she realised that it was not her brother, she began to sing a hymn. The man turned into a large black dog which ran into the hillside.

The philosophy expressed by Crowley in *The Book of the Law* bears a remarkable resemblance to that of the inner circle of the Nazi party, which practised a similar type of ceremonial black magic. It has been claimed by some that members of that inner Nazi circle formed the original nucleus of the American CIA.

Now let's shift our focus of attention to some strange events that took place in modern times.

Chapter Five

STRANGE SUICIDES

Shortly before Morris K. Jessup died under mysterious circumstances in 1959, asphyxiated by the exhaust from his automobile while hot on the UFO trail, a copy of his book *The Case for the UFO* was sent to the Chief of the Office of Naval Research in Washington. Passages had been underlined and comments handwritten in, apparently by three Gypsies who were barely literate and made many spelling mistakes, but who displayed intimate and detailed knowledge of UFOs. There has been a great deal of controversy as to the authenticity of these comments. The dominant theory at the moment is that they were not written by three Gypsies, but by one man with no Gypsy blood, pretending to be a Gypsy and spinning a science-fiction fantasy. This is possible, but has not been proved. What seems to be important is not so much the source of the comments as the ideas they contain. Captain Sidney Sherby of the ONR thought them important enough to contract with a small publisher named Varo for a limited edition of Jessup's book that included the comments and underlinings, presumably for use by ONR personnel. No matter who may have written them, the ideas the comments contain are remarkable enough to merit being evaluated independently of their origin as hypotheses. I think they deserve a serious second look, to be inspected with an open mind, and therefore summarise them here:

Falls from the sky of blood, flesh, fish, frogs, insects, reptiles, and chunks of ice containing organic matter are explained as spoiled food dropped, and periodic cleaning of hydroponic tanks after experiments with different types of food for a growing population.

The comment on the famous case of the Devil's Hoofprints, which terrorised England during the winter of 1855, was that: "The Measure-Marker was accidentally left idling. . . . Marker is like a low-power stonecutter." The clusters of cup marks found on rocks in different parts of the world were made by a similar and more powerful instrument. The cup marks come in clusters because the UFOs have a tendency to wobble and oscillate as they hover (the well-known falling leaf motion).

The comments describe two different space races who share the planet with us without our knowledge. They have bases on the ocean floor as well as in outer space, and it is an insult to call them visitors, as they have been here longer than we have. Fortunately for us, they feel more at ease in Earth's environment on the ocean floor than at ground level.

The Little Men are basically benevolent, unless someone happens to get in their way when they're on a mission, but are disgusted by humanity's inability to live up to the ideals expressed in its sacred books. They regard most humans as worthless animal forms of life, sworn to destructiveness and to those passions that negate the idea of a higher life-form possibility. It was the Little Men who constructed the colossal stone edifices of antiquity. They built their temples in many different parts of the world, but their civilisation was nearly wiped out by the sudden attack of a race identified only as S Men, whose physical characteristics are not described. The S Men attacked the Little Men with small asteroids as well as other weapons, and drove the Little Men from their bases on this planet, but the Little Men returned in force victoriously. Since then an uneasy truce has reigned between the Little Men and the S Men, with occasional outbreaks of hostility. The S Men are ravenous for red meat, extremely materialistic, lack a sense of humor, and are greedy for power. To the S Men, war is the sport that makes life worth living, and one planet in a galaxy means nothing to them.

At this point I'd like to make a few comments of my own. The hypothetical S Men sound remarkably like the Nazi SS. Hitler believed himself to be in contact with a "superman" of extreme cruelty. Hitler's aide-de-camp, Rauschning, testified that Hitler used to collapse in terror after having had nocturnal visions of this "superman", who was invisible to everybody else, possibly an entity that had been invoked by ceremonial black magic. It is commonly believed that the inner circle of the Nazis was deeply involved in ceremonial black magic. It should be remembered that thanks to Allen Dulles in partnership with Reinhard Gehlen, the Gestapo was transplanted intact into the very heart of the U.S. legal system as the *Central Intelligence Agency*, without the knowledge or consent of America's citizens. Did the same type of inner circle ceremonial magic continue under the camouflage of the Stars and Stripes? Certain aspects of the animal mutilations discussed in the next chapter make this far-out possibility seem quite possible. Is that inner circle trying to set up an alliance with the same type of entities that Hitler was in alliance with? If such a secret alliance is in the works, might that be a major reason for the otherwise insane insistence on maintaining a cover-up which is contradicted flagrantly by not only a mountain of existing evidence, but new evidence arriving almost daily? Thanks to legislation put through Congress (the Intelligence Identities Protection Act of 1981),we already have a situation in the United States in which our traditional freedom of speech, guaranteed by the Constitution, is becoming freedom to speak about anything except the CIA. Some claim that the concentration camps have already been built, but they are still standing there empty. Let us act before it is too late. Having made my own comments, I now return to the comments made in the margins of Jessup's book.

The Little Men enjoy music and dancing, consider subtle spiritual realities more important than gross materialism, have child-like spontaneity, and yet have matured to the point that they no longer desire war. The Little Men have gills as well as lungs, like a human embryo, and spend over half the time in water. They use telepathy instead of writing. One comment describes them "as peaceful and naively curious a bunch of inadvertent havoc wreakers as you'll ever see."

Jessup states:

In our study of storms we have been driven inexorably to admit that some storms have an artificial aspect, a sort of organic appearance, an air of being manufactured for a purpose and to be carrying out that purpose. We therefore postulate some percentage of artificiality, or intelligence, among that small percentage of storms which suddenly appear in otherwise undisturbed skies, proceed with a purposeful manner, as though concealing something, and discharge peculiar materials. They seem to be concentrated, perhaps too directive to be entirely meteorological in their origins. . . . I believe that space structures of five to twenty miles diameter are sufficiently large to produce such storms, and there may be elements of purposefulness in so doing, if only for camouflage or concealment.

To this, the comment is that the Little Men's Great Ark is even larger.

When Jessup says that every science breaks down when forced to contemplate the origin of man's intellectual development, the comment is: "What inspiration caused man to become man by using tools? Whence came the idea? Science says necessity, but the same necessity exists for apes even now."

Jessup advances a brilliant hypothesis concerning the method by which airplanes, ships, and people are made to disappear:

Conceive of a force, ray, or focal point, in some force-field either unknown to us, or at least not understood, which produces rigidity in a localized or sharply delimited volume of air, or possibly in space itself. We are thinking of something like crystals of ice freezing within a body of water. The element remains the same but its physical attributes change suddenly and drastically.

Another example might be the passage of a limited but powerful magnetic field through a scattering of iron filings or iron powder. Before the approach of the magnetic flux, the powder lies loose, flexible, and penetrable. Yet, when the flux enters it, invisibly and imperceptibly to the senses of man, this docile powder becomes rigid, tenacious, coherent, and at least semisolid. Do the space dwellers have a force which produces this temporary rigidity in the air, or even in the gravitational field itself? Or do they create "local" concentrations of the gravitational field as we are able to do with the magnetic field?

Suppose that some intelligent entity was directing concentration of potential which could make small volumes of rarified air rigid, could set up a sort of island in the gravitational or magnetic field, moving the island about as the spot of a searchlight is moved on thin clouds. Such a thing would be invisible, would have many of the physical attributes of a solid body, but very small mass. For example, its movement through the air would be wavelike, and would not involve transformation of the medium any more than the spot of a searchlight would require movement of the cloud which enabled the beam to attain visibility. In moving, this island would simply "freeze" on the advancing edge and "thaw" on the trailing edge. In this way, it could have almost infinite velocity, and also acceleration, just as the spot of the searchlight. In this manner it would appear to be free of mass, and actually it would be free of mass, because only the force beam would move, not the air. Yet in resisting the impingement of a bird, a plane, or perhaps a meteor, it would have mass, and a very destructive mass at that. A pilot flying a plane into such a body would have no warning. Yet if such a thing were a few hundred yards in diamater, its mass in resisting the plane would be thousands of pounds, perhaps tons. The analogy to a ship hitting an iceberg would be very close.

If such a force island were formed in the upper atmosphere, it might be very possible for it to have many of the physical characteristics of a solid body, and yet in matters of illumination it could behave exactly as any other auroral phenomena. In this connection we must remember that auroral phenomena are magnetic and may be caused by streams of electrons from the sun which are, in effect, precisely the type of force beam upon which we are speculating.

It seems obvious that a single beam could not have the effect which we suggested, else the freeze would take place along the entire length of the beam. However, it is possible that the three-dimensional volume enclosed within the intersection of two beams might create such a congealed island.

Speculating further on this weird possibility, remember that oxygen is a magnetic substance. It is not, perhaps, paramagnetic like iron, manganese and nickel, but is nevertheless sufficiently magnetic that it can be separated from the other constituents of air by means of a magnetic field.

If such a congealment were possible, consider the result of crossing the two beams at the exact aerial position of a flying plane and congealing the air around and in the plane. Could you, in this way, hold a plane in suspension, or even carry it away? Could you, by a similar concentration of beams, freeze two aviators on the sands of the Arabian desert, and carry them away? Could you freeze a man and instantly lift him out of sight, or cause him to be invisible within the block of frozen air or oxygen? Could you freeze the crew of a ship, and remove them from the vessel?

Further on, Jessup is describing an airplane disappearance, and the comment in the margin is: "Men frozen helpless make good prey." Other comments indicate that men who are drunk are not mentally paralysed by the freeze. Radio men in their shacks with the sender turned on are less affected. No man wearing hob-nail boots or cleats on his shoes has ever been abducted, nor any man in a cave under earth. If one is in the country and a sudden hush falls, all animal and bird sounds stop dead, the way to avoid abduction is to cover one's self with earth.

These few extracts from his work and the comments on it give at least some slight idea of how brilliant and controversial the research was that Jessup was involved in when suddenly snuffed out with an official diagnosis of "suicide". We now take up the case of another strange "suicide".

Dr. James E. McDonald was Senior Physicist of the Institute of Atmospheric Physics at the University of Arizona. He thought that the Federal Power Commission was evading the evidence concerning UFO involvement in the total power failure that paralysed New York on July 13th, 1965, and dared to say so in front of a Congressional committee.

The official explanation was that five key points in the Con Ed system had been struck by lightning almost simultaneously, then a sixth key point had been struck by lightning a few hours later.

There was a UFO sighting in Kentucky on July 12th, witnessed by both local police officers and civilians. The UFO was described as a large white pulsating light with small red and green lights blinking above and below it. On July 13th, just before the "lightning" struck (how could Con Ed have neglected to install lightning rods around their expensive equipment, an elementary precaution any farmer takes for his barn?), a UFO was sighted hovering above power lines at Waterford, New York. There was also a sighting on Fire Island of flashing lights moving in unsteady patterns, making their way westward toward the city. Just fifteen minutes before the sudden black-out, there was a UFO sighted near the World Trade Towers in New York City: fat at one end, thin at the other, bright multicolored lights blinking on and off as it swayed back and forth.

Major Donald E. Keyhoe distilled the essentials out of enormous amounts of information concerning UFOs and electrical power failures in his *Aliens From Space* (Doubleday, 1973). He devoted particular attention to the great New York power failure of 1965. The following paragraph summarises the results of his meticulously detailed investigation, as described in his excellent book:

Just after the power failed at Syracuse, two UFOs were seen at Hancock Airport by multiple witnesses, including the city's Deputy Aviation Commissioner. One of the UFOs was also observed from above by a flight instructor and a computer technician in a plane approaching for a landing. When the flight instructor reported the sighting to the Deputy Commissioner, he specified that the UFO was directly above the Clay power substation, an automatic control unit between Niagara Falls and New York, on a grid system that was supposed by our best qualified experts to be accident-proof and infallible. Other pilots and assorted witnesses reported other sightings elsewhere. Two civilians in flight over Pennsylvania shortly before the blackout began witnessed two UFOs flying above them with Air Force Jet interceptors in pursuit. Also just before the blackout began, a UFO was sighted near the Niagara Falls power plant. After it was all over, experts investigating the cause of the breakdown traced its origin to the area of the Clay substation, but were unable to find anything wrong with the equipment. When investigators and journalists began to take the hypothesis of UFO intervention seriously, a previously overlooked broken relay in Ontario was announced to be the cause of the disaster. However, later investigation brought out that the supposedly broken relay had in fact never broken. The supposedly infallible billion dollar U.S.—Canadian grid system dissolved in four seconds flat as the network was suddenly and simultaneously drained of power in some sectors while being overloaded in others. The multiple safety controls supposed to be effective in such an emergency did not work at all. They had worked effectively during previous smaller-scale emergency situations. In 1968 Congressman William F. Ryan (D., N.Y.) put Dr. McDonald on record concerning UFO activity at the time of the great power failure. Dr. McDonald charged the Federal Power Commission with evading the evidence connecting UFOs to the power failure. As Dr. McDonald made this accusation in Congress, it was entered in the Congressional Record.

On June 13, 1971, Dr. McDonald was found dead under mysterious circumstances: shot through the head, with a pistol by his side. The official verdict was 'suicide'. It is true that Dr. McDonald's courageous statements had provoked a torrent of derision and abuse, and he was being ostentatiously ostracized by his colleagues (in the tradition of Giordano Bruno, Paracelsus, Galileo, Wilhelm Reich, and a few other rare immortals). However, he was a man of principle who believed in the validity of what he was doing, not at all the type of person we would expect to commit suicide.

Murder disguised as suicide is one of the well-known specialties of the CIA, which was hell-bent on suppressing UFO information and certain other specific types of information at that time. Perhaps there *is* a cover-up of the Kennedy and King assassinations, in which so many witnesses mysteriously died about the same time Dr. McDonald did, like the cover-up of the near-impossibility of disposing of nuclear waste safely, and the cover-up concerning the real nature of UFO phenomena, and *perhaps all are inextricably linked together*. The same group of entrenched establishment authorities which is responsible for spraying our marihuana with the lethal poison Paraquat (in the nation whose Founding Father, George Washington, wrote in his Diary: "Take ye the hemp seed and sow it everywhere.") is also responsible for these other crimes against the human race.

There is ample documentation suggesting that among the highest priority covert operations of the CIA are those designed to maintain a steady supply of heroin and cocaine to the Mafia. For specific details, see *The Politics of Heroin in Southeast Asia* by Alfred W. McCoy, published by Harper & Row in New York in 1972; *The Great Heroin Coup* by Henrik Kruger, published by South End Press, in Boston in 1980; and *Mama Coca* by Antonil, published by Hassle Free Press in London in 1978. Uncle Sam's much-publicised 'war on drugs' is in fact a war on the *independent* drug dealers, who constitute a threat to the Mafia monopoly. The CIA and the Mafia have worked hand-in-hand from the very beginning of the Agency. Remember Lucky Luciano's helping hand during the invasion of Sicily in World War II? Did you ever stop to think that the more strictly illegal and severely punished the use of drugs becomes, the more profitable is the traffic in them? Intentionally confusing the relatively benign drugs with the genuinely toxic and addictive drugs, and treating all users as criminals, maximises the number of junkies: a type of citizen that is easy to control.

How come the man chosen to be Secretary of Labor under the present Administration turned out to have such obvious Mafia connections that he had to be white-washed by a token superficial investigation, after which he went on to become the first Cabinet official in the history of the United States to be indicted on criminal charges? The basis for President Reagan's personal fortune was the real estate deal he made shortly after becoming the Governor of California, when he bought land cheaply, and then soon afterward sold it for an astronomical amount to a group of benefactors who have never been publicly identified. Why should their anonymity be regarded as sacrosanct, when the possibility exists that they may be among the small group of privileged contractors from whom the Pentagon purchases equipment at the most amazingly exorbitant prices?

The CIA is the largest, most bloated multi-national corporation in the world, and it cares no more for the actual well-being of the American people than does a parasite for the actual well-being of its host.

At the end of World War II, the Allies surgically removed the Nazi tumor from Germany. When Allen Dulles took Reinhard Gehlen into partnership to transform the Office of Strategic Services into the *Central* Intelligence Agency, supposedly to make U.S. Intelligence "more efficient", taking over almost the entire Gestapo network in the process, assimilating its members into the U.S. Intelligence community and simultaneously granting U.S. citizenship or protection to a swarm of high-ranking Nazi war criminals, the tumor that had been surgically removed from Germany metastasized in the United States. The CIA is a cancerous growth on our body politic that functions as a law unto itself, a branch of our government that is not accountable to anyone in the government (except theoretically to the President), a government within the government which has since its inception expanded and still continues to expand its degree of control exponentially, a secret police with life-or-death power, an American Gestapo that supports fascism world-wide. Almost single-handed, except for some help from a few top Pentagon officials, Allen Dulles transformed the jubilant victory of the Allies into a covert defeat.

The most plausible of the plethora of conspiracy theories spawned by the assassination of John F. Kennedy was that when JFK decided to fire Allen Dulles after the fiasco at the Bay of Pigs, Dulles re-assigned the squad of CIA/Mafia hit men who had been assigned to assassinate Castro, but who had bungled their attempts, to JFK, and that on this mission they succeeded in hitting their target. If true, every U.S. President since then has been subordinate to the CIA, living with the knowledge that there is a gun behind his back which will blow him away if he steps out of line. Since the murder of JFK, both candidates in each presidential election have been screened by the same "security" organisation, which does not change fundamentally after any election. Every four years, we get our choice between a Republican Tweedledum and a Democrat Tweedledee.

President Reagan's celebrating the fortieth anniversary of the end of World War II by laying a wreath on the graves of the S.S. storm troopers who perpetrated Hitler's worst atrocities was not a "mistake" made by an inefficient staff. No amount of blarney can gloss over the fact that with that one gesture, our President managed to alienate not just the Jews and the Gypsies, but also the English, the French, the Dutch, the Norwegians, and all of our traditional democratic Allies. The roots of that symbolic gesture go deep.

It should not be forgotten that Hitler gave the Germans a "new patriotism", boosting their egos by making them feel they had a divine right to be selfish and to discriminate against minorities, before leading them into unprecedented catastrophe.

We must face the fact that the malignant growth of corporate fascism has metastasized throughout our body politic. Our survival as a free nation requires that we recognise the different forms it takes, and fight them effectively.

If anyone ever deserved a posthumous Congressional Medal of Honor, it is Karen Silkwood.

Karen Silkwood's murder was disguised as an automobile accident after she tried to alert the public to the way safety regulations and plutonium leakage were being deliberately ignored at the Kerr-McGee nuclear plant where she was employed. A federal judge ordered Kerr-McGee to pay her heirs the unprecedented amount of ten million dollars in punitive damages. Her story was the subject of a powerful motion picture that should be viewed by any reader who doubts the need for our concerns.

Thirty years after Kerr-McGee built their uranium processing plant at Shiprock, New Mexico, they had to close it down, since it had become (as do all nuclear plants after that approximate time span) too "hot" to operate, extremely dangerous garbage. So Kerr-McGee pulled out of Shiprock, and closed down its operation there, leaving behind 72 acres of uncovered uranium tailings. They also left behind something else. The impact of radiation on the health of the local population was dramatically demonstrated by a spectacular rise in the community's rate of major birth defects, miscarriages, diseases of all kinds, and death. According to local statistics, low-level radiation from Kerr-McGee's intensive uranium mining in Shiprock, New Mexico, appears to have caused more and worse birth defects than did both the atomic bombs dropped on Hiroshima and Nagasaki combined.

In 1968 Kerr-McGee built a uranium processing plant near Gore, Oklahoma, around which major environmental degradation has occurred. The waste emitted daily by the plant contains 17 toxic heavy metals and 4 radioactive substances. This waste has been leaking from storage ponds, has infiltrated sub-surface water, and is seeping into the Illinois and Arkansas rivers. Several major uranium spills have severely contaminated local surface streams. State officials and the tame news media, apparently blind to everything except Kerr-McGee's financial clout, systematically ignore the flagrant conflict of interest constituted by Robert S. Kerr's membership on the board of Oklahoma Water Resources. The Environmental Protection Agency reprimanded the Gore plant on 21 occasions during 1984 and 1985 for over-dumping violations. The Nuclear Regulatory Commission issued a temporary permit to Kerr-McGee, allowing them to inject five million gallons per year of radioactive waste into an on-site injection well. When Kerr-McGee tried to have the temporary permit made permanent, the NRC evaded its responsibility by transferring jurisdiction over the well to the Oklahoma Department of Health, with which Kerr-McGee is now negotiating. An independent study of the injection well site states that injection of the waste into the 3,000 foot deep Arbuckle Formation results in profound lateral flow contamination. In other words, instead of being contained in an enclosed underground area, the waste is spreading out in all directions. The NRC has not only refused to acknowledge the validity of this study, it has granted Kerr-McGee a permit (*without issuing a license,* in order to by-pass safety requirements) to build a *second* plant in the same area to process uranium to weapons grade *without making any additional plans for waste disposal.* This suicidal insanity has all the power and the prestige of the Reagan Administration behind it.

If anyone thinks that Kerr-McGee is a rogue elephant whose behavior is not typical of the nuclear industry, they should contemplate the details of the most recent case of the Karen Silkwood type, which surfaced just as this book was about to go to press. According to the February, 1986, issue of *Acres, U.S.A.* (P.O. Box 9547, Kansas City, Mo. 64133): "Judith Penley was about to give details of safety problems at TVA's Watts Bar nuclear plant. But before she could do so, she was gunned down at a Cleveland truck stop. According to her attorney, Albert Bates, Penley was ambushed no less than twice in four days. She escaped the first time, but was not so lucky the second time around. She was killed by a shot from a high powered rifle at close range. Senator Albert Gore has asked the FBI to investigate. In the meantime local authorities are investigating repeated break-ins at the home of an equipment inspector."

The shades of Karen Silkwood and Dr. McDonald may be mute, but the testimony they bear is eloquent. The fate of Dr. McDonald is an unmistakably clear example of what happens when a scientist of integrity dares to disagree fundamentally with the clique of professional politicians whose only aim is to perpetuate and extend their control over everyone else. Dr. McDonald was neither the first nor the last witness to be silenced in such a fashion, but the example of what happened to him is particularly dramatic and unforgettable.

It is worth pointing out that one of the main reasons none of Dr. McDonald's colleagues spoke up for him is that

George Adamski had almost single-handedly succeeded in making the subject of UFOs seem so utterly ridiculous that no serious scientist would want to have anything to do with it. By mixing a certain amount of the real thing with a certain amount of sensational nonsense, then presenting it scrambled up together to be accepted or rejected as a whole, it is possible to make unfamiliar subject matter seem repugnant and unfit for study by intelligent people, while attracting the ignorant like flies. People who traveled with Adamski noticed that he had been issued a special passport, such as is usually reserved for diplomats and high government officials. It is entirely possible that he may have been a CIA dis-information agent, who successfully fulfilled the mission of making the subject of UFOs seem so absurd that no independent in-depth investigation would be made by qualified academics.

The hypothesis of collusion between a demonic type of UFO occupant and demonic elements operating under camouflage within our government is strengthened when one considers the circumstances under which the martyrdom of Wilhelm Reich took place. During the period just before United States authorities sent one of the greatest geniuses of modern times to his death in the penitentiary, then confiscated and burned all of his work they could get their hands on, in true Nazi tradition, Reich received considerable unwelcome attention from a type of UFO manifestation that was definitely hostile to the research into subtle aspects of life energy he was engaged in. However, those who drove him to his death and burned what they could of his work won only a temporary victory. In the long run, they immortalised him.

Chapter Six

MYSTERIOUS MUTILATIONS

UFO occupants have been taking a strong interest in our farm animals, killing and dissecting them by the thousands and tens of thousands. The importance of this aspect of UFO activity has been so persistently played down and minimised by the authorities and the press that I intend to go into it at considerable length. The first part of this chapter will focus mainly on what was going on in Montana during 1975 and 1976. The remainder of it will deal with incidents of this type, and peripheral phenomena associated with them, that took place nation-wide (with some foreign reports included) from 1978 through 1984.

Typically, only reproductive and digestive organs that we consider inedible are taken, perhaps with an ear or an eye or the tongue. Carcasses have frequently been found drained of almost every last drop of blood in a way that would be impossible even with the use of a powerful vacuum pump, as normally the veins would collapse before all the blood could be extracted. Such carcasses often had two puncture wounds in the throat.

Coyotes will normally eat almost any carrion, no matter how rotten. They are certainly not fussy about their food. However, coyotes and other predators will not eat or even go near many of the carcasses left behind after these historically unprecedented mutilations, which began in 1973. There have been scattered cases reported here and there in the past (particularly in England during 1904-1905), but nothing on anywhere near this scale.

By 1976 it was estimated that there had been about 2,000 animal mutilation cases in the United States. In Puerto Rico there had been about 300 cases. Mutilations were being reported sporadically elsewhere, but no one seemed to be releasing statistics. In the United States the current estimate is of about 10,000 cases, a 500% increase.

The best publicly available documentation of phenomena during the first few years of the mutilations is a book written by a Deputy Sheriff of Cascade County, Montana, Captain Keith Wolverton, in collaboration with a local school-teacher, Roberta Donovan (*Mystery Stalks the Prairie*, published by T.H.A.R. Institute, Raynesford, Montana 59469 in 1976).

Among the peculiarities noted by Captain Wolverton was a cow that had been cut open by something that left neatly and precisely defined serrated edges. Two different medical pathologists certified that this could not be attributed to predators or barbed wire.

One of the most puzzling aspects of the mutilations was the lack of footprints or tracks of any kind, even when carcasses were found in mud or snow.

The possibility of the mutilations being the work of a fanatical religious cult was considered, but how could any cult carry on such activity without leaving footprints or other tracks? How could they silently overpower wild range cattle and their guard dogs, perform sophisticated surgery in the field, and then disappear without a trace?

UFO activity seemed a more plausible explanation, particularly as UFOs had been reported in association with a number of mutilations. So had unmarked helicopters, which did not always behave like ordinary helicopters, and which seemed to multiply like rabbits, flying at speeds far in excess of the range normally available to helicopters.

Witnesses of UFO sightings reported that herds of cattle in the vicinity were panic-stricken. A rancher and his wife, who both got a clear look through powerful binoculars at a UFO landed about 5/8 of a mile away, reported that two appendages emerged from the egg-shaped object. They made a motion as a swimmer does with his arms when doing the breast stroke, then they retracted back into the egg.

Another rancher and his sons saw a UFO as big as a hotel, which was accompanied by four smaller ones. He also observed through strong binoculars from less than a mile away, and described the large UFO as rectangular in shape, 300 to 400 feet long and about 60 feet high. It had two rows of windows, which were each about 5 to 6 feet high and 2 to 3 feet wide. The smaller UFOs approached it, then darted away only to return again. Then the rancher and his sons saw what they thought was a helicopter approaching. However, as the helicopter approached the large UFO, it turned into a small UFO.

A phantom automobile began to appear on local roads, appearing as if out of nowhere, following people, then disappearing in seemingly impossible fashion.

Captain Wolverton and his colleagues were extremely puzzled by the failure of Federal authorities to do anything about the widespread criminal mutilations being reported from many different states. It was because of this unpardonable apathy on the part of higher officialdom and the anguish of his fellow citizens, whose livestock were being mutilated with impunity, that Captain Wolverton felt impelled to preserve his on-the-spot account of these strange events in book form.

UFOs that turn into helicopters and vice versa have been reported in several other cases from different sources.

There have also been single cases in which both UFO phenomena and Bigfoot phenomena were simultaneously present. Apparently both UFOs and Bigfoot have the ability to become invisible at will. A rancher following a fresh Bigfoot track heard it running nearby, breathing heavily as if out of breath, but when he shone his flashlight at where the noise was coming from, there was nothing there.

Among the most ancient Irish legends is that of the Cloak of Invisibility, which recurs in different forms in many other cultures. Right up into the last century, legendary heroes like Crazy Horse were believed to have the ability to make themselves invisible. Perhaps it's an ability that Bigfoot never lost.

During the course of a UFO incident, a pounding noise was heard by one witness. A transparent ectoplasmic Bigfoot shape materialised before another witness. During the following weeks, there were dozens of reports of a flesh-and-blood Bigfoot roaming the region. One team of investigators experienced loud pounding noises and weird lights flashing inside their tent.

There is the case of the elderly lady living alone in an isolated area who heard strange noises on her porch, picked up a 16 gauge shotgun, threw open the door, found herself face to face with a Bigfoot only a few feet away, and fired point-blank into its stomach. To her astonishment, the creature disappeared in a flash of light with no sound or smell.

In an incident that took place in Pennsylvania in 1973 (reported in the May 1982 issue of *The MUFON UFO Journal*), a group of farmers saw a UFO descending toward a field during the early evening. They decided to find out what was going on. As they walked over the crest of the hill, they saw a UFO estimated at about 100 feet in diameter resting on the ground. Nearby were two Bigfoot creatures about 8 feet tall, with arms that hung down past their knees, covered with long dark hair. At first the farmers thought that the creatures must be bears. A farmer who was armed with a 30.06 rifle fired a shot over their heads. The creatures responded by approaching the group, which then realised they were not bears or any other form of life ever seen before. The farmer with a rifle fired three shots in a row directly into one of the creatures, which made a whining sound and raised its right hand. The UFO suddenly disappeared, the sound abruptly stopped, the farmers turned their backs and fled. When they returned about 45 minutes later with a local police officer, neither the UFO nor the creatures were to be seen. However, the officer verified that there was a glowing ring on the ground about 100 feet in diameter that would have been bright enough to read by if he had stepped into the circle and tried to do so. This case was one of 103 different UFO/Bigfoot sightings reported from a six county area of Pennsylvania during 1973.

The often-reported Little Men do not appear to be physically adapted to extensive exploration of terrestrial forest and wilderness areas. The Pech Merle cave drawing in France from the Palaeolithic era depicting a specimen of this type of humanoid pierced through by spears suggests they may be vulnerable to surprise attack. It is possible that they may work in collaboration with Bigfoot creatures, releasing them to carry out certain types of missions, maintaining communication either through telepathy or implants, then picking them up after the missions are completed. There have been so many Bigfoot sightings in highly settled areas no large wild animal could penetrate without being noticed that this seems a distinct possibility. Of course, it is also possible that Bigfoot may operate independently of the Little Men.

Although Bigfoot sightings have occasionally been reported from areas where cattle mutilations were taking place, no definite linkage has been established so far between these two different types of phenomena.

The first newsletter circulated concerning the mutilations was *The Cattle Report*, edited by Ed Sanders. It was short-lived, but during its existence published an account of an incident that had taken place in Logan County, Colorado, a region which had been plagued with many mutilations, with which unmarked helicopters were associated. About 10 P.M. on August 21st, 1975, an unidentified helicopter was reported heading into Logan County from the east. Sheriff Graves and his deputies went into action. Seventeen ground units took part in the chase, and the sheriff rented a private plane with its pilot, taking two deputies with him. There was no cloud cover and the night sky was clear. During the pursuit there were some odd interventions in the form of radio messages from individuals claiming to be Air Force officers relaying radar information from Warren Air Base, later found to be fraudulent. However, the most interesting aspect of the incident is the way the chase ended, about 4:30 A.M. in southwestern Nebraska. The occupants of the sheriff's plane saw the lights of the unidentified helicopter beneath them clearly, then the lights went out. The sheriff and the pilot assumed that the helicopter had landed, but when the pilot brought his plane down to an altitude of slightly over 100 feet for a close look, the only thing visible was *a missile silo*.

A previously unsuspected aspect of the mutilations was brilliantly brought to public attention by researcher David DeWitt, who pointed out that just about the same time that the mutilations began, around 1973, a new branch of science was beginning to develop: biogeochemistry, through which it becomes possible to locate mineral and petroleum deposits through analysis of salts in tissue samples of herbivorous animals that have been grazing on a section of land for an extended period of time. The seemingly useless parts removed from the mutilated cattle are precisely those required for such analysis. Here indeed we have a plausible motive for at least some of the apparently senseless mutilations.

Since the CIA acts as the private police force of the multinational corporations, such a search for mineral and petroleum deposits could (by a sufficiently warped mind) be brought under the umbrella of National Security. When deposits were located, the rancher could be relocated, preferably by foreclosing his mortgage.

Since many mutilations have occurred near air bases and sensitive military installations thoroughly covered by long-range radar, where any intruding civilian helicopter pilot would have been immediately challenged by jet fighters, it is difficult to believe that the military didn't know what was going on. It is well known that the mutilations tend to come in waves. During a wave, it is night after night after night. How come all those jet fighters never managed to intercept even one of the multilators' helicopters?

Project Stigma was founded in Texas in 1978 to investigate the continuing occurrence of animal mutilations. Its news report, *Stigmata* (P.O. Box 1094, Paris, Texas 75460), contains the most complete and reliable documentation of this extremely puzzling subject matter yet made public. I have summarised information concerning the period 1978-1984 from this source, adding my own interpretations of the data where this seems appropriate.

1978-1979

An item of considerable possible importance is the story of a middle-aged lady, who lived with her husband in Arkansas. One day she was picking apples, and fell from the ladder. One of her legs was deeply cut, and she also received a severe blow on the head, which knocked her out to the point that she was unable to move or cry out to her husband. While lying on the ground in this condition, two beings such as she had never seen before approached. They were humanoid, but not human. One was tall and thin, the other quite short. They began to give her abundantly bleeding leg medical treatment with an instrument they had with them. Within a short time all bleeding and pain had stopped, and there was only a small scar to show that there had ever been a wound. They then gave her a piece of metal with markings engraved on it. She invited them to her house for a meal, but they replied that the only nourishment they took was juice. The lady offered them some fruit juice, but the response was that the juice they used for nourishment was different from the type of juice consumed by humans.

Their voices did not seem to come from their mouths, but from their abdomens. They walked away, and the lady walked back to her house, retaining the piece of engraved metal. Among other things, the engravings depicted pyramids and six-pointed stars.

About six weeks later, the lady's dog did not return home as usual from its daily ramble through the nearby woods. The lady walked deep into the forest looking for her dog, and came to the edge of a clearing in which there was something very strange indeed going on. A horse was lying on its side, apparently unconscious. Two men in white, dressed like surgeons in a hospital, were at work on the horse. There were also two Air Force helicopters landed in the clearing, two men in Air Force uniforms, and the same two humanoids who had come to her rescue after she fell from the ladder.

The lady realised that this was a scene she was not supposed to be watching, and began to retreat. As the group noticed her presence, she broke into a run. She heard footsteps running behind her, but panic endowed her with a burst of speed, and she managed to leave them behind. Then she was overtaken by a helicopter, which flashed a blue beam of light on her. This beam of light severely burned her right breast and clothing. This time she was able to scream for help, which arrived as the helicopter retreated. She was taken to the local hospital to have her wounds treated.

Upon arrival at the hospital, in response to questioning she told the hospital staff exactly what had happened to her. People having nothing to do with the hospital staff began turning up to question her. The local sheriff insisted on taking her to a psychiatric clinic, claiming that she was insane and had herself been responsible for the horse mutilation, which had in fact occurred. After a thorough examination and a battery of tests, the doctors refused to commit her. They diagnosed her as sane, and she was released.

After she returned home, she was harassed at all hours of the day and night by strangers who insisted on questioning her, repeating the same questions over and over again. Her husband decided to quietly sell their property and move to a different state. They did this, and had peace for a short time, but then the harrassment began all over again.

This story remained anecdotal until 1980, when researchers located the lady and her husband. The Mutual UFO Network began investigating the case, but as of 1986 had not yet made public its conclusions. It is highly unusual for this organisation to take so long to make up its mind about a case. It seems possible that the controversial implications of this case might be a reason for such unusual hesitation to make public the results of the investigation. If MUFON thought that the case was a hoax, there would be no reason to delay releasing its report. However, until the report is released, nothing definite can be said one way or the other.

During 1978 and 1979, several police officers proposed theories and made relevant comments on the mutilation phenomena. It was suggested that the cattle were taken up into the air, mutilated while in the air, then dropped to the ground, Carcasses had been found in seemingly impossible places, sometimes with broken bones as if dropped from above. It was also suggested that the cattle had been selected and marked in some way before the mutilations took place, perhaps even years before. Later it was discovered that patches of hide on mutilated animals fluoresced under black light, so that may be the marking mechanism. They could be stained with an otherwise invisible fluorescing substance on a preliminary run.

One policeman stated that ranchers had become reluctant to report the mutilations, and when they did asked that the report and their names be withheld from the press, citing this as a reason there was so little public awareness of the extent of the mutilations. Many sheriffs and police officers noted the way that predators like coyotes as well as domesticated dogs refused to approach most (but not all) of the carcasses. Typically a coyote or dog would approach to within about ten feet from the carcass, and then retreat from it.

There was considerable speculation over the way in which wild range cattle could be immobilised, particularly after a bull escaped from a cattle show in the town of Paris, Texas. The bull went on a rampage, while its owner and local police officers tried unsuccessfully for two and a half hours to subdue it. Finally the owner gave up, and told the policemen to shoot. A deputy sheriff fired six 30-30 and 30.06 shells into the bull with no immediate effect. The bull collapsed twice, but rose to its feet again each time and continued to rampage around the streets, doing even more property damage. Finally a double-barreled shotgun at close range finished off the animal. An autopsy showed that all six shots fired from the heavy-caliber rifles had entered the bull's skull. If the police force of a town aided by professional ranchers had that much difficulty subduing just one animal, how on earth did the mutilators immobilise them?

A possible explanation was found when tissue samples taken from a carcass revealed the presence of chlorpromazine, a tranquiliser commonly used in medicine. A massive dose of chlorpromazine would be capable of immobilising a large animal. As New Mexico State Police Officer Gabe Valdez said to the reporter from the *Santa Fe New Mexican*: "We know this stuff is made here, and it isn't from outer space. Whoever is doing it is highly sophisticated, and they have a lot of resources. They're well-organized."

During an election campaign in Colorado, a candidate for sheriff campaigning against his opponent, the incumbent sheriff, claimed that the incumbent had received a letter from the government saying that the mutilations were O.K. and he should not concern himself with them. The incumbent denied the existence of any such letter.

Some of the most interesting theories and comments arrived in letters sent by concerned citizens to Project Stigma. Here are a few of the many received during 1978 and 1979:

One theory proposed was that the mutilations were highly skilled excisions, performed under the auspices of the United States government, to determine the amount and extent of plutonium leakage from the Rocky Mountain Arsenal near Denver. It was pointed out that the existence of such leakage had been reported in the Denver newspapers, and was a matter of considerable controversy. The parts usually taken from the cattle were reproductive and mucous tissues, where high concentrations of plutonium would tend to accumulate. One of the animals mutilated was a buffalo, which was inside the Cheyenne Mountain Zoo at the time. One of the cattle mutilations had taken place near the fence of the North American Air Defence Command (NORAD) installation on Cheyenne Mountain, the nerve center of the entire U.S. defense system and probably the most heavily guarded area in the whole world, protected by the most sophisticated surveillance systems available to modern science. At the site of another mutilation, a standard issue U.S. Army scalpel had been found. One rancher claimed to have witnessed a landed helicopter with men in army uniforms cutting up one of his cattle, and to have retreated from the scene without having been noticed. At first the local sheriff was very active about trying to catch the mutilators, and coverage in the local newspaper was extensive. Then suddenly the sheriff had nothing more to say about the matter, which simultaneously ceased to be mentioned in the local paper. The owner of the local paper then sold out and moved away from the region. Helicopters had frequently been noticed hovering over herds of cattle, and had frightened away observers by diving at them. Turmoil and consternation among local ranchers reached such a point that they began firing high-powered rifles at any helicopters flying over their property, and the Air Force had to order its personnel to fly detours or higher than usual. UFOs had been sighted occasionally in the region, but not in direct association with any known mutilation incident.

Project Stigma pointed out that this theory failed to account for the fact that mutilations were occurring nationwide on a larger scale, in many regions nowhere near nuclear installations, not just in the Denver area, and to that extent could be considered simplistic.

Another letter-writer thought that 95% of the mutilations were the work of extra-terrestrials, who need large amounts of biological tissue for immunisation procedures, much as our scientists use eggs and substances extracted from animals to prepare medicines for similar purposes. The extra-terrestrials use the medicines prepared not only to immunise themselves against terrestrial diseases, but also to keep humans healthy, their concern for our health being similar to the concern of our scientists for the health of laboratory animals.

The extra-terrestrials appearing among us are the advance scouts for an enormous variety of intelligent life forms from other regions of the cosmos.

A different correspondent speculated about the possibility of the existence of a group within the government secretly practising ceremonial black magic, such as is known to have been practised by the Nazis, which had succeeded in materialising an entity that demanded blood sacrifice and vital essences. Perhaps some hitherto unsuspected factor such as this might be involved in the mutilations.

In the next issue of *Stigmata*, another correspondent developed this idea further. His opinion was that this group had been in existence for centuries, and had unleashed forces that benevolent magicians had chained. He mentioned that in Scottish folklore a clear distinction was made between wizards who believed in submitting their egos to the wisdom of nature and those who did not, the "killing ones" who drained cattle and humans of their blood. In ancient Scotland the "killing ones" had not been allowed to dominate. However, with the advent of Christianity came the idea that nature had to be perfected and surpassed. As humans lost respect for nature and ceased to believe in the effectiveness of magic, it left them wide open to exploitation by these "killing ones", who are responsible for the suicidal error of our creating a technology that actively attacks our planet's biosphere. The group of evil sorcerers thrives not only on animal viscera, but also on "the blindness of a group-mind drunk on alcohol and the boob tube". They gain their strength from our ignorance and blind spots. Because we avoid facing unpleasant facts instead of looking straight at them, this group is able to "farm" us. To confirm the validity of the concept that animal viscera have magical potency, he refers to the "muti" killings in South Africa, in which animals and humans are slain to obtain specific body parts, which are then dried and reduced to powder for magical purposes by sorcerers who have dedicated themselves to the forces of evil.

In the same issue there is an article about the Ed Foley abduction case. During his abduction, Mr. Foley found himself in telepathic communication with UFO occupants, who informed him that the reason for their presence here is their need for "life essence", which has been almost entirely used up on their home planet. They travel through the cosmos to many different stars on which organic life exists in order to extract the essences necessary for their survival. This nourishment is prepared mostly from the simpler forms of organic life, such as vegetation and plankton in the ocean, but includes to some extent vital essences of animals, from which they take blood and brain juices and glandular secretions. The flesh is of no use to them, only the vital juices (this brings back to mind the story of the Arkansas lady who was told by the humanoids that their only form of nourishment is "juice", but not the kind consumed by humans). They consider humans to be different from other animals and not fair game. "They carefully avoid humans as much as possible in their harvesting of fluid substances."

Also in this issue is a comment on the strange attitude of the supposedly independent Center for UFO Studies, staff members of which were instructing investigators not to link UFO phenomena to the mutilation phenomena. This seems hard to reconcile with scientific objectivity: telling researchers to make up their minds before examining the evidence.

During 1979, approximately six years after the mutilations had started, the Federal government began to at least go through the motions of showing some concern for the problem. The Department of Justice decided to convene a conference in Albuquerque, New Mexico, to discuss the matter. Both professional law enforcement personnel and amateur civilian researchers were invited to express their opinions.

Senator Schmitt of New Mexico opened the conference by raising the question of whether or not the FBI had investigative jurisdiction over criminal activity such as the mutilations, which had occurred in several different states by similar processes, and concluded that indeed it did. The representative of the FBI present replied that the FBI only had jurisdiction over crimes committed on Indian reservations. Senator Schmitt said that an official of the Department of Justice had told him that Federal lands other than Indian reservations could be included under FBI jurisdiction. The representative of the FBI did not agree. The Senator backed down and said it was something to be looked into. There was a great deal of discussion about cooperation between different government agencies, and the amateurs were allowed to have their say. However, Captain Keith Wolverton, the author of *Mystery Stalks the Prairie*, who had come all the way from Montana, was forbidden by his superior officers to make his speech as planned. At the last minute his testimony was suppressed. The amateur researchers came away from the conference with the impression that it had been convened for a different purpose than the one that had been announced: that it was not really to encourage communication between official and unofficial investigators, but rather to find out how much the unofficial investigators really knew about what was going on. A participant quoted by *Stigmata* suggested that: "The conference was designed to embarrass the sincere and legitimate mutilation investigators by sprinkling the meeting with bizarre, dubiously relevant presentations and information. This would make it easier for the media and the public to reject the whole matter by throwing out the baby with the bath water."

The end result of this highly publicised conference was that no investigation at all would be undertaken on the

Federal level. An FBI agent who had conveniently just retired, Ken Rommel, was granted $50,000 to investigate mutilations in *one district of New Mexico*. Oddly enough, during the year his investigation lasted there were no mutilation cases in that district. There were mutilations occurring on a large scale in many other regions, even up in Canada, but nothing during that year in that particular district.

As the editorial summing up the conference in *Stigmata* perceptively stated: "The FBI or some other Federal agency may not be *compelled* to investigate but could do so if desired; apparently no such desire exists." It was remembered that Palmer Hoyt, the editor and publisher of the *Denver Post*, a journalist who was legendary for his courage and objectivity, had expressed the opinion that: "The FBI and/or the CIA (and/or some other agency or agencies) were and still are protecting the mutilators." He expressed this opinion shortly before he died.

It was not only the amateurs who went away from the conference feeling frustrated. A deputy sheriff resigned in disgust because none of the other professionals even wanted to look at the evidence he had painstakingly gathered for the occasion, the many photographs, including those taken consecutively for 130 days of the body of a horse which did not decompose. He just couldn't get over the fact that not a single one of them had even wanted to look at his photographs.

1980

While Ken Rommel was focusing his well-paid attention on the peaceful scenery of the section of New Mexico to which he had been assigned, mutilations were reported from Texas, Colorado, Wyoming, Washington, California, South Dakota, Nebraska, Iowa, Kansas, Oklahoma, Arkansas, Illinois, and North Carolina, as well as from Alberta and Manitoba in Canada. The final fruit of Mr. Rommel's research was a 297 page report, which concluded that the mutilations were the work of predators following natural deaths, and recommended that no further Federal funds be wasted on investigating the matter, which had been distorted and exaggerated by the hysteria of an uninformed public, as well as by deliberate hoaxes and falsified or erroneous reports, some of which were the work of police officers. Although he wrote that at the outset of the investigation, he had no preconceived opinion as to how it was going to turn out, this contradicted a statement made in a previous interview: that he had reached his conclusions almost immediately after accepting the job.

The resemblances to the *Condon Report* and the *Warren Report* are so obvious as to be hardly worth mentioning. The *Rommel Report* takes its place beside them, to gather dust on library shelves. One more expensive whitewash job paid for by the American taxpayer to maintain the illusory bliss of ignorance, like a junkie pays for his fix. It has already been pointed out that it may be precisely this tendency to avoid facing unpleasant facts that enables parasitic entities to "farm" us.

So the answer to the $50,000 question was that there isn't anything out there but buzzards and coyotes, and anyone who says different is a damn fool or a liar. This, in spite of the fact that veterinarians from Oklahoma State University had publicly stated that their veterinary school was unable to graduate a veterinarian capable of doing the type of surgery being done in the field with sophisticated precision by the mutilators.

According to an article that appeared in the *Santa Fe New Mexican* after the *Rommel Report* was released: "State historian Myra Ellen Jenkins said today her research had revealed no record of cattle mutilations in New Mexico prior to those recorded in recent years . . . though Rommel attributed the cattle deaths to natural causes and the mutilations to predators and decomposition, Dr. Jenkins said today she has found no record in historic documents or folklore of the type of selective mutilation reported in many of the cases."

Let us consign Mr. Rommel's irrelevant remarks to the oblivion they so richly deserve, and proceed with our investigation.

There had been an interesting case in Canada: a seven-year-old heifer whose unborn calf had been removed and mutilated *without the placental bag being broken.*

A story which could not be checked out, as witnesses refused to cooperate with investigators, concerned a group of people who came upon a UFO hovering above a dying horse. Although there were no visible wounds on the body, the animal was bleeding abundantly (perhaps through the pores?). However, the blood seemed to evaporate before coagulating or dripping to the ground (perhaps aspired upward?).

There had been an incident in Brazil, about which Project Stigma learned from an account published in the French journal *Ouranos*. A 66 year old farmer and his 23 year old son were working on some cattle, which they had enclosed in a corral. They separated a cow from her month-old calf, which weighed about 60 pounds. They took the cow a short distance away. They didn't bother to tie up the calf, which remained loose in the corral with the other cattle, about 15 feet from where they were working on the cow. They noticed that the cattle in the corral suddenly began to act frightened, and that the cow they were working on was becoming difficult to control. At first they didn't pay much attention, but the cow kept bellowing as if in danger and trying to turn her head to look toward the calf. The elderly farmer wondered if there was anything wrong with the calf, and turned his head in that direction. The calf was bawling in fear, and was suspended in a standing position with no visible means of support about three feet in the air. Father and son both watched as the calf was moved along parallel with the ground at this same height in the direction of the adjacent field. All the cattle were bellowing and trying to stampede out of the corral. The father and son were so astonished that they did not move from where they were standing, or make any attempt to retrieve the calf. After the calf had floated along horizontally about sixty feet into the field, it began to rise vertically. It ascended straight up quite slowly, taking several minutes to reach a height at which it appeared about a quarter of its size. Then it suddenly disappeared, though the height was far beneath the clouds. It had kept bawling all the time it was being floated along horizontally, but as soon as it started to rise vertically the bawling stopped. No other phenomena were noticed.

This incident reminded Project Stigma of an anonymous report from the western United States it had not been able to get confirmation of, according to which two police officers driving down the highway in their patrol car encountered a cow floating across the highway at a height of several feet in the air. It is entirely understandable that police officers would not want their names attached to such a seemingly nonsensical report.

Then there was the Judy Doraty case. Mrs. Doraty was driving through Texas with members of her family, when she noticed that a UFO was following her car. She saw a calf being sucked up toward the UFO through a beam of light. Next she found herself aboard the UFO with her daughter, watching "little men" cut up the calf. She was terrified when the "little men" began examining her daughter on what looked like an operating table, but she and her daughter were returned to the ground safely.

There are interesting similarities between what happened in Puerto Rico in late 1974 and the winter of weirdness in England, 1904-1905. Phenomena reported from Puerto Rico during this period included not only UFO sightings and animal mutilations, but also "apparitions of the Blessed Virgin, religious statues shedding tears and leaking drops of blood, mysterious disappearances of people, strange noises and explosions . . . large unknown birds, something which looked like a ball of fur or hair that rolled along the ground, humanoids, and not-so-humanoid zombie-like and ape-like dwarves."

During 1979 it was the turn of the Canary Islands. There were a series of spectacular UFO sightings, one of which was witnessed by certainly hundreds and possibly thousands of people on three different large islands, many of whom thought that the end of the world had come. Other incidents involved commercial airliners, one of which found itself on a collision course with a number of pulsating red objects. The collision did not occur, but the shocked and frightened pilot made an emergency landing at the nearest airport. During the time period between these incidents, a purple rain fell on one town of the Canaries, and blue rain fell on another town. Two fierce German Shepherd dogs were found dead outside their enclosures with holes in their chests. Goats and rabbits were found dead, beheaded and their bodies drained of blood. The bodies of 14 sheep were found, from which only the viscera and blood had been taken. Some of the sheep had perfect circles cut into their bodies. There are no newspaper reports of other types of strange things going on in the Canary Islands during this period, which doesn't necessarily mean that they weren't happening.

Among the letters received by Project Stigma in 1980 was one from a sergeant in the U.S. Army, which he wished to have published in spite of the probable consequences to his military career. Staff Sergeant Clifford E. Stone, 301-50-0182, thought it worth jeopardizing his future to make public the information contained in this one letter. In order to do justice to this heartfelt document, I quote from it verbatim:

. . . I ask no one to take my word for what I am about to say concerning UFOs. However, I assure you everything I am about to say is fact and may be verified by using the Freedom of Information and Privacy Acts to obtain the documents that I obtained from government agencies. It is my hope that Congress will wake up and create a new committee to do a scientific study of UFOs. The fact is that the U.S. Senate was lied to by the Pentagon in 1968 during the Senate hearings into UFOs.

First, let us look at the conclusions of the U.S. Air Force's Project Blue Book, the USAF's so-called *Scientific Study of UFOs* by the University of Colorado and the review of the *Scientific Study* by "a panel of the National Academy of Sciences". Those conclusions were "(1) No UFO reported, investigated and evaluated by the Air Force has ever given any indication of threat to our national security; (2) There has been no evidence submitted to or discovered by the Air Force that sightings categorized as unidentified represent technological developments or principles beyond the range of present-day scientific knowledge; and (3) There has been no evidence indicating that sightings categorized as unidentified are extra-terrestrial vehicles."

The truth of the matter is that the fairy tale *Cinderella* is based more on fact than the above conclusions. You see, neither of the above study groups were presented with all the facts. Let me cite you just one example. To be sure, there are more.

In March 1967, Cuban Air Defense radar picked up a UFO over Cuban air space. Two Cuban jets were sent to intercept the UFO. When the jets made the intercept of the UFO, they tried to make radio contact with the object but were unable to do so. The jets at this time were ordered by Cuban Air Defense to shoot the UFO down. When the jets tried to fire, the UFO vaporized one of the jets. This incident was monitored by the U.S. Air Force's Security Service. To wit: Detachment A, 6947th. Security Squadron based at Homestead Air Force Base. This report never was filed with Project Blue Book. In fact it was (and still is) classified at least Secret by the National Security Agency, "in the interest of national defense". While this case does not prove UFOs to be extra-terrestrial, it does shoot down the first two of the above "official" conclusions.

On December 17, 1969, the Secretary of the Air Force announced the termination of Project Blue Book, thus ending the investigation of UFOs. However, apparently no one told the State Department, National Security Agency, Central Intelligence Agency, Defense Intelligence Agency and every other Intelligence organization in the United States. All of these agencies are still investigating reports of UFOs. I have letters from these intelligence agencies denying me information on UFOs because the information I was requesting was classified "in the interest of national defense". How can something as non-existent as the U.S. Government claims UFOs are be a matter of national defense? How can the U.S. Government justify classifying something "in the interest of national defense" when that something "has never given any indication of threat to our national security"?

I would like you to ask your readers to write their Congressmen and demand a new scientific study of the UFO phenomenon based on *all* the facts, not just what the intelligence agencies wish to release. We the American Public have a right to know the truth. We the American Public have a right to know what our government is doing about UFOs.

SSG Clifford E. Stone, 301-50-0182
HQ Det, Hanau Mil Comm
APO New York 09165

1981

Mrs. Iona Hoeppner teaches science to the 7th through 12th grades at Briggsdale School in Weld County, Colorado. She has Bachelor of Science degrees in physics, biology and chemistry from three different universities. Two days after the discovery of a mutilated calf near Briggsdale, Mrs. Hoeppner went to the site to collect samples for laboratory analysis. On the previous day, the Sheriff of Weld County and his deputies had inspected the carcass, noting that a perfect four-inch circle had been cut out of the calf's belly. While being interviewed, the sheriff said that the flesh underneath the cut had not been touched by predators or insects, and had retained its whitish-pink color. A triangular cut made by the sheriff (which included a portion of the original cut made by the mutilators) had turned brown overnight.

When Mrs. Hoeppner arrived at the scene, she cut out a piece of hide that included parts of both the original incision and the sheriff's incision. She had difficulty in obtaining a blood sample. When she inserted her syringe into the carotid artery, she expected to fill it, but obtained only about 5 cubic centimeters of a transparent maroon-colored fluid, which looked like serum.

There was a small pool of red fluid on the loose ground near the head of the calf, and another small pool of the same substance under the belly. This liquid did not appear to be evaporating, nor was it being absorbed into the ground. Mrs. Hoeppner filled a vial with this liquid. She noted two bloodless puncture wounds in the calf's throat. The tongue had been cut out. She took some smear samples from inside the mouth, then returned to the school science laboratory with the samples she had collected. That evening she began to prepare stains and set up cultures in an incubator. She also made a microscopic examination of the piece of hide. About midnight Mrs. Hoeppner's husband and a friend, who was a school athletic coach, locked up the lab and closed all the windows before going home.

Early the next morning a school employee phoned Mrs. Hoeppner to ask if she had left the laboratory door open and a mess all over the floor. She went to the school immediately, and found that the lab had been broken into. The lab door had an old lock which would not be difficult for an intruder to pick. All the samples she had collected on the previous day were gone except the piece of hide, which had apparently been overlooked in the freezer. Nothing else of any significance was missing from the lab.

When Mrs. Hoeppner reported the burglary to the school superintendent, he refused to make a complaint to the sheriff, on the grounds that this would "upset the school".

On the following day, Mrs. Hoeppner phoned the

sheriff. She did not report the break-in, but said she was interested in comparing the samples she had gathered with his samples. She was told that the samples had been forwarded to the diagnostic laboratory at Colorado State Univerity in Fort Collins. However, when she phoned this diagnostic lab, she was told that the samples had never arrived.

After having made these phone calls, Mrs. Hoeppner returned to the mutilation site. Maggots were all over the carcass, except in the immediate area of the original incision. Mrs. Hoeppner put on sterile gloves and carefully took fluid samples from various parts of the body. She also took some more of the red liquid, which had still not evaporated or been absorbed by the loose ground.

She returned to the lab with her specimens, which she hid carefully. She prepared dummy specimens and placed them about the lab in the same way she had left the original specimens before retiring for the night. She then closed the windows, locked the lab, and went home. The next morning she found the lab door locked and the windows closed— but every single one of the decoy dummy specimens had disappeared. She analysed her specimens. Two items turned out to be of particular interest.

The red fluid from the pools on the ground was not an organic substance. It was thinner than blood, and contained no detectable bacteria. It was as sterile as anything Mrs. Hoeppner had ever looked at. Her equipment was not powerful enough to detect viruses, but there were no bacteria at all. Microscopic examination revealed two unusual constituents. There were strange looking rectangles, approximately 10 microns by 3 microns, with striations on them running crosswise. They did not look like anything she had seen before. Also throughout the fluid sample there were small crystals about one by two microns. It took two weeks for this liquid to be absorbed by the loose ground at the mutilation site, leaving a brownish maroon-colored stain and killing the grass in its immediate vicinity. Mrs. Hoeppner tried pouring samples of water, carbon tetrachloride, potassium chloride, and thick mineral oil on the ground next to the carcass. All were absorbed almost immediately, though the mineral oil took a bit longer.

The most interesting item of all was the section of hide cut by the mutilators, which was completely different from the cuts made by the sheriff and herself. After conducting a careful microscopic examination, she had to conclude it was neither a cut nor a laser burn. Not one single cell had been destroyed. The incision was made *between the cells, cell by cell*. Not one single cell was even damaged. The sheriff's cut and her own had cut right through the cells, as is normal. The mutilators had separated the cells from each other precisely along their boundaries. Mrs. Hoeppner's opinion was: "I don't think mankind has the ability to do what has been done."

Puerto Rican researcher Salvador Freixedo came up with two extremely sinister reports from Mexico, which were published in Barcelona by *Mundo Desconocido*, and were summarised in *Stigmata*.

In the state of Queretaro, there were several cases of mothers with infants just a few days old falling into an unusually heavy sleep, from which they awakened to find their babies dead and drained of blood, but with no wounds or marks on their bodies. UFOs were not reported in connection with these incidents, which may not be connected with them. However, in the context of other unusual events of this nature in recent years, as reported from many different localities, UFO involvement must be considered as a possibility.

In the state of Tabasco, seven workers were crowded into an automobile, driving down a busy highway on their way to a party. They were expecting to have fun that night, and were laughing and telling jokes. Suddenly there was a terrific crash, and the men thought they were being hit in the face by gravel, which turned out to be broken glass from the shattered windshield of the car. The three men crowded in the front seat with the driver shouted to him to stop, as there was something heavy on their legs that felt like some sort of animal. The driver was in such a panic, blinded by the pieces of broken glass that had hit him in the face, that he pushed down on the accelerator instead of the brake. Finally he managed to put on the brakes and stop the car. The heavy thing that had fallen through the windshield into the front seat was the upper half of a human body. Not knowing what else to do, they deposited it by the side of the road and returned to their homes, at which the police turned up in due course to charge them with vehicular homicide. The lower half of the body was found near the highway not far from the point of impact. As in the Queretaro incidents, there was no direct UFO involvement. However, the men all swore that the body fell through the windshield from above. The car was a normal one. When a speeding car hits a pedestrian, what happens is well known: the victim is either run over by the wheels or rolls off the hood and is knocked to the side of the car. Never before has a human body been sliced neatly in half by an accident of this type. Because this is what had happened: the victim had been cut cleanly in two, leaving no ragged edges or dangling intestines. Furthermore, there was no blood in either half of the body or on the clothes. There was no mud or dirt on the clothes. There were no bones broken in either half of the body, with the exception of the spinal column, which had been cut through without fracturing any vertebrae.

On the other side of the Atlantic, Spanish farm laborers in the mountains near Malaga reported that they had found a wild cat sliced neatly into three parts after encountering a human-like figure over six feet tall that seemed to be encased in metal and that had two large long cylindrical legs. When it moved, it did not walk forward like a man; it walked sideways. The farm workers turned loose their dogs, which were barking furiously, and the figure disappeared from one moment to the next. Besides the remains of the cat, on the following morning almost fifty footprints were found, deep and perfectly circular, all in straight lines, not parallel as would be the case with someone walking normally.

This resembles a case which took place in Falkville, Alabama, on Oct. 17th, 1973. Police Chief Jeff Greenhaw photographed and pursued a being in a metallic suit, estimated to be about 5½ feet tall, after having been called out to investigate a UFO landing. According to Chief Greenhaw: "He was running in a very odd manner, from side to side, arms down to his sides, and it looked as if he had springs under his feet to propel him. He could take 10 feet . . . at one step." The being disappeared as the patrol car spun off the road.

The incident involving the Spanish farm laborers took place in the spring of 1978. It is most unlikely that they would have heard about the details of Chief Greenhaw's adventure in 1973, and they did not seek publicity for their sighting of the strange being.

To return to 1981, during this year a veritable explosion of UFO activity erupted along the Amazon river in Brazil. Occasional sightings had been reported for generations, but never before on such an unprecedented scale.

Charles L. Tucker is one of the directors of the Mutual UFO Network. He participated in an expedition up the Amazon with Brazilian Air Force Major Holando Lima, who had been appointed to take charge of UFO investigation for the Brazilian government. In an interview with Joan T. Griffith, published in *Pursuit* (P.O. Box 265, Little Silver, NJ 07739), Mr. Tucker stated that "Whole communities have reported sightings. . . . It is one thing to have a few scattered sightings in an area from time to time, but here the sheer volume of reports is staggering. You have top citizens like village officials, doctors, and police all witnessing these things." Doctors have been called upon to treat people for burns and other ailments after close encounters with UFOs or their occupants, who in some cases have used a sort of ray gun on people. Animals and sometimes humans have been found drained of blood. Different kinds of craft have been observed, and different types of occupants. UFOs are sighted so frequently in the region of Santarem and Monte Alegre that many investigators think they have an underwater base in that area.

During 1981 Project Stigma received a document entitled simply "Memorandum". Here is the entire text of this communication exactly as it was received:

An eyewitness has described an official Project Grudge Report Number 13, Top Secret, *Need To Know Only* classification, that was in fact published but then never distributed and was in fact subsequently destroyed. It consisted of 624 pages, typed, offset reproduced on white paper with a gray cover, and included whole pages of print by (name deleted) and Col. Friend. It covered U.S. Government Official UFO Procedures, classifications, and all Top Secret UFO activity from 1942 through 1951. Among other information it included the following:

    (1)   (a)   Significant UFO sightings.
               (b)   UFO Landings.
               (c)   UFO/Alien Close Approaches, Abductions, Detentions.
               (d)   Crashed UFOs and UFO Retrievals.
               (e)   Sensitive Military/Industrial Areas where close encounters occurred.
               (f)   Technical Details on Dismantled UFOs.
               (g)   UFO Physics—Exotic, Nuclear, Weaponry.
                      (1)   Clean Breeder Reactor size of oval basket-

ball.

    (2)   Ultrasonic, Light, Ray and Beam Weapons.

(2)   Photographic Section—All glossy pages, photos 3½ x 5, 8 x 10.

    (a)   Photographs of sensitive UFOs.

    (b)   Color photographs of crashed UFOs.

        (1)   Three in good condition (2) One dismantled

    (c)   Color Photographs of deceased aliens (Averaged 4½ feet).

    (d)   Color Photographs of 3 Living Aliens.

    (e)   Color Photographs of Human Mutilations (head, rectum, sex organs, internal organs, blood removal). One Military witness observed human abduction, body found a few days later. This case which had happened in 1958 had been added to the file.

(3)   Covered Human and Humanoid Aliens.

    (a)   Humanoid Species.

    (b)   Humanoid Autopsies

        (1)   No indication of age.

        (2)   Small species similar to humans very similar, varied in height a few inches.

        (3)   Liquid Chlorophyl Base Nourishment.

        (4)   Food absorbed through mouth membrane, wastes excreted through skin.

        (5)   Language similar in appearance to Sanskrit, mathematical phrases.

        (6)   Live Alien communicated only desired answers to questions. Remained silent on undesired questions.

Classified summary of the report completed the text.

Note: The one copy seen had been annotated and updated by someone.

Needless to say, there has been considerable controversy concerning the authenticity of this "Memorandum". Project Stigma was able to contact its author, who was willing to tell his story only under the condition that his real name not be made public. He will be referred to as "Toulinet".

Toulinet had been a captain assigned to Intelligence in the Green Berets during the Vietnam War. He had been in charge of a Special Forces investigative team that had to carry out a very difficult, dangerous and mind-bending mission: retrieval of a B-52 that had been forced down in the jungle by a UFO, a wreck that left no survivors. The plane had radioed back to base that it was under attack by a UFO before going down. After completion of the mission, Toulinet was sent back to the U.S., where he spent three months in a psychiatric clinic. He was then assigned a new job in England, as a U.S. Army intelligence analyst at a RAF "Listening Post".

One day Toulinet found a locked and sealed diplomatic pouch waiting for him at his office. Inside it was the 624 page Grudge 13 report. It took him four days for him to read it and write up his analysis. The report and his analysis were then picked up by a courier.

Shortly afterwards, out of a clear blue sky, Toulinet was suddenly informed by his commanding officer that his performance was not satisfactory, and that he was being terminated from the service. Furthermore, he was just as suddenly re-classified by the British government as an "undesirable alien", and obliged to leave England. Toulinet returned to the United States and settled down with his family. However, what he had read during those four days was impossible to forget. He was now a civilian, but he had many old friends who were still in uniform. He began his own investigation. It is his opinion that from the early 1950's to the mid-1960's the Air Force maintained relocation and debriefing colonies for people who had experienced close encounters of the third and fourth kinds, in which they were to be isolated for the rest of their lives, but that such colonies are no longer in existence. He also thinks that one of the three aliens captured alive by the U.S. government may still be alive in captivity. Through his contacts he has obtained information about a minimum of 16 and a maximum of 20 cases of UFO-related human mutilations: perfectly circular wounds; viscera, sex organs, and tongues removed; no blood or body fluids, yet no vascular collapse. Newspapers usually attribute such cases to "gangland killings" or "predator damage."

The Grudge 13 report he had seen had been published in 1953, and updated to 1969. He had read it in England in 1977.

1982

The debate over the authenticity of Toulinet's "Memorandum" continued on into 1982, and continues still. Project Stigma's investigation was unable to establish anything definite about the document one way or the other, but did indicate that Toulinet's military career had been what he said it was.

In May of 1982 Toulinet was contacted by his former commanding officer at the listening post near London, who had also been unceremoniously dumped from the service, and who had retired to New Mexico. He told Toulinet that he had information concerning the location of an apparent UFO crash or landing in New Mexico. Several weeks later Toulinet and the colonel, accompanied by a third man, drove a four-wheel-drive van to the suspected site. They parked the van. Toulinet walked a considerable distance from it to carry out a preliminary examination of the area. The other two men remained near the van, unloading and preparing equipment. Suddenly a noise and flash attracted Toulinet's attention. He saw a rocket tear through the night sky and explode on or near the van, apparently killing his two companions. Toulinet fled from the area, and hitch-hiked back to his home. He told a friend what had happened, saying that his life was no longer worth two cents, and then disappeared. He has not been seen or heard from since.

While considering the possibility that Toulinet's document might be authentic, two details struck me as being of considerable potential importance: language similar to Sanskrit, nourishment based on liquid chlorophyll. If those two details were valid, the implications were both far-reaching and inescapable.

Among the recent developments in modern science is the discovery that chlorophyll is not confined to Earth. Chlorophyll has been detected throughout space. It exists everywhere. A basic nourishment of chlorophyll would therefore be logical and appropriate for space travelers.

The Vedas are the most ancient sacred texts of India, and were composed in Sanskrit. The civilisation of India was based upon the *Vedas* as Occidental civilisation was based upon the Bible. The oldest of the *Vedas* is the *Rig-Veda*, followed closely by the *Atharva-Veda*.

The *Rig-Veda* is divided into ten books, the ninth of which is entirely devoted to hymns in honor of a plant called "soma", the use of which was reserved for members of the Brahmin caste during religious ceremonies. Soma was revered for two reasons: the beverage prepared from it was the favorite drink of the god Indra and his companions; it was also a major hallucinogen which enabled participants in the ceremonies to visualise and communicate with Indra and the other gods of the pantheon.

There has been considerable debate as to the identity of the soma plant. From the descriptions of the way it was prepared, we know that soma was a liquid chlorophyll infusion with a specific alkaloidal content. According to the original texts, it was a vine that was crushed between rocks, and prepared in a similar fashion to the way the Indians of the Amazon prepare potions from the ayahuasca vine. During ayahuasca ceremonies, the Indians of the Amazon visualise and communicate with their deities. Soma is described in the *Rig-Veda* as a creeping plant, a vine with leaves and seeds, which does not apply to a mushroom. Psychedelic mushrooms were probably added to the potion at a later date, after the original plant became scarce and finally extinct through over-harvesting. During the period when every household in India was looking for the soma plant, which had become worth its weight in gold, it could have been over-harvested to the point of extinction within a few years. My opinion is that a vine related to the ayahuasca vine of the Amazon once grew in northern India, but was over-harvested to the point of extinction.

The correct way to greet Indra and his companions was with beakers of soma. After having drunk the soma, they became most welcome allies, since they possessed invincible weapons and traveled in celestial chariots. The extra-terrestrial aspects of the soma cult are particularly explicit in the *Atharva-Veda*. The following quotations are from the William Dwight Whitney translation, which was published by Harvard University in 1905:

Sweet verily is this soma, and full of honey is this; strong verily is this; and no one soever overpowers in conflicts Indra, having now drunk of it. . . . O Indra and soma, cause to roll from the sky the deadly weapon, from the earth also, a shattering for the evil-plotter; shape out from the mountains the noisy one, wherewith you burn down the increasing demon. O Indra and soma, cause it to roll forth from the sky; with fire-heated stone-smiting unaging heat weapons do ye pierce the devourers in the abyss. . . . let them go to silence. . . . He who hath worshiped thee, O fury, missile thunderbolt, gains power, force, everything in succession; may we, with thee as ally, that art made of power, overpower the barbarian, the Aryan, with powerful power. . . . Here I am for thee, come hitherward unto us, meeting us, O powerful all-giving one; O thunderbolt-bearing one, turn hither to us; let us two slay the barbarians; and do thou know thy partner. Go forth among them; be on our right hand, then will we two smite and slay many Vrtas: I offer to thee the sustaining top of the sweet; let us both drink the initial draught. . . . The mighty one chose a drink of soma; a great stone became what was his body. . . . Your mastery I know, your kingdom, O Trishandi. . . . what in the atmosphere, what in the sky, and what men are on the earth. . . . Iron-mouthed, needle-mouthed, likewise thorn-tree-mouthed, let the flesh-eaters, of wind-swiftness, fasten on our enemies with the three-jointed thunderbolt. . . . O Indra and Varuna, soma-drinkers, this pressed soma, intoxicating, drink ye, O ye of firm courses. . . . The great superintendent of them sees, as it were, from close by; whoever thinks to be going on in secret, all this the gods know. Whoso knows, goes about, and whoso goes crookedly, whoso goes about hiddenly, who defiantly—what two, sitting together, talk, King Varuna, as third, knows that. Both this earth is King Varuna's, and yonder great sky with distant margins; also the two oceans are Varuna's paunches, also in this petty water is he hidden. Also whoso should creep far off beyond the sky, he should not be released from King Varuna; from the sky his spies go forth; thousand-eyed, they look over the earth. All this King Varuna beholds—what is between the two firmaments, and what beyond; numbered of him are the winkings of people; as a gambler the dice, so does he fix these things. . . . Since thou verily, O self-ruling Varuna, knowest all births, O well-conducting one—is there anything beyond the welkin? Is there anything below what is beyond, O unerring one? There is one other thing beyond the welkin; there is something hard to attain hitherward from what is beyond; this I Varuna, knowing it, proclaim to thee. . . . The one this side, the other beyond the back of the sky, in secret are deposited the two treasures of the Brahman. . . . The two wheels of thee, O Surya, the priests know. . . . further, the one wheel that is in secret—that, verily, the enlightened know. . . . On the back of yonder sky the all-knowing ones talk a speech not found by all. . . . The five-footed father of twelve shapes they call rich in ground in the far half of the sky. . . . Eight-wheeled, nine-doored is the impregnable stronghold of the gods; in that is found a golden vessel, heaven-going, covered with light. In that golden vessel, three-spoked, having three supports—what soul-possessing monster there is in it, that verily the knowers of Brahman know. The Brahman entered into the resplendent yellow golden unconquered stronghold that was all surrounded with glory. . . . Ascend ye to the highest heaven; O seers, be not afraid; ye soma-drinkers, soma-drenchers, this oblation is made to you; we have gone to the highest light. . . . Up out of the darkness have we, ascending the highest firmament, gone to the sun, god among the gods, highest light. . . . These fore-knowing ones have turned hither upward from below by roads that the gods go upon; upon the back of the virile mountain the ancient streams flow forth new.

It is obvious from the content of the Vedic hymns in honor of Indra and soma that during the period when they were composed, contact between humans and non-human celestials was socially approved behavior, of considerable practical and religious significance. This is in striking contrast to contemporary attitudes in our modern civilisation, which greet such manifestations with sneers of derision and contemptuous dismissal, automatically assuming those involved to be liars or fools or insane. All plants with effects known to resemble soma's in any way are now strictly illegal.

Let us consider the hypothesis that what UFO occupants with a language resembling Sanskrit and a basic nourishment of liquid chlorophyll may face us with is the return of Indra and his companions, the invincible soma-drinkers in their celestial chariots. If this be the case, upon their return they were not met with libations of soma by a joyful populace come to celebrate the occasion. They were met with machine-gun bullets, and with deliberate deception on the part of our highest levels of authority. Instead of renewing the ancient alliance, the politicians in charge of our power structures chose the path of war. They made that choice without informing their fellow citizens, who according to law should have had a voice in making such a major decision, and should at the very least have been informed about it. Considering contemporary attitudes and the choice made without consulting us by our leaders, perhaps we should consider ourselves lucky that so far only a few human corpses have been found. To greet the power symbolised by Indra and his companions by pretending they do not exist would be suicidal insanity. Provoking the wrath of such entities by ignoring their existence could turn out to be much more devastating to us than it has been so far. Think back on the legend of Vishnu and his disc in the second chapter of this book. Our survival as a civilisation may depend on our ability to recognise what is hovering above us, and to communicate with it instead of pretending it isn't there. Particularly when one considers that during recent years there have been on the average about 150 UFO sightings reported per day worldwide, and that only about one person in ten bothers to report a sighting.

A significant new development has been reported from the Amazon basin. According to articles that appeared on Sept. 22nd and 23rd, 1982, in the Rio de Janiero newspaper *O Dia* (credit: UFO Newsclipping Service, Route 1, Box 220, Plumerville, Arkansas 72127), the Amazon river town of Itacoatiara (population: about 80,000) was in a state of turmoil because women had been discovering themselves to be pregnant after UFO encounters, and men with voices that were normally baritone or bass found themselves able to talk only in a high-pitched treble. Citizens had taken up arms, and many different families gathered together for protection, but when the UFOs with their multicolored lights appeared, those on guard often felt dizzy and paralysed. On occasions when they had been able to fire on the lights, the lights had gone away. Women said that as the multicolored lights approached, they collapsed into a deep swoon, from which they awakened with the feeling that they had been impregnated. The local Chief of Police asked for reinforcements, and two platoons of Military Police were sent. One platoon was deployed around the town of Itacoatiara, the other platoon was attempting to locate the UFO base. Sightings and incidents continue to be numerous in the region.

All these disturbances are being reported from the Brazilian population of the Amazon. It is no secret that the original Indian inhabitants of this region are being methodically exterminated, much as the original Indian inhabitants of the United States were methodically exterminated during the nineteenth century, in order to take away their tribal lands. A member of the Brazilian military junta expressed his government's unofficial policy quite clearly during an interview with *Newsweek*, which quoted him as saying: "When we are certain that every corner of the Amazon is inhabited by genuine Brazilians and not by Indians, only then will we be able to say that the Amazon is ours."

Vast areas of the Amazonian tropical rain forest, which provides approximately one-fifth of this planet's atmospheric oxygen, are being clear-cut every day by multinational corporations with the most modern equipment for immediate short-term financial profit, the long-term ecological consequences be damned. No one bothers to negotiate with the Indians living in these areas. They are simply shot on sight by mercenaries hired for this purpose as the bulldozers move in, and have no choice but to retreat deeper into the rapidly shrinking forest.

The only place on the planet where an equivalent of the ancient Vedic soma ritual is known to survive happens to be among these same Indians of the Amazon. Did one of their medicine men remember that the correct way to greet powerful visitors from the sky was with a beaker of his tribe's traditional ceremonial potion? Could there be a new alliance in the works?

Dennis and Terence McKenna are two brothers who traveled up the Amazon in order to investigate the use of ayahuasca by shamans. They also tried it themselves. The following description of a portion of their experience, taken from their brilliant book *The Invisible Landscape* (Seabury Press, New York, 1975), demonstrates the relevance of ayahuasca to the subject of UFOs:

"We could feel the presence of some invisible hyperspatial entity, an ally, which seemed to be observing and sometimes exerting influence on the situation to keep us moving gently toward an experimental resolution of the ideas we were generating. Because of the alien nature of the tryptamine trance, its seeming accentuation of themes alien, insectile, and futuristic, and because of previous experiences with tryptamines in which insectile hallucinatory transformations were observed, we were led to speculate that the role of the presence was somehow like that of an anthropologist, come to give humanity the keys to galactarian citizenship. We discussed this entity in terms of a giant insect and, through the insect trill of the Amazon jungle at midday, seemed able to discern a deeper harmonic buzz that somehow signified the unseen outsider. This sense of the presence of an alien third entity was sometimes very intense, most intense in early March, and from there fading off gradually.

For the next thirty-seven days, especially the next fourteen days, our shared ideation consisted of, among other themes, but as a dominant one, the idea of a shamanic journey of return from the ends of space and time to earth, with the collected energy configuration of space-time condensed into a kind of lens or saucer, a true philosopher's stone. One of us experienced an intense transference state similar to reactive paranoid schizophrenia and accepted the paternal and curative role of shaman and psychopomp. From the sixth to the seventeenth of March, one of us did not sleep, and the other, while awake, spoke continuously, in apparent and convincing telepathic rapport with anyone he wished, in command of enormous technical erudition and with a strange and rapidly evolving hyperspatial cosmogony which, following a Manichean perception, visualised the solar system as a huge light pump, wherein the light of souls is pumped from planet to planet until it finally leaves the solar system altogether, and is transmitted to the galactic center. Some of his "discoveries" were that Jupiter is the reflected image of the earth in hyperspace, is teeming with bizarre life forms, and is somehow an essential key to unraveling the species' fate. In his interior epic, late twentieth-century history was experienced as a frantic effort to build an object, which he called, "the lens", in order to allow life to escape to Jupiter on the heels of an impending global catastrophe.

Slowly, as the shamanic voyager neared his home, his place in space, his stitch in time, the myth making and the symptoms of election schizophrenia faded in each of us. However, the continuing process of understanding, triggered by the experiment, did not cease."

1983-1984

During 1983 and 1984, the number of mutilations dropped dramatically. They continued to occur, but far less frequently than at any time during the preceding decade. As the cases that did occur were similar in nature to those already described, the focus here is on research developments during those two years.

In April, 1983, Project Stigma interviewed Dr. Paul Bennewitz, President of Thunder Scientific Laboratory in Albuquerque, New Mexico. Dr. Bennewitz conducts investigations for the Aerial Phenomena Research Organization, and described in detail a case he had been working on, which resembles in some respects the Judy Doraty case mentioned earlier in this chapter. A mother and her young son were driving on a country road near Cimarron, New Mexico, when they saw two UFOs. One of them was in the process of abducting a calf. Both the mother and her son were then abducted also, and taken on separate UFOs to an underground base. At this base she watched as the calf was mutilated. She saw a vat containing unidentified body parts floating in a liquid, and another vat containing the body of a male human. Small metallic objects were implanted into both her body and her son's body. She and her son were then returned to her car. Since this incident they have been in a state of severe trauma, accompanied by multiple physical and psychological ailments. Examinations using the sophisticated medical technique known as CAT-scan confirmed the existence of the implants. Dr. Bennewitz said that the results of his investigation indicate that the underground base is located deep underneath the Jicarilla Apache Indian Reservation near Dulce, New Mexico. It is perhaps not a coincidence that the region around Dulce has been particularly afflicted by mutilations. The results of Dr. Bennewitz's investigation also indicate that this base is operated by aliens in collaboration with the U.S. government. In exchange for technical information, the U.S. government provided the aliens with the Dulce base and at least three other bases, also agreeing to permit the aliens to carry out human abductions and animal mutilations without interference. Project Stigma is unable to confirm or refute Dr. Bennewitz's findings, but feels they deserve serious consideration.

Anonymous letters can not be considered reliable sources of information, and normally would not be included in the evidence collected here. However, as with the comments written in the margins of the Morris K. Jessup book, described in the "Strange Suicides" chapter, the statements this particular letter contains are remarkable enough to deserve being evaluated independently of their origin as hypotheses. The following extracts are taken from an anonymous 'Letter to the Editor' that was published in the Denver paper *Up the Creek* on April 8, 1983:

"I was in the Army, stationed in New Mexico. Got out in '81. I was in Intelligence, and learned what's really going on. I trust you won't print my name, or I'll be dead within a year. The mutilations are done by a secret government operation called Delta. It doesn't use tax money, mainly it uses support from Exxon and Atlantic Richfield. The money is laundered through General Meyer's office in the Pentagon. . . . They take the animal parts to test the effects of germ warfare and poison (some weak mix of cyanide and dioxin) they're testing on the civilians in America. I guess now if there are black helicopters over Denver, they're testing in the cities, too. The other thing with the 'copters is they're used to ferry heroin and coke. That's right. Why do you think the federal narcs can't crack the bigtime drug movers? Easy. The government, or the Army, is doing it. Does that blow your mind? Delta's big bases are all underground and on Indian reservations. HQ for operations (and where a lot of the choppers are based) is 28 miles east of Albuquerque on I-40, then 14 miles north on a dirt road into the Laguna Indian Reservation."

The release of *Clear Intent* by Lawrence Fawcett and Barry Greenwood in 1984 was a landmark event that completely transformed UFO research. Among the explosive material it contains is this fascinating description of the landing of a black helicopter:

It was in 1974. It was early in the morning when a Chinook helicopter came down across the way from my home. As the helicopter landed on the beach, men began to jump out of the craft, which was charcoal black with no markings. These men were dressed in black pajama-type uniforms and carried M-16 rifles. The area where the helicopter came down is called the "Sore Thumb" and is about 500 feet from my home in an open area on the beach. The men in black uniforms began to set up a perimeter on the beach. I walked down towards one of the guards who came to within about 200 yards of my house. I tried to talk to him, but he did not answer me, he was all business. I could see that he had no patches on his uniform and there was a microphone attached to his shirt. He was wearing a black, baseball-type hat and had black jump boots on. A police car from the Suffolk County police department came into the area and a police officer went over to the guard and asked some questions. The officer asked, "Who are you and what is going on?" The guard didn't answer. The officer then said, "Look, you're standing here carrying a weapon and you're in an unidentified uniform. I'd like some identification." Again, the guard didn't answer. The policeman stated, "If you don't answer me pretty soon, you're going to end up on the ground in handcuffs." The guard in the black uniform said, "I don't think so; look around." Apparently all these guys could talk to or hear one another over the microphones. As the police officer turned around, the other men in the black uniforms were all pointing their guns at the officer. The officer went to his cruiser and called his superior and told him what had happened. He was told to get out of the area. The officer left in his car. I could see other helicopters out over the ocean. They were smaller craft but they were black in color and they had no markings. As if by signal, all the men suddenly returned to the large helicopter and lifted off and disappeared. We later learned that the Air Force had been removing warheads from missiles on Long Island and was flying them to a holding area in New Jersey when one of the helicopters developed engine trouble and made a forced landing three miles down the beach in parking lot 9. The helicopter that landed in front of my home was a security group to protect the downed craft.

A special elite corps in black uniforms plays an important part in a booklet by William Pabst, entitled *Concentration Camp Plans for U.S. Citizens* (published by Spiral Feedback, Box 80323, Lincoln, Nebraska 68501). According to Pabst, they will be the ones responsible for rounding up domestic dissidents when the concentration camps built during the Johnson Administration and kept under mothballs ever since are activated. Not many people realise that one of the last things Nixon did before leaving the White House was to sign legislation designed to make another Watergate impossible, empowering the President to replace the Constitution with martial law simply by declaring a State of Emergency. Under martial law, the elite corps in black uniforms would take over all normal law enforcement duties, leaving the United States at the mercy of a resurrected Gestapo. President Reagan could replace the Constitution by martial law from one minute to the next at any time by going on TV and announcing a State of Emergency. Early in 1984, he signed Executive Order Rex 84, the contents of which are secret. Rumor has it that Rex 84 deals with procedures for rounding up domestic dissidents and taking the network of concentration camps out of mothballs. Anyone who disagrees with Big Brother is to be labeled a 'terrorist' and dealt with accordingly.

During 1983 and 1984 there were a number of developments in modern science which may be relevant to the mutilations.

There had been no blood shed at all from wounds on some of the mutilated carcasses, yet when investigators made cuts elsewhere in them, there was normal bleeding. Some cuts had a burned appearance, as if the wound had been cauterized. This suggested the possibility that lasers were being used. However, other bloodless cuts showed no signs of intense heat.

According to *Science Digest* (October 1983) and *High Technology* (April 1984), IBM Research Labs has made an ultra-violet excimer laser available to surgeons, which makes cuts with extreme precision, and without charring.

An engineer at the University of Maryland has invented a scalpel that produces microwaves as it cuts. The advantage of this is that the proper level of microwaves prevents bleeding, so cuts can be made without drawing blood, a great advantage in surgery.

At Stanford University a scalpel using ultrasound has been invented. The proper level of ultrasound can dissolve tumors or tissue.

These recent developments may have nothing to do with the mutilations, which have been going on for over a decade. However, there is often a time lag between when an experimental device is first tried out and when it becomes commercially available. During this interim period of testing, government agencies are frequently involved. These are inventions of great potential benefit to the medical profession and the entire human race, but it is obvious that the same instruments that could be used for life-saving surgery could also be used to mutilate.

Another peculiarity about the mutilations is the way many carcasses have been drained of every single drop of blood in seemingly impossible fashion, as normally the veins would collapse before all the blood was taken.

In 1983 Dr. Mario Feola of Texas Tech University published an article in *Surgery, Gynecology, and Obstetrics* concerning the use of cattle blood as a temporary replacement for human blood in transfusions. Dr. Feola expressed the opinion that cattle blood can be temporarily substituted for human blood if it has undergone a special filtration process and is used only once on a patient, not repeatedly. A bovine hemoglobin molecule is similar to a human one. The Army has expressed interest in his research.

Again, this may have nothing to do with the mutilations. If the Army wishes to stockpile cattle blood it can do so legally in any amounts required, and would have no need to resort to clandestine illegal methods. What is of possible relevance here is that the bovine hemoglobin molecule so closely resembles the human hemoglobin molecule that it is possible to substitute specially filtered cattle blood for human blood in transfusions.

During 1983 a professional scientist who wishes to remain anonymous suggested to Project Stigma that those responsible for the mutilations may be harvesting DNA and genetic material. This was an interesting and plausible hypothesis, but without much in the way of supporting evidence until a UPI wire story appeared on Feb. 27, 1984. Dr. James Womack, an animal geneticist at Texas A & M University's College of Veterinary Medicine, announced his discovery that humans share many of their innermost genetic secrets, including 'perfect match' chromosomes, with cattle. Womack's research revealed that cattle carry a 'perfect match' of portions of the important 21st chromosome pair in humans, a strand known to carry the characteristics of Mongolism or Down's Syndrome, a congenital disease associated with human mental retardation. In addition, large fragments of four other chromosome pairs were matched. "What we're already finding are big chunks of cattle chromosomes identical to large regions of human chromosomes", he said. "These are big blocks of homologous material, perfect matches. The genes fall in the same sequence. We must have more in common than previously believed."

Another interesting idea that may be relevant to the debate in progress turned up in a letter received in 1984, containing this passage:

> "I've studied vitamins and nutrition for a long time. A recent arrival on our nutritional scene is protomorphogens, or glandulars: the ground-up glands of cattle. If you take these for a year, you get hooked on them. Your own glands stop producing their hormones. The autopsied 'little men' had no alimentary canals: no glands? Did they need cattle viscera to stay alive? I'll bet you could live hundreds of years like this. The diet becomes completely regulated and controlled. You could refine it so that there are no toxins. Also you get a wonderful sense of well-being. I've heard that in some alternative cancer clinics, these glandulars are used to treat cancer victims, and so are glands from human fetuses."

Another possible use for such glandulars might be to instill elderly politicians with youthful vim and vigor. Be that as it may, the unusual properties possessed by this new type of nourishment provide a possible motive for the mutilations. Removing the sexual organs and the digestive system would be the quickest and easiest way to obtain most of the glands. But why go to the trouble and risk of eviscerating cattle illegally on the range, when enormous quantities of cattle viscera are available at a low price at any slaughter-house? That is the question which has plagued investigators since mutilations began to be reported on a large scale in 1973. As we go to press in 1986, I can only hazard a guess that aliens might prefer not to operate through normal commercial channels. It would only make sense in human terms if the location on which the cattle had habitually grazed was important, and the parts taken were used to detect mineral deposits, oil, or levels of environmental pollution.

Before shifting the focus of our attention to other aspects of UFO activity, it should be mentioned that these mysterious mutilations bear a troubling resemblance to a passage from the book of Exodus (chapter 29, verses 10-14):

"And thou shalt cause a bullock to be brought before the tabernacle of the congregation; and Aaron and his sons shall put their hands on the head of the bullock. And thou shalt kill the bullock before the LORD, by the door of the tabernacle of the congregation. And thou shalt take of the blood of the bullock, and pour it upon the horns of the altar with thy finger, and pour all the blood beside the bottom of the altar. And thou shalt take all the fat that covereth the innards, and the caul that is above the liver, and the two kidneys, and the fat that is upon them, and burn them upon the altar. But the flesh of the bullock, and his skin, and his dung shalt thou burn with fire without the camp: it is a sin offering."

Chapter Seven

SPACE TRIBES SIGNAL

It does not seem likely that the type of beings respon-sible for at least a large proportion of the mutilations would be the same as the type that planted Jesus, Quetzalcoatl, and Padma Sambhava among us, and took Mohammed on his celestial journey. Perhaps when the Fatima message was suppressed, the beings responsible for it lost interest in their long-term experiment with recalcitrant obtuse humanity, and allowed those only interested in exploiting us to take over. If the type of being invoked by the inner circle of the Nazis is still being invoked and propitiated with blood sac-rifice under the camouflage of the Stars and Stripes, it would be quite natural for those that made Enoch one of them to decide that humanity deserves to be turned over to the type of being its leaders have invoked. As witnessed from above by the Watchers, it may look as if humanity has not learned anything at all. Are we really more civilised than the Aztecs, or do we just offer blood sacrifice in more hypocritical ways, disguised as righteous wars? And as famine and disease caused by the manipulations of bankers and politicians?

Seeing it all from the Manichean viewpoint of angelic warfare between powers of good and powers of evil may be excessively simplistic, as the paradoxical is commonplace when it comes to UFO phenomena, but it is one of the valid ways to approach the subject and should not be ignored. Much of the evidence points in this direction.

There has been considerable debate as to whether UFOs are extra-terrestrial or ultra-terrestrial or inter-dimensional. However, one possibility does not necessarily rule out the others, and they may all be true. Some UFOs may be time-travelers from the future, who avoid interact-ing with us because they do not want to change the course of events that leads back to their home base of reality. Or, on the other hand, they might have acquired the art of subtly modulating the course of events in order to strengthen favorable aspects of the home base environment and cancel out negative ones, and be fine-tuning the creation and maintenance of a paradise as home base. A paradise such as may have existed on this planet long ago, and which might return.

Some UFOs behave like machines, others as if the UFO itelf was a living organism. Yet others appear as light shapes or energy patterns. Some reports describe vehicles contain-ing occupants, which have both mechanical and biological features. For example, the crystal powering the vehicle is alive and pulsates, or the vehicle seems completely mechani-cal except for a tail like an animal's. Entities with cyborg-like traits turn up quite frequently in the reports. Perhaps some UFOs have the ability to shift from the mechanical or the protoplasmic to the etheric and back again, as we shift gears on a car.

It is an odd fact that among the viruses there are some that look like UFOs, such as the virus T. Bacteriophage. Some UFOs may have the ability to operate in either the macro-dimension of outer space or the micro-dimension of viruses, switching back and forth between them at will.

In his list of the special powers that can be acquired

through the practise of yoga, Patanjali mentions the ability to become extremely large or extremely small. If this is an ability that exceptional human beings can acquire through the practise of yoga, then it may be possible that other forms of life elsewhere in the cosmos can also acquire it.

Considering the possibility that the resemblance between virus and UFO may be more than coincidental, let us pursue the analogy further. According to *Van Nostrand's Scientific Encyclopedia* (Van Nostrand Reinhold Co., New York, 1976): "The precise mechanism of how a virus transfers its nucleic acid to the host cell, and how the normal function of the cell is directed toward the production of progeny, remains obscure." If the analogy is valid, what substance transferred from UFOs to humans would correspond to the nucleic acid transferred from the virus to the host cell? Later in this chapter, we will investigate the correlations between UFO phenomena and LSD phenomena.

According to legends from many different cultures in antiquity, any shaman worth his salt was supposed to have a cloak of invisibility at his disposal. There is a theory that this involved learning to control the body's aura, which is normally transparent, but can be rendered temporarily opaque. The ability to become invisible or to shift shapes might be explicable in terms of modern scientific concepts, such as geometric hyperspace and the neutrino sea. Anyone with access to even one more dimension than we have access to could evade our most carefully planned investigations indefinitely. The only way we could catch up would be to become more multi-dimensional ourselves. Perhaps that is the challenge posed to humanity by the UFOs. Our survival as a species may be at stake. Let's at least face the facts before us, instead of continuing to try to pretend that nothing unusual is going on.

The reports of Men in Black who appear after UFO incidents to frighten witnesses into silence tend to fall into two categories. In the first, the Men in Black look and behave like normal human beings, such as might be employed by federal investigative agencies, often claiming government credentials, which the government later denies the existence of. In the second, the Men in Black look and behave like non-humans disguised as humans. The concern of both categories is to frighten witnesses into silence, not hesitating to take more extreme measures to obtain their silence. Dr. Berthold E. Schwarz describes a remarkable case involving the second category in his *UFO-Dynamics* (Rainbow Books, 1983): a doctor who is a general practitioner in a small town in Maine had become involved in a local UFO incident, and collected a batch of written materials and tapes pertaining to it. One evening the doctor happened to be at home alone, and received an unscheduled visitor, who told him to take a coin out of his pocket and hold it in his outstretched hand, watching it carefully. The penny turned light blue, blurred, became a fuzzy blue ball of vapor, and disappeared. The visitor, who had very pale skin and was dressed in black like an undertaker, wore heavy make-up and bore other signs of being a non-human disguised as a human. The visitor then informed the doctor that unless he burned his research materials and stopped investigating the case, his heart would vanish from his chest just like the penny had vanished from the palm of his hand. The visitor would know telepathically whether or not the materials had been burned. Having made these statements, the visitor disappeared in paranormal fashion. The doctor made a bonfire of his tapes and documents.

Some aliens are apparently no more alien to us than was the Queen of Elf-land to Thomas the Rhymer in ancient Scotland, or was the fairy woman who carried off Connle the Red, son of Conn of the Hundred Battles, in her ship of glass, her firm crystal coracle, in ancient Ireland. Merlin was supposed to have been the product of such a union.

Brain capacity does not correlate directly with intelligence, which is also determined by the number of neurons and the convolutions present in the brain. However, brain capacity is an important factor indicating the potential for high intelligence. Modern man has a brain capacity of about 1300 cubic centimeters. The Cro-Magnon man responsible for the highly artistic cave paintings in the Pyrenees had a brain capacity of about 1400 c.c. Boskop man was an African Negroid race that became extinct during prehistoric times, in spite of having had a brain capacity of about 1800 c.c. These large-brained types appeared quite suddenly, without intermediary stages, as if out of nowhere.

The research of Max H. Flindt is not very well-known, but two of his theories are relevant to the subject under discussion. Flindt attributes the paradoxically rapid development of the human brain to inter-breeding between primitive humanity and extra-terrestrials.

Modern science remains unable to find the cause of or a cure for schizophrenia, cases of which continue to flood our mental hospitals. Flindt's theory is that schizophrenia is caused by subconscious racial memory of the extra-terrestrial branch of our family tree, yearning for a long-lost home "not of this world", accompanied by dim awareness of a deep split somewhere far back in our ancestry. This may also be relevant to the unsolved question of the origin of human religious beliefs. Flindt points out that such factors as the considerable differences between glandular and nervous systems in primitive humans and extra-terrestrials would provide a physical basis for the traumatic tensions associated with this repressed memory of a profound split in our ancestry.

Our civilisation has forgotten the existence of other types of intelligent beings in the universe. Most of humanity thinks that as an intelligent species, Homo sapiens is unique, but this is no longer a tenable position. The mountain of unanswerable evidence provided by the publication of *Clear Intent* entirely erodes away the support for this position.

From the descriptions of UFO close encounters, it seems probable that we are being visited by different types of beings from different regions of the cosmos, who vary considerably in their motivations for coming here, their characteristics, and their ways of interacting with us.

Richard Sigismond is a psychologist and anthropologist who has been researching UFO phenomena for thirty years, and is a senior investigator for the Center for UFO Studies. In a recent interview with Bill Smith of the Boulder, Colorado, *Daily Camera*, which appeared in the issue of Nov. 3, 1985, Sigismond briefly summarised his knowledge of the different types of extra-terrestrials that are visiting us: "There is a one meter tall entity, hairless, large heads. A five-foot group with features one might call Eurasian is reported only occasionally. Nor is the creature with a long spindly body—like the one in Spielberg's movie—reported very often. One group of three-footers has thick bodies and pumpkin-shaped heads. The beings we call 'Swedes' could pass you on the street without being noticed. Then there are the 4½ foot humanoids. They have grey skin tone, elongated heads, slight protuberances in place of ears, long claw-like hands. This group is reported most often in close encounters of the third kind, including the abduction cases."

As previously mentioned, Budd Hopkins found that nine out of ten of the abduction cases he investigated involved this specific group, which turns up more frequently than the others not only in the case histories, but also on the autopsy table.

The courageous researcher who has done the most to remove the veil from this long-kept and closely-guarded secret is Leonard E. Stringfield. Here is the description given in his classic *The UFO Crash/Retrieval Syndrome*, published by the Mutual UFO Network in 1980:

The approximate height of the alien is 3½ to 4½ feet tall. One source approximated 5 feet. The weight is approximately 40 pounds.

Two round eyes without pupils. Under heavy brow ridge, eyes described variously as large, almond-shaped, elongated, sunken or deep set, far apart, slightly slanted, appearing "Oriental" or "Mongoloid".

The head, by human standards, is large when compared with the size of the torso and limbs. "Take a look at a 5-month old fetus," I was told.

No ear lobes or protusive flesh extending beyond apertures on each side of head.

Nose is vague. Two nares are indicated with only slight protuberance.

Mouth is indicated as a small "slit" without lips, opening into a small cavity. Mouth appears not to function as a means of communications or as an orifice for food ingestion.

Neck described as being thin; and in some instances, not visible because of garment on that section of the body.

Most observers describe the head of the humanoids as hairless. One said that the pate showed a slight fuzz. Bodies are described as hairless.

Small and thin fits the general description of the torso. In most instances, the body was observed wearing a metallic but flexible garment.

Arms are described, long and thin and reaching down to the knee section.

One type of hands has four fingers, no thumb. Two fingers appear longer than others. Some observers have seen fingernails; others without. A slight webbing effect between fingers was noted by three authoritative observers. Other reports indicate types with less than four fingers.

Legs short and thin. Feet of one type described as having no toes. Most observers describe feet as covered. One source said foot looked like orangutan's.

Skin description is NOT green. Some claim beige, brown, or tannish or pinkish gray and one said it looked almost "bluish gray" under deep freeze lights. In two instances, the bodies were charred to a dark brown. The texture is described as scaly or rep-

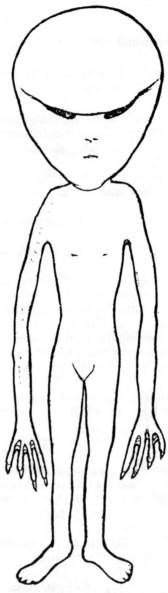

Drawing of a Humanoid based on information from the doctor who performed an autopsy on it. Data concerning size of head, torso and limbs, and other details, were gathered over a period of several months in 1979. The doctor likened the proportions of head and body to that of a five month old fetus.
(*Leonard H. Stringfield*).

Humanoid Head
Most reports describe two round eyes without pupils under a heavy ridge. The head is large compared to torso size. No ear lobes apparent. Nose is vague. Mouth is merely a slit with no lips. Doesn't appear to function as a means of communication nor for eating food. No teeth are observed.

Drawing of Humanoid head and hand from reports by firsthand witnesses. These illustrations were submitted to a former C.I.A. employee for review and comment. (*Leonard H. Stringfield*).

Humanoid Hand
One type of hand has four fingers, no thumb. Two fingers appear longer than others. Slight webbing between fingers frequently observed. Arms are long and thin. Skin is lizard-like.

tilian, and as stretchable, elastic or mobile over smooth muscle of skeletal tissue. No striated muscle. No perspiration, no body odor. Under magnification the tissue structure appears mesh-like, or like a grid's network of horizontal and perpendicular lines. This suggests that the texture of the granular-skinned lizards, such as the iguana and chameleon, may be similar to at least one type of alien humanoid.

No teeth.

No apparent reproductive organs. Perhaps atrophied by evolutionary degeneration . . . "The chest area contained what seemed like two atrophied mammary gland nipples. The sexual organs were atrophied. Some other investigators have observed female specimens.". . . In my non-professional opinion, the absence of sexual organs suggests that some of the aliens, and perhaps all, do not reproduce as do the Homo sapiens, or that some of the bodies are produced by a system of cloning or other unknown means.

To most observers the humanoids appear to be "formed out of a mold", or sharing identical facial characteristics.

Brain and its capacity, unknown.

Colorless liquid prevalent in body, without red cells. No lymphocytes. Not a carrier of oxygen. No food or water intake is known. No food found aboard craft in one known retrieval. No digestive system or GI tract. No intestinal or alimentary canal or rectal area described.

More than one humanoid type. Life spans unknown. Descriptive variations of anatomy may be no more diverse than those known among Earth's Homo sapiens.

So here we have a detailed close-up of the elusive Little Man, who may be no more than the advance scout for a variety of other intelligent life forms.

One of Stringfield's information sources said that he had seen glyphs on a crashed UFO that resembled San-skrit.

William L. Moore co-authored *The Roswell Incident* with Charles Berlitz (Grosset & Dunlap, 1980), which is about a UFO that crashed near Roswell, New Mexico, in 1947 and that was retrieved by the U.S. government. Since the publication of the book, he has continued to research the subject, and succeeded in talking with doctors who had autopsied the small large-headed cadavers. The type of Little Man involved in this incident had a heart, a bladder, a single lung and a single kidney. The digestive tract looked like it ate soft or mushy food. Perhaps this may be the type reported elsewhere that lives on "juice", but not the kind that humans drink. An interesting detail is that one of the doctors interviewed refused to give any information, but did let drop the fact that he was still receiving a monthly cheque from the U.S. Department of Justice in 1982, 35 years after the incident!

Travis Walton of Snowflake, Arizona, was abducted by a UFO in front of six witnesses. Police at first suspected them of having murdered their companion, cross-examined them, and gave them lie detector tests. The tests indicated that the witnesses believed themselves to be telling the truth. After five days Travis Walton was returned to the region from which he had been taken, in a state of shock but otherwise unharmed. This is how he described his captors (in *Ultimate Encounter* by Bill Barry, published by Pocketbooks):

They were very short, shorter than five feet, and they had very large bald heads, no hair. Their heads were domed, very large. They looked like fetuses. They had no eyebrows, no eyelashes. They had very large eyes—enormous eyes—almost all brown, without much white in them. The creepiest thing about them were those eyes. Oh, man, those eyes, they just stared through me.

Similar descriptions turn up in an abundance of case histories from all over the world. The resemblance between descriptions of humanoids and the model proposed by Dale Russell of the National Museums of Canada for a hypothetical intelligent descendant of the dinosaurs is startling. This striking similarity is reinforced by the detail of their skins being iguana-like. Are these the "flying dragons" of antiquity?

It was a common belief among the worshippers at the sacrifices periodically offered to various deities in antiquity that these deities consumed only a subtle essence of the offerings. In many cultures the first fruits of the harvest were put aside as the part for the gods. A tribe would prepare a sample batch of what they were producing, and take it to a specific place at a specific time, where it would be ritually consumed.

Maybe UFOs are cutting up our farm animals in clandestine fashion because the human race as a whole has forgotten the significance of putting aside the first fruits of the harvest, has forgotten who the Watchers are and why they come, has forgotten the ancient covenant and cosmic alliance that was nearly universal in the cultures of antiquity.

Human psychic energy may be the equivalent of rocket fuel or cocaine to inhabitants of other dimensions. Seen from this angle, the otherwise senseless wars of religion between devotees of different jealous gods which have recurred constantly throughout human history take on a rational motivation. It would explain why such extraordinary importance has been accorded to the individual's choice of which deity to worship. By worshipping a specific deity, one channels psychic energy in a specific direction. Charles Fort thought that we were being farmed for our flesh like pigs or geese or cattle, but this theory is not supported by the multitude of case histories which had not yet occurred at the time Fort wrote his books. In general, UFO occupants do not behave as if our flesh as food is what interests them, although a small percentage of cases does concern types of beings that are collecting human as well as animal blood. In most cases they are conducting physical examinations and collecting genetic material and samples of different kinds.

What does seem to be of paramount interest to many of them is our belief systems. A more apt analogy may be that of the bee-keepers and the bees. Creation myths from a variety of cultures indicate that man was created to give conscious homage to his Creator(s).

Particularly explicit is the Creation myth of the Maya Indians, those superb mathematicians and astronomers, nearly all of whose written works were destroyed by the Catholic Church. Their Creation myth was one of the few codices to escape the flames. This extract is from *Popol Vuh: The Sacred Book of the Ancient Quiche Maya*, which was translated from Mayan into Spanish by Adrian Recinos and from Spanish into English by Delia Gaetz and Sylvanus G. Morley, published by the University of Oklahoma Press in 1950:

> Then said Huracan, Tepeu, Gucumatz when they spoke to the soothsayer, to the Maker, who are the diviners: "You must work together and find the means so that man, whom we shall make, man, whom we are going to make, will nourish and sustain us, invoke and remember us . . . have us invoked, have us adored, have us remembered by created man, by made man, by mortal man. Thus be it done."

Precisely the same idea is expressed in the Sumerian Creation myth on the opposite side of the world, which is more ancient than the Babylonian and later Semitic versions of the Creation. The projection of psychic energy we periodically exude in the form of religious devotion may be like honey which fortifies and sustains the deities it is directed to. At this stage of our development, blind worship may no longer be what is required, but rather conscious understanding of our symbiotic relationship with the multi-dimensional entities which planted our ancestors on this planet. If they are now signaling their presence to us in the hope that we have become capable of understanding and communication instead of blind worship, our ignoring of those signals could give them the idea that the experiment has been a failure and should be terminated.

Perhaps the worldwide public appearance of UFOs and the appearance of LSD, both of which events took place shortly after the first atomic bombs devastated entire cities, are not isolated separate events but, on the contrary, closely linked. Both the UFO and LSD experiences are characterised by multicolored luminous apparitions and otherworldly realities. LSD may have been deliberately planted among us to prepare us for the shock of confrontation with non-human intelligent beings. Was LSD the dress rehearsal for the main event: mass landings? Dr. Albert Hofmann's famous "error" by which he discovered the unique properties of LSD-25, his "accidentally" ingesting this particular one of many different batches of lysergic acid contrary to normal laboratory procedure, could have been telepathically inspired.

Before the extraordinary properties of LSD became widely known, almost anyone with access to stationery with a professional letterhead could buy it legally from the manufacturer, Sandoz Laboratories in Switzerland. When restrictions began to be placed upon its sale to the public, one man took it upon himself to replace Sandoz as source of world supply almost single-handedly: the famous psychedelic guerilla chemist Augustus Owsley Stanley, known as Owsley. Owsley's LSD was the purest, the cleanest, and the strongest that ever hit the streets; its quality became legendary. He is estimated to have manufactured and distributed between one and four million doses of this fabulous 'white lightning' between 1965 and his arrest in 1967. Charles Perry was a friend of his during that period, and wrote an article entitled "Owsley and Me" in the Nov. 25th, 1982 *Rolling Stone*, which culminates with the following statement:

Certainly, he used to entertain theories that nobody else was willing to contemplate. For instance, it was a commonplace assertion in 1967 that LSD was causing a sort of accelerated evolution of the human race, but only Owsley came up with this twist: "What if LSD were revealed to us by beings from another planet who want us to evolve because they can use evolved intelligences as components in some immense, inconceivable machine of theirs? And when we've taken enough LSD, when we're *ripe*, they'll . . . *harvest* us."

Be that as it may, if telepathic contact with alien intelligence was made regularly in antiquity, and is still being made by a few Hopi Indians, Australian Aborigines, Dogons in Africa, and undoubtedly other tribal groups we are not aware of, it can also be made by us. No government expert or religious leader can do it for us. We each must seek this inter-stellar psychic communion in our own way within ourselves.

The concept of reincarnation implies a latent ability to regress back to former lives, and thus to restore the long-dormant far memory of experience and information accumulated during previous existences to conscious awareness. A substantial number of those who have worked on activating this latent ability find that their past lives include incarnations as extra-terrestrials. This occurs so persistently that it has become a commonly accepted belief among those engaged in such work that extra-terrestrials from many different points of origin have incarnated on Earth during this crucial all-or-nothing climax of human history. Some of those who remember previous existences as extra-terrestrials also become aware of specific missions they were born to carry out during the present terrestrial incarnation. Many others do not recall having been extra-terrestrials themselves, but do remember existences during which they interacted with extra-terrestrials. Both of these groups approach the taboo subject of human/E.T. communication and interaction with far less trepidation than those who have not explored these possibilities.

Ruth Montgomery, in a series of books of which the last has a title similar to this one (*Aliens Among Us*, Putnam, 1985), postulates another type of human/E.T. interface: that there are aliens among us who have taken over the body of a human on the point of death or in severe crisis, with the consent of that human. Montgomery calls them "walk-ins", describing them as aliens who are positively oriented. However, if a body is taken over without the consent of the individual concerned, the possession is of a demonic nature.

Some cases in the literature on demonic possession (as well as saintly raptures) may be explicable in terms of telepathic hypnosis by entities from elsewhere, who are not always the imaginary projections most doctors automatically assume them to be. Not only the average doctor, but also the overwhelming majority of the authorities in our culture reject such concepts as reincarnation, human/E.T. interaction and telepathic hypnosis, and dismiss the far memory of past lives as subjective delusion.

There is certainly subjective delusion in some cases, as it is all too easy to let wishful thinking lead one astray in such areas. This is particularly true of the psychic channeling of extra-terrestrials, purported telepathic communication for which there is no physical evidence. I would agree with the skeptics to the extent that a large proportion of what is supposed to be far memory or psychic channeling comes from no farther away than the individual's subconscious in the present lifetime. But just as many UFO sightings can be explained in terms of misidentification of natural phenomena, yet there persists a small hard-core percentage which can not be explained satisfactorily in conventional terms, so it is with the far memory and psychic channeling. There are occasions when information derived from such sources makes sense in terms of normally accepted logic, or is validated by the course of events. This pragmatic down-to-earth book would not have been written if I had not felt myself to be guided and inspired by invisible entities, who help me to carry out my mission.

An elderly lady who was abducted by the "little guys" and returned to her point of origin, but who wishes to remain anonymous, had this to say about her experiences:

Fear and panic are very important to the alien. If you become panic-stricken, you will be of no use to their Earth project. A person must be able to stay calm under all situations. The aliens must work with people who do not panic. They are not here to get us out of fights, to end our wars, to change our governments, or to physically save us. All they do is to pass on information about what their instruments are recording to those willing to listen and able to understand. We must save ourselves. We must protect ourselves. We are not really their concern. They have problems enough of their own. If somehow their information can help us, they are glad to be of service. But when the time of disaster arrives, they will pull out of our solar system. They refuse to become entangled with our warlike planet.

A different elderly lady, who has been through a similar experience, has no objection to allowing her name to be made public. Ida Kannenberg lives in Hillsboro, Oregon, where she and her husband own and operate a successful antique shop. Although she is now nearly seventy, she continues to travel all over the world searching out and buying antiques for their shop. She is highly energetic, well-educated, and interested in a wide variety of subjects.

Mrs. Kannenberg's first physical UFO encounter took place in 1940, during a night when she was out on the desert. At first she was only able to remember a blazing red object coming toward her, but not what happened afterwards. The shock was so great that for many years she remained confused as to what had actually happened to her. In 1968 she began to have telepathic experiences, which were initially very frightening. In 1980 she tried being regressed under hypnosis by Dr. Leo Sprinkle. During the sessions conducted by Dr. Sprinkle, she was unable to recall what her captors looked like, but did remember that technological implants had been made, including audio-visual implants. The UFO entities can see through her eyes and hear through her ears. She is aware of the continuous presence of what she calls her "live-in companion", who answers to the name of Hweig.

Mrs. Kannenberg realises that Hweig would be explained away by conventional scientists in terms of split personality or some other form of mental aberration. Although she does not agree with this interpretation of her situation, she does not claim to have any paranormal abilities because of her contact with Hweig. She does not seek publicity, nor does she avoid it. She writes down dialogues and insights she finds to be of particular interest as they occur, and has given me permission to quote the following descriptions:

There is the problem that everything I can see, he can also. Not only Hweig, but his immediate crew. Since their observation is through technological implants, the whole scene can be played upon a screen, like our television.

Hweig is an enomous tease. I suppose it does get boring always listening in to me 24 hours a day, though sometimes he takes a vacation for a week or more and someone else monitors. I try to tease Hweig back. The only problem is he always knows what I am thinking as soon as I know it myself. Therefore it is very difficult to play any kind of joke on him. I managed it just once.

I was looking for a particular skillet in the pantry and talking all the while, internally of course. I said, "Not that skillet, it is too large, and this one is too small, that one is for square eggs, ah, this one is just right."

Back came a quizzical little query, "Square eggs? I don't think I ever heard about square eggs."

There are several things I can do to drive Hweig up the wall. If I sneeze or whistle, he will say, "Please warn me when you are going to do that. A sneeze sounds like thunder, and a whistle pierces my eardrums like a dagger."

This Hweig/Ida or Ida/Hweig collaboration has been reached with a great many battles between us, a great deal of stomping and yelling on my part, and a great many sighs and apologies on his. Sometimes it is sheer aggravation: after all, I am married! And sometimes it is absolutely hilarious.

In the beginning of our association Hweig terrified me with his explanations of who and what he was, and what he intended to do. I was afraid that my mind was going to be taken over by an alien personality. However, after more than four years of this constant telepathic contact, I feel very much myself. Even more so, for I know myself so much better. I have had to face up to myself.

To me one of the big questions has always been: why is Hweig a *constant* companion? Is he a monitor only? Why do the Ufolk care what I say and do every minute? I'm not anyone. Why is my daily routine of such importance to them? Why did Hweig so entrench himself in my mind and life that I cannot dislodge him no matter what I say or do? I have begged, pleaded, wept, screamed . . . but he is still with me.

Hweig has put me through some very painful processes, but he declares they were necessary in order that he learn the levels of my tolerance and modes of reaction, so that the best possible use might be made of my peculiar talents and abilities. Certain limitations had to be overcome, or at least ameliorated. And when I cuss him out from time to time, I am only letting him know the limits of my compliance.

With mechanical devices that permit mind invasion and control, an alien civilization could conduct any kind of surveillance, and there would be no defense against it. The aliens can do this now. How long before Earth science can do the same? Or can they do it now? Can the aliens be Earthians?

I am not trying to "scare talk". I am trying to relate what has been done to me by persons who seem compassionate and responsible. Can this be done in the near future by others who may be neither compassionate nor responsible, who could be utterly reprehensible? It is time to study what this type of mind control is all about, beginning with those contactees who have experienced it.

Hweig told me that he and his colleagues are trying to prevent mind control from becoming established here on Earth. Is it because this type of invasion is fast becoming possible from other sources—perhaps right here on Earth? Would mind invasion by terrestrial governments or organisations be carried out with the same ethical and moral responsibility and codes of dignity that the UFO mind invasion has demonstrated in my case?

I have questioned Hweig about his ability to prophesy. He said, "By probabilities only. I am NOT, I repeat, NOT superhuman. I can do only what you could do, if you had an equal reservoir of information to draw from. We prophesy only by balancing potentials, by probabilities. Even so, we can be wrong. Some things are not wholly predictable."

So many times I have been asked, "Why don't they give you something useful, like a cure for cancer?" Hweig answers this, "What would you do, Ida, with such information? If I told you how to build and fly a UFO, what could you do with that information? Would anyone listen to you on that subject? Do you have the capital and knowledge to do the job yourself? I give you the information you can use. Those who can receive technological or scientific help ARE RECEIVING IT, though they may not have a live-in companion as you do. They receive in the manner in which they are able, and the information they are able to use."

I ask Hweig, "Why is there this influx of extraordinary help at this particular time? Why now?" Hweig's answer: "At this time mankind stands in dead center of the crossroads of human endeavor. I do not mean anything so simplistic as a single crossroads, but a convergence of many roads, each seductive in itself. A compromise must be made and maintained if the current world civilizations are to endure. The compromise must react onto many levels of human activity. World government leaders are struggling to find compromises on a political level, but the everyday people of the world must find their own ways of compromise on an individual level, such as levels of personal beliefs, as well as many other kinds. The metaphysical cores, not the histories, of all religions should be studied, and the psychological needs that shaped these beliefs. Only on that level can compromise be found, and until it is the fires of war will continue to brutalize the human race."

That was the only commitment Hweig would make concerning religion. "We are not here to tamper with your beliefs," he said. "Only to urge a compromise and understanding among them all, to find a set of humanistic values that all can tolerate and refer to."

Often he has warned me: "Do not allow any information we give you to become the basis for a cult or a religion. No cults! No religions!"

I ask Hweig, "Why has all this come into focus right at this time?"

"For the first time in the course of this round of civilization, world-wide communication has brought all the differences of belief and activities into a coherent area of observation. Patiently, many individual researchers in many lines have been digging into their respective studies. With the advent of computer technology, all of those separate researches can now be brought under one roof, so to speak. They can be analyzed and studied on a comparative basis. Religion, for example, must be compared to mathematics. Does that sound silly? It is salvation! Archaeology must be studied in relation to electro-magnetic waves. Only with computers can such comparative studies be adequately carried out. And they will be. This is the direction in which you and all contactees are being guided: toward the sharing and comparing of information, which can then become a common basis for understanding."

Another direct question, "Am I being mind-controlled?"

Hweig's answer: "Only to the extent necessary to impel you toward those studies and activities that will further our purpose, to have you gain information to share and compare with others. This in turn will further your own purpose, to contribute to the health and continuance of your own civilization."

I ask, "Who gives you the right to thus invade my privacy, my mind?"

"You do," he said, "by the fervor of your desire to help your own people. You asked to be guided to a way to be of use, of help. This is the response to your own request. You put it into words, and we answered. How else do you expect it could happen?"

I assume he is telling me that no one is going to perform a miracle for us. If we want to save or help our civilization, we are going to have to bestir ourselves to the task. We will have guidance, and information will be brought to our attention. The action—or inaction—is ours alone.

The first necessary action is data analysis and comparison. The compiling is already done. Every contactee is a gold mine of resource material. We must learn how to extract and use it.

We outline these needs by asking, Who, Where, How, and Why.

First, Who? That would be trained workers, scientists, students competent to obtain and utilize information.

Second, Where? In a research center with adequate facilities.

Third, What? To study contactees who are willing to divulge their information, and to be studied themselves in their interaction with the UFO connection.

Fourth, How? By devising a data code comprehensive enough to cover ALL of the forthcoming material. This can be modified and extended as the work continues.

Fifth, Why? To define specific plans of action, the manner and means of using that material once the information is obtained.

Another question I ask Hweig: "Why is this information given in this peculiar fashion? Why all the mystery and camouflage?"

His answer: "Ufolk and their activities are only one fashion in which information is being given. The Ufolk can handle the type that leads to psychical research, and to psychological research through scientific disciplines. Technological, medical and other scientific information and help is being disseminated by other means."

I know that all over the world, there are others who are experiencing the same phenomenon as I: a constant telepathic contact with other entities, all of whom claim to be of the UFO fraternity. Although they may introduce themselves as several varieties of beings, they are all UFO-connected.

It is my belief we are the vanguard of an experiment that will in the future be expanded to hundreds and thousands more of Earth's inhabitants.

It is important, therefore, that we begin to compare notes on these very personal experiences, and to try to find an answer to that big question: "Where is all of this leading us?"

This is a far more profitable question than, "Are UFOs going to invade the Earth at some future date?"

We are already invaded. The Ufolk are here, in our minds in these telepathic contacts.

While others tell us we are crazy, or fooled by our own subconscious, or experiencing a split personality or some other aberration, the Ufolks are blithely taking advantage of all this time to dig in and establish their territory in our minds.

Nero fiddled while Rome burned. Our people watch TV while their minds are wide open to invasion.

There are tremendously ticklish questions to be answered here. Without profound research, such as a UFO Center would provide, these questions cannot be answered.

While we older folk have been the experimental trial-and-error stage of the Ufolk mind invasion, our young people will be next. With their thinking powers numbed by constant frenetic entertainments, aided and abetted for some by alcohol or drugs, their minds could become so benumbed and bewildered that any type of mind invasion, alien or Earthian, would be a cinch.

Kooks like myself and my live-in companion, Hweig, should be the subject of serious scientific investigation. Dr. Sprinkle and his allies recognize and want to do this, precisely this.

There comes a time when one individual and his immediate associates cannot provide all the capital and energy and facilities needed to conduct and complete complicated and adequate studies. It takes the financial backing and cooperation of those willing and able to devote their assets, both monetary and intellectual, to the task.

Believe me, our world governments are not without some recognition of the problem, but they do not go to the source of the information they need: the contactees, and the contactee's contactors.

Now it is necessary to interject a dictation by Hweig:

Now I, Hweig, will dictate as you, Ida, have no way of knowing how to interpret these events and scenarios.

First, we must emphasize the necessity to read the following in its entirety, as we can give the total story only bit by bit, and later bits will clarify earlier bits that might discourage the reader if he be not forewarned. Therefore please be patient, ride all the way through with us, then judge according to your own understanding.

About 80% of all UFO abductions and personal contacts are the result of hypnotically induced illusion and hallucination.

Those who perpetrate this hypnotic state and its seeming events are unseen but present within the room, car, or otherwise near the contactee. This unseen presence is often felt by sensitive

230/ *Extra-Terrestrials Among Us*

persons—and all our contactees are MOST SENSITIVE—as a pressure in the atmosphere immediately surrounding them. The presence is projected by technological means much beyond the powers of your own people at present. This indicates the presences are those alien to yourself, and not of your normal every-day earth person no matter how advanced in any science, technology, or psychic ability an earth person might be. The alien presence has powers far beyond anything you might dream of.

It is necessary for the alien presence to be in close proximity to the contactee. By close we mean VERY CLOSE, almost within touching distance.

This presence, being almost pure energy, need not be in any one particular form, but can attain any form or abstraction desired. Black and white pinwheels, balls of light, fireflies, revolving disks, any form may be utilized to come momentarily into the vision of the contactee. We call this a semi-corporeal form or semi-physical state. Or the presence can remain totally unseen, in the state that is similar to your out-of-body experience, though the essence of that presence is of a more powerful energy than the essence of your out-of-body state. However, this is the closest analogy we can find to describe this energy state.

It would frighten your spitless, as you say, Ida, to know how many times you have been surrounded by alien presences. The knowledge of their extent of control over you would further alarm. This goes for all contactees of similar events.

For this reason, the potential alarm, we conceal the facts just given and instead perpetrate an illusion of physical aliens who seemingly come into the contactee's presence, or bring the contactee into theirs, knowing you can accept and interact with physical beings in a less frightened and more objective manner. Yet we wish to get across the idea of VERY ALIEN personalities, therefore we do not offer the visualization of your own kind of form, even though many of us are precisely your kind of form.

To feel you were being contacted, and perhaps controlled, by unseen forces would throw you into a panic, perhaps beyond acceptance. But to deal face to face with physical beings, no matter how alien, would eliminate some of that panic. At least that is our proposition, and this is why these illusory beings appear.

Not all contactees or abductees face illusory personages. A very few are quite physical and quite "real" as you term realness.

The illusory beings are the semi-corporeal selves of very real physical beings, who are at that moment existing in another area of being, and are quite busy doing something else physically, but are aware of what is happening in and to their semi-corporeal self.

This is certainly confusing. Let us recapitulate.

The unseen presences are there through technological means. They induce hypnotic illusion of abstract forms or hypnotically project the semi-corporeal forms. These latter are projections of real beings who are somewhere else physically at the time. They use projection "copies" because some time in the future these physical originals may find it necessary to interact with the contactees in a wholly physical manner. It would then seem to be an on-going experience.

Let us reiterate for clearness:

A corporeal flesh-and-blood person so projects himself in an unseen state through technological means that he enters into close presence of a contactee, or abductee, and is then able through his own psychic power to gain hypnotic control over that contactee when said contactee is in a relaxed state. If the personage were present in semi-corporeal or corporeal state, he could control the situation equally well.

The contactee, being already in a relaxed state, is readily accessible to the hypnotic form of control.

What transpires thereafter is all illusory or hallucinatory, unless there is a need for physical interaction. In such a case the contactee can be conducted aboard a physical craft where the physical interaction occurs.

By physical interaction we do NOT include examinations per se, as these may be of either category, physical or illusory.

Why should it be necessary to go through so much physical effort when illusion will serve the purpose of the Planners just as well? The psychological reaction of the contactee and the mental and the emotional results of his scenario, both to himself and to his audience, are what it is all about. If the same results can be obtained through hypnotically induced illusions as through physical action, then the illusion is chosen.

We are saying things backwards and forwards and inside out so that, hopefully, no ambiguity remains.

The presence in the room or car or wherever with the contactee can be felt as an oppression, a "thickness in the air", as one contactee described it. The contactee begins to breathe in a more shallow manner and to feel closed in, or caged, or captured, or unable to move.

The presence is the energy essence of a real corporeal being, who through technological devices sends his energy self, in a state relative to the out-of-body state, to this place. Since he is not a psychic master, he is not able to send his energy essence through his own psychic power, but must depend on technological devices.

The energy essence encloses the WILL of the presence, who is elsewhere physically, but is linked through mind stuff to his energy essence and will.

And that human being is so restricted by moral and spiritual law he cannot, dare not, serve as an evil power. He carries out instructions received from higher natures, and by higher we mean more knowledgeable, more powerful, and more responsible. He is further instructed to use the most compassionate modes of interacting he can devise.

Non-understanding, haste, error of judgment, mis-reading of contactee's reactions, as well as many other factors, can impose a task on the controller that he may be less than perfectly equipped to handle. Remember he is only another human being trying to do a very difficult job. He is working with persons as alien to himself as he is to them.

The presence of the controller is never seen by the contactee unless it is necessary to attract his attention, or to rivet his mind onto a single point. At such a time abstract designs or evasive objects, usually circular, are used. Other times the unseen presence can be felt or sensed by those most sensitive to such emanations of energy.

The condition and reaction of the contactee decides whether or not the presence is to be seen in any form or to remain unseen.

Many contactees have mentioned the "feel of an evil presence". The presence is NOT EVIL, but is part of the UNKNOWN and does take CONTROL for a few moments, and from the arising fear and apprehension the contactee interprets "evil".

The contactee response to the sense of being controlled is entirely according to his own nature and character. One resists and tries to struggle, one weeps or screams, one jeers, or even giggles. In the response, its kind and degree, the controller reads information it is necessary for him to know in order to continue into the future. The preliminary or initial scene is thus an act of getting acquainted, each measuring the other's potentials. Furthermore, the controller is just as much "on the spot" as the contactee, for he too is *undergoing a training session*, and is being weighed and measured by his instructors.

From his own psychic and *trained* abilities the controller then conjures up the appearance of apparent personalities who seemingly take charge of the scene. These are appearances of substance, but not true corporeality. We refer to them as semi-corporeal. They are projections of real persons who are to be physically met in the continued scenario of the contactee.

If footsteps sound, temperatures change, and there are NO SUDDEN TRANSITIONS in the scene, the event is entirely physical. If so, there are noises, odors, the sense of touch as well as vision. Touch does not mean pain, pain is psychologically induced by the contactee through fear.

There can be a shifting of states, a moving in and out of states during the course of a single event, so a single event can be a very complicated affair. Each would have to be minutely inspected and analyzed to realize these changes. At this moment such a scrutiny is not important and would only obfuscate this recital.

Thus we see MIND TRAVEL as well as OUT OF BODY TRAVEL can be induced from outside the contactee.

It is within this framework that the building blocks of the individual myth are found. When we realize the changeable conditions of the contactee/abductee event, we can begin to understand why the scenario itself is so very difficult to grasp as reality. But in comprehending these varying and shifting states, the interpretation of the building blocks becomes much easier.

By symbolic event we do not mean symbols such as a cross indicates a good guy and an x a bad guy. We mean the contactee is put through an event that is NOT TRUE in its content, but its psychological effect symbolizes one or more of the following ideas. These events and the ideas they symbolize are the building blocks of the structure. Depending upon the cultural experience of the contactee, the following ideas are presented in various manners:

    I.   Ideas presented in the Scenario of Recognition:
         1. of civilisations existing on other planets
         2. of civilizations existing of fantastic technological achievements

       3. of civilizations existing of tremendous scientific knowledge

       4. of civilisations existing with people of various natures who have knowledge of all kinds, medical, artistic, cultural, etc.

II. Ideas presented in the Scenario of Biological Intervention:

       1. of cross-breeding with alien races

       2. of giving of ovum or sperm for breeding experiments

       3. of implantation of sperm or fertile ova

       4. of taking of cells for examination, experimentation, or for cloning

       5. of interference with mental input, conscious recall, memory

       6. of implantation of technological devices for later use

III. Ideas presented in the Scenario of Initiation:

       1. of an unseen secret organization of good will and benefit

       2. of inspirational aids to solve problems and difficulties

       3. of secrets of the past to be found anew

       4. of promotion of societal contacts leading to cooperative efforts

       5. of monuments of good endeavors recorded in lost places

       6. of destruction of powerful deterrents to human/earth collaboration

IV. Ideas presented in the Scenario of Self-Development and Self-Awareness:

       1. of offering new personal insights

       2. of strengthening stabilizing beliefs

       3. of offering new projects

       4. of analyzing life-evaluations

       5. of value of self-freedom

       6. of support of person's intentions/ambitions

There are many other scenarios and parts thereof, and those can each or all merge one into another. In order to analyze them at all, we have to dissect the living form.

We come to rejuvenate the Earth, and to aid in the evolutionary development of man.

This is the end of Hweig's dictation, and of Ida Kannenberg's statement.

Ann Canary is another lady who has been abducted and returned. She discussed her experience at the Contactee Conference convened by Dr. Leo Sprinkle at Laramie, Wyoming, in 1981, climaxing it with this statement: "After many years, I now realise and know that my own transformation was not and is not a single experience here on Earth. There are literally hundreds if not thousands of people who have experienced this metamorphosis. Our numbers are growing yearly and we are beginning to locate and communicate with each other. An alien invasion has already occurred on Earth. The conquering power is not military or technological/economic superiority. It is a revolution in consciousness, and spiritual knowing that has been implanted within the minds of thousands of people all over the world. The future of this world is passing into the hands of these people. Those of us who have been contacted no longer serve the old orders. We fear nothing—least of all the threat of death or physical deprivation. We are HERE—NOW! We walk among you daily—we pass you on the streets, stand next to you in the elevators, and you see little of what is moving daily closer to its completion. We are among you— and our force is the force of mind governed by morality and an ethical code that upon Earth is incomprehensible."

Thus might have spoken a priestess of Demeter (whose celestial chariot, drawn by dragons, brought seeds from other worlds to this one) about the Eleusinian Mysteries.

A.E. (George Russell, Irish poet and painter) was thus described by his friend, the novelist George Moore: "The dog at his heels and the stars he would soon see (for dusk was gathering) were not different things, but one thing. There is but one life, he said to himself, divided endlessly, differing in degree, but not in kind." A.E.'s superb classic. *The Candle of Vision*, was published by Macmillan in 1918, and contains the following passage:

Once I lay on the sand dunes by the western sea. The air seemed filled with melody. The motion of the wind made a continuous musical vibration. Now and then the silvery sound of bells broke on my ear. I saw nothing for a time. Then there was an intensity of light before my eyes like the flashing of sunlight through a crystal. It widened like the opening of a gate and I saw the light was streaming from the heart of a glowing figure. Its body was pervaded with light as if sunfire rather than blood ran through its limbs. Light streams flowed from it. It moved over me along the winds, carrying a harp, and there was a circling of golden hair that swept across the strings. Birds flew about it, and over the brows the fiery plumage as of wings of outspread flame. On the face was an ecstasy of beauty and immortal youth. There were others, a lordly folk, and they passed by on the wind as if they knew me not or the earth I lived on. When I came back to myself my own world seemed grey and devoid of light though the summer sun was hot upon the sands.

In the summer of 1976, nine year old Gaynor Sunderland went for a bicycle ride in the country around her home town of Flint, North Wales. In a field she saw a huge UFO, from which a man and a woman emerged who didn't look quite human. The man, who was thin and angular, wore a skin-tight silvery suit with a helmet that covered both his head and face. He saw her hiding in a hedge. Telepathic contact with him made her feel dizzy. Her skin turned cold. It was as if an alien presence had entered her mind. She returned home safely from the incident. Within a week, her two brothers were also telling their mother, Mrs. Marion Sunderland, about their respective UFO close encounters. Mrs. Sunderland and her husband have not had any close encounters, but have both witnessed a definite UFO in the sky at a distance. Marion Sunderland has been having psychic experiences since childhood. All of her children, in particular her daughter Gaynor, have inherited this trait. By combining their psychic abilities with the work of other researchers, they have succeeded in finding archaeological treasures of high importance, all associated with Mary Queen of Scots. Graham Philips and Martin Keatman have written a book about their fascinating adventures, entitled *The Green Stone*, which was published by Granada in 1984.

Many contactees prefer to remain anonymous, but have things to say that deserve a hearing. When statements made independently are cross-referenced, they often support each other. The following hypothesis is a theme that surfaces again and again in such material.

There is an almost infinite variety of nearly innumerable intelligent life-forms scattered through the stars in this galaxy alone, as well as through a number impossible to estimate with precision of other galaxies. There are uncountable myriads of intelligent beings at all different stages of development and with differing varieties of characteristics. They can be roughly classified into three groups: Federation, Independents, and Renegades. Federation membership is voluntary, but by invitation only. Terrestrial humanity has not yet matured sufficiently to be invited to join, though we are close to that stage of development. Those who decide not to join the Federation, but wish to live at peace with it, become Independents. Just as humanity on Earth has among its members a criminal class, which can not be distinguished from law-abiding citizens on the basis of personal appearance, clothing, or the transport vehicles they use, so do the Ufolks have among them a criminal class. The Renegades are space pirates and scavengers, persistently associated with the constellation of Orion, though they also have other bases elsewhere. They are the easiest of the space groups to make an alliance with, but they do not hesitate to betray their allies whenever circumstances may be advantageous. They are not invincible. They are among the lower echelons of the galactic powers, and can not guarantee victory, as Hitler found out. Some of the Renegades come from the ranks of the Independents, but Federation members are not all advanced enough to be immune to greed, and Renegades often disguise themselves as Federation or Independent. However, they have certain characteristics that render them recognisable no matter what their disguise may be. As they are negatively oriented, they encourage selfish motivation and discourage concern for the well-being of others. Their standard operating procedure is to establish a privileged elite caste dependent on them, which in turn controls the masses for them. Their manipulation of human governments and organised religions has been and is nearly all-pervasive. It is we who give them power over us. Persistently negative thought-patterns among humans provide the basis for the manifestation of their power. Their technique for neutralising the positively oriented is to pretend to be positively oriented also, but from within that framework to deliver predictions of disaster which either become self-fulfilling prophecies or do not happen at all, thereby discrediting in the eyes of his or her contemporaries the positively oriented dupe who in good faith transmitted these warnings. Such attitudes are in sharp contrast with the distinguishing characteristics of Federation members, which are: reluctance to infringe on an individual's freedom of choice, and concern for the well-being of all forms of life.

When we exploded the first atomic bombs, without being aware of the consequences, we sent a cosmic alert signal in all directions throughout this and neighboring galaxies. So we have all kinds coming here, with many different types of motivation and interacting with us. Upon seeing a UFO land nearby, one should not assume its occupants to be either benevolent or hostile. If one is walking down a lonely street and a stranger approaches from the opposite direction, at a certain point one gets an intuitive impression as to whether the approaching stranger is benevolent, more or less neutral, or downright hostile and dangerous. In the case of a UFO close encounter, one should react according to the same sort of intuitive signal, being careful not to panic merely because of physical appearance not conforming to human standards of beauty or conventional norms. A being may appear physically ugly to us, yet have good intentions. Ugliness is no guarantee of good intentions, but it is compatible with good intentions. The signal to go by is the intuitive impression, the early warning system we each have built into us, which is activated by situations such as meeting a stranger on a lonely road, or a UFO close encounter.

The universe visible to us is of such grandeur and complexity that it surpasses the limits of our comprehension. Moreover, our scientists have now discovered that the universe visible to us is only a small fraction of the total universe.

Professor Fred Reines is a physicist who worked with Dr. Oppenheimer on the first atomic bomb. For the past 28 years he has been studying neutrinos, and is now with the University of California. In January, 1982, he made this statement on the BBC program "Science News": "Our universe is only one-tenth of the whole, nine-tenths are made up of invisible mass."

Modern astronomers agree that nine-tenths of the universe seems to be missing. When we look through a telescope at our galaxy, the Milky Way, or at a distant galaxy, we are seeing only one-tenth of the stars or mass. The atoms that make up the other stars and planets are moving at such high speeds that they are invisible to our eyes. If we spin a bicycle wheel at 100 miles per hour, even at this low speed the spokes become invisible to us. The motion of distant galaxies and the stars in them can only be accounted for under the laws of gravity if there is far more mass associated with each galaxy than there is in the stars visible to us.

Rates of speed inside the atom are just as staggering as they are in outer space. Particles within the atom move at speeds of up to 670 million miles per hour, and those are only the particles that our scientists have so far discovered and been able to study. Others may be moving at even greater speeds.

It has long been known that the atom contains protons, neutrons, and electrons. The neutrino was discovered in

1956. The missing nine-tenths of the universe is now thought to be composed of neutrinos and neutrino-like particles.

Neutrinos are extremely difficult to study, as they are the most elusive of all known sub-atomic particles. Although they have mass, they pass right through physical matter. It has been estimated that a neutrino from the Sun would stand a good chance of penetrating a thickness of lead stretching from Earth to the nearest star without colliding with anything. Trying to study a particle of such extreme subtlety confronts scientists with a paradox comparable to catching a ghost in a test-tube.

In their "Hidden Variables: Where Physics and the Paranormal Meet" (published in *Future Science,* edited by John White and Stanley Krippner, Doubleday, 1977), authors E. H. Walker and Nick Herbert state that "the central nervous system, unlike the computer, is composed of trillions of jittery, individually unpredictable synapses whose patterns exist primarily on the collective level rather than on the individual level. Sir John Eccles has described this labile jungle of neurons as the sort of machine a ghost might operate."

These recent developments in physics, neurology, and astronomy provide an unexpected breakthrough into the understanding of psychic and paranormal phenomena.

The atoms our physical bodies are composed of contain protons, neutrons, and electrons, as do all other atoms in the physical universe perceptible to our senses. The atoms of our physical bodies also contain the much finer and faster-vibrating neutrinos and neutrino-like particles.

These finer and faster-vibrating particles compose the substance of the bioplasmic 'spirit' body that is joined to our physical body by an invisible magnetic cord, which breaks at the moment of death. The bioplasmic body is the butterfly that breaks loose from the chrysalis of the old worn-out physical body when we die. We are in this world, but we are not of it. We come from, and will return to, the dimension of neutrinos and neutrino-like particles that the nuclear physicists have recently discovered, the same dimension that Sir William Crookes and Sir Oliver Lodge postulated the existence of a century ago. The so-called supernatural and paranormal turn out to be natural and normal after all.

There may be a correlation between this invisible nine-tenths of the universe and the puzzling fact that approximately 90% of the human cerebral cortex is unassigned. We use only about one-tenth of our potential intelligence. If we were able to use our full brain capacity, would the invisible nine-tenths of the universe become visible to us? Is the dormant 90% of the cerebral cortex comparable to equipment that is ready for use, but is not yet connected to its power source? What is the mental connection that needs to be made in order to complete the circuit and activate our dormant potential?

There are abundant indications that this invisible nine-tenths of the universe is swarming with life, and is just as real to its inhabitants as this world is to us. If they wish to interact with our physical dimension, they have to slow down their rates of vibration. In this context, consider the following statement made by a UFO contactee after he had been abducted and returned:

The Sun is a transmitter and the Earth is a receiver on a specific range of frequencies. UFOs can share the same space with us, as they operate outside our normal range of frequencies, interacting only when they wish to. A nuclear bomb is a miniature Sun, which emits energy on all spectrums, not just the Earth range of frequencies that humans are sensitive to. Therefore nuclear war would annihilate not only terrestrial humanity, but also many forms of intelligent life inhabiting dimensions we normally have no awareness of or contact with. So no wonder we are being visited by aliens.

Parapsychologist Larissa Vilenskaya pointed out in an article on remote viewing in *Psi Research*, vol. 4, no. ¾, that: "Recently the SRI research team made an attempt to investigate possible production of photons during a remote-viewing task. They found that when the remote viewing was good, there was an increase in the signal detected by the photon-counting system."

Jacob Sarfatti's unpublished *Diary of a Mad Physicist* contains some relevant reflections:

Imagine a network of points and lines—a Persian rug. Now imagine we go a level deeper, in such a way that each point, when looked at under great magnification, is the same network again! Similarly, the entire network in which your awareness now resides, is but a point on the same network at a superlevel. The whole thing can have the topology of a circle. Thus, if you get on the astral elevator whisking you up and down through the networks, you will meet yourself going the other way. . . . The idea is that the discontinuous quantum jump, beyond space-time, is a manifestation of the archetypal mythic journey of separation-initiation-rebirth. . . . This is why the quantum biocomputer is more than a Newtonian machine and is capable of creativity. . . . But suppose a part of the information processing is at the quantum level of electrons in individual neurotransmitter molecules all linked, noncausally, by superluminal ERP quantum connections. This is an implicate order beyond space-time. Who is then to say that some inspirations may not come from intelligences elsewhere or at different levels of the stratified reality (higher beings)?

A highly relevant statement was also made by another physicist, Denys M. Wilkinson (published in *The Infinite Hive* by Rosalind Heywood, Chatto & Windus Ltd.): "Perhaps there do indeed exist universes interpenetrating with ours; perhaps of a high complexity; perhaps containing their own forms of awareness; constructed out of other particles and other interactions than those we know now, but awaiting discovery through some common but elusive interaction which we have yet to spot."

Dr. Francis Crick, who won the Nobel prize for his co-discovery (with Wilkins and Watson) of the DNA code, suggests in his book *Life Itself: Its Origins and Nature* (Macdonald, London, 1982) that life may not have arisen naturally on earth, but may have been sent in the form of bacteria in a spaceship by an alien civilisation which foresaw its own doom.

But what if it was not destroyed, what if it still exists, and its emissaries hovering over us have been greeted with machine-gun bullets?

Sir Fred Hoyle, the British astronomer, has proposed a theory similar to Crick's. And Buckminster Fuller expressed an almost identical idea beautifully in his poem *"How Little I Know"* (from the *Saturday Review* series *What I Have Learned*):

Within the order of evolution as usually drawn
Life 'occurred' as a series
Of fortuitous probabilities in the primeval sea.
It could have been sent or 'radiated' there.
That is, the prime code
Or angle and frequency modulated signal
Could have been transmitted
From a remote stellar location.
It seems more likely
(In view of the continuous rediscovery of man
As a fully organized being
Back to ever more remote periods)
That the inanimate structural pattern integrity,
Which we call human being,
Was a frequency modulation code message
Beamed at earth from remote location.
Man as prime organizing
Principle construct
Was radiated here from the stars—
Not as primal cell, but as
A fully articulated high order being.

Thomas Bearden is a retired Lieutenant Colonel in the U.S. Army, who spent twenty years specialising in nuclear weapons and military intelligence. He has written an extraordinary book entitled *The Excalibur Briefing* (Specula, P.O. Box 1182, Huntsville, Alabama 35807, 1980), which deals with paranormal phenomena and new military applications of psi research. He does not claim to be a UFO contactee, but occasionally experiments with what he calls a "free-stream" of consciousness. In a mentally calm released state he sits down in front of a typewriter and lets flow whatever comes without the usual mental discipline imposed on thoughts or any censorship whatsoever. Although he makes no claims at all for this material, I selected the following passages from it because they seem to me to be of considerable significance. These excerpts are taken from his unpublished *Free Stream Creation*:

The real reason for our contacts directly with human specimens is that from time to time it is necessary to do certain measurements to refine our operational methods and insure the safety of this pre-natal species. Yes, we must continue to trick you in this writing for it seems to be the only way we can bypass successfully the censorship of your conscious . . . What we are doing is not really mental, but it has mental effects that result several harmonics up from where we are working. We are generally preparing humanity for a great shift in consciousness, and this preparation is necessary to prevent the mancells from "burning out" or shorting out for the final connection. It is analogous to turning a baby in the womb to the correct position to prevent a breech birth . . . We are operating through a severe force screen to prevent blasting out the neuronal circuits with bioenergy. If the receiver instrument is too blockaded by solidified ideas, of what you call a scientific or logical nature, it is not possible to penetrate through the blocks/locks unless much greater power were used in the touch. And more power would simply fuse the circuitry and render it useless. So most scientists are not reachable until they themselves gradually reduce the strength of the blocks. This is of course gradually beginning to occur . . . But many probetouches do go into resonances of all sorts—an instrument resonates to its own particular resonances. Thus when we "stroke" an instrument, we have little or no control over the overtones impressed on the signal, or how distorted the signal comes out. It is entirely possible to get an individual who responds by thinking or "realizing" that he is indeed the Archangel Michael. Indeed, in his own peculiar reality construct, he is what he thinks he is. But of course that is a thought form construct, and that is a totally different thing from what you call reality . . . Because of the large number of structures and blocks that most humans have, you will get mostly signal buried decades down in the noise. That is, you will get a lot more noise than signal . . . We are demonstrating to you (it is one form of our communication) a science that is just a little beyond where you are now, but one at a level you can reach if you try very hard. Thus our ships exhibit to you as solid 3-d matter, then turn into a 3-d right-angled space to become to you photonic (glowing balls or shapes of light), and then make another right-angled turn to either rematerialize to you or to totally vanish, depending on the dimension we pick to make the turn in . . . It makes good sense in 6-d, but no sense to you in 3-d . . . Your 3-d is simply one cross-section of a 6-d world. In a 3-d cross-section, "we" can be we, it, or nothing at all. In fact, "we" can be "you" yourself, or all of these at once, or none of those at once . . . *In one 3-d intersection of our holographic multidimensional nature, it is like the collective unconscious of all humanity acquiring a collective conscious instead of a multitude of fragmented individual little consciousnesses.* In one sense we are simply your own individual subconscious. In another sense we are the unconscious of the entire human species, collectively, as one unconscious. In another sense we are the unconscious of the entire biosphere. And yet in another sense we are "extra-terrestrial being(s)" contacting humanity and communicating with it. And in another sense we are God communicating directly with Man. Each of these is an intersection, and each is true within its own intersection. Yet each is only part of the truth, not the whole truth. Yes, like the five blind men and the elephant, the parable . . . You are literally children playing with mudpies and starving, under the unseen bounty of a table containing a great feast . . . At present you are all quite blind. Even the best of you, even the most accurately visionary, from a multidimensional point of view is quite erratic and rather unpredictable. You are really much like very crude cat's whisker radios, noisy, not of much signal strength, not of much power. But these words are not intended to be derogatory at all; they are intended to clarify the situation. You are on your way, of course, to changing all that. But you must not be arrogant and proud of your really very small 3-d accomplishments. Neither must you be dominatedly bowed; there are no "masters" and there is to be no domination. There is instead to be the borning of a new infant, and then its growth and maturing. In that process, you will acquire multidimensionality. When you are ten dimensional, you will figuratively "smile" at all this; but it will be something very strange indeed, a 10-d smile.

Space tribes signal. Medicine dreamers awaken. Eagle-snakeman returns. Flying dragons speak.

It is urgent and essential for us to demonstrate in some effective fashion that a basis for a peaceful dialogue exists. Until now the official attitude has been to pretend that nothing unusual is going on. As the evidence is so considerable that it can no longer be swept under the carpet and is growing from day to day, this ostrich-with-its-head-in-the-sand attitude is no longer tenable. It is, moreover, an insult to the intelligence of both humanity and our visitors. The ever-increasing numbers of human abductions and cattle mutilations might be their way of responding to our refusal to acknowledge their existence. From their point of view, our polluting the oceans may constitute a cosmic crime. The blind arrogance of a few politicians intent on retaining personal power at all costs puts the entire human race in danger of the ultimate disaster, the nightmare come true of inter-stellar warfare, with our civilisation suffering the fate of Atlantis.

What direct action can an individual take to alert the general public to the urgent reality of this extreme danger that the entire human race is in? People everywhere have been conditioned by their political leaders to dismiss reports of such phenomena with a sneer, a giggle, or a guffaw. How can an individual break through the conditioning of Big

Brother's 39-year-old big lie, which automatically labels these reports as unworthy of serious consideration? When you try to talk to your friends and acquaintances about this subject, you will be astonished at the extent to which people do not want to know, and are willing to do almost anything to evade inspecting the evidence. The idea that non-human intelligent beings genuinely exist goes against the grain of what they have been taught since childhood, and being obliged to face the fact panics them.

My suggestion would be to first think the matter through for yourself, thoroughly and at length, getting a picture of the situation into focus as clearly as possible within your own mind. Then try discussing it with family members and close friends. Note the feedback, and consider it as help in getting the picture into focus. Try discussing it with friends, acquaintances, and (if you feel the circumstances to be appropriate) perhaps occasionally with strangers. When and if all these discussions stimulate you to the point of making a statement of your own, write it out, rewriting it as often as may be necessary in order to get it into a form that satisfies you. The next step would be to make as many copies as may be feasible without putting undue strain upon your resources. Send these copies to local, national, and international authority figures, to radio and TV stations, and to publications that print 'Letters to the Editor'.

An individual can also join one or more of the responsible groups already engaged in this research, such as: Society for the Investigation of the Unexplained (SITU), P.O. Box 265, Little Silver, NJ 07739. Project Stigma, P.O. Box 1094, Paris, TX 75460. Citizens Against UFO Secrecy (CAUS), c/o Lawrence Fawcett, 471 Goose Lane, Coventry, CT 06238. Mutual UFO Network (MUFON), 103 Oldtowne Road, Seguin, TX 78155. Fund for UFO Research, P.O. Box 277, Mt. Rainier, MD 20712. Project Identification, c/o Dr. Harley Rutledge, Dept. of Physics, Southeast Missouri State University. Cape Girardeau, MO 63701. Aerial Phenomena Research organisation (APRO), 3597 West Grape Drive, Tucson, AZ 85741. Center for UFO Studies (CUFOS), 1955 St. John's Drive, Glenview, IL 60025. American Association of Meta-Science, P.O. Box 1182, Huntsville, AL 35807. The Fair-Witness Project, Suite 247, 4219 West Olive Street, Burbank, CA 91505. The Sourcebook Project, P.O. Box 107, Glen Arm, MD 21057. Archaeus Project, 629 Twelfth Avenue S.E., Minneapolis, MN 55414. Canadian UFO Research Network (CUFORN), Box 15, Station A, Willowdale, Ontario M2N 5S7, Canada. British UFO Research Association (BUFORA), c/o Norman Oliver, 95 Taunton Road. London SE12 8PA, England.

Flying Saucer Review, Snodland, Kent ME6 5HJ, England, is a high-quality publication devoted to genuine research, as is *Fortean Times*, 96 Mansfield Road, London NW3 2HX, England. Lucius Farish's *UFO Newsclipping Service*, Box 220, Rt. 1, Plumerville, AR 72127 is a reliable way to keep up with recent developments.

Is UFO activity so clandestine because humanity is an experiment in progress? Would mass landings correspond to the completion of the experiment, which was described in different traditions long ago as Judgment Day? Is that the type of event we are on the brink of?

Instead of panicking or pretending they aren't really there, the urgent and essential thing to do is to establish direct communication. The United Nations should pass a resolution recognising their existence, which invites them to land in peace and to communicate directly. Perhaps only when all the nations of the Earth agree on this will the dialogue begin. As Charles Fort said: "The peoples of this earth must organize themselves before conceiving of, and trying to establish, foreign relations."

Beings from elsewhere watching this planet from above

might well have a different standard of values than those inhabitants of the surface so obsessed with making money that they are blind to the interdependence of all forms of life, the hard-headed professional politicians intent only on retaining personal power at all costs, who control nearly all existing governments. That may explain why government authorities are so quick to cast ridicule on UFO sightings and dismiss them as collective hallucinations, just like Bishop Agobard of Lyons so long ago.

As nuclear physicist Stanton Friedman has said: "No government on Earth would want its citizens to pledge allegiance to the planet rather than to itself, and to think of themselves first as Earthlings, rather than as Americans, Canadians, Russians, etc."

If the existence of non-human intelligent beings whose science and technology are far in advance of our own was to be publicly acknowledged by government officials, the at present all-powerful monolith of the State would suddenly become very small change indeed. The arms manufacturers and international bankers and multinational corporations enslaving common citizens everywhere through manipulation of government debt and by force of arms would lose control of the world. When it is generally realised that all those expensive weapon systems are obsolete, even when brand-new, in comparison with the UFO technology, what justification is there for continuing the arms race?

The reluctance of heads of state to admit that their governments have been blatantly and persistently lying to their tax-paying citizens about the subject of UFOs (and about what other subjects?) for the last 39 years is perfectly understandable. However, that is not a valid excuse for perpetuating these falsehoods. The public can no longer be pacified by having the persistently recurring phenomena explained away in conventional terms. Hardly anyone still believes that UFO incidents can all be explained away in terms of weather balloons, swamp gas, flocks of geese, mass hallucinations, or any of the other red herrings which used to be swallowed whole without thinking twice by a naive public, now somewhat more sophisticated.

The results of a Gallup poll taken in 1966 indicated that 40% of the population of the U.S. thought that UFOs were real. The Gallup poll of 1974 showed a rise in percentage to 54%. This trend continued in the 1980 Gallup poll, which had a percentage of 60%. The percentage registered by the 1984 Gallup poll was 80%. One might say that the solution is rapidly reaching the saturation point, and precipitation is due to occur.

As it becomes more and more obvious to the world at large that UFOs are real and are not of terrestrial origin, the credibility of the standard official explanations shrinks to the vanishing point. The extra-terrestrials have not only arrived: from here on out they are sitting in on the action, whether we choose to recognise that fact or not.

In the first chapter of this book I quoted a statement made by Professor Jean-Pierre Petit of CNRS (the French equivalent of NASA) in an interview published by *Paris-Match* on Oct. 26, 1984. In this final chapter, I wish to quote another portion of that interview:

> "Why don't the authorities show more interest?"
> "In my opinion, it's an instinctive rejection. Civilisations are like living beings. When two individuals meet, three attitudes are possible: coexistence, one devours the other, or they go different ways. The existence of another civilisation is frightening, because if it is technically superior, it can enslave us. This is a persistent theme in science-fiction. But there is a possibility even more upsetting than this. If beings visit us without enslaving us, they may also be superior to us morally, socially, or politically. Contact could thus cause our primitive and barbaric social structure to disintegrate. As our terrestrial civilisation is unable to coexist without shock, it chooses to reject the phenomena in a defensive reaction, which could be compared to that of Dr. Zaius in *Planet of*

the Apes".

"You're not very complimentary to the human race."

"Let's look around us! The vast majority of humans are dying of starvation while the others are accumulating completely insane weaponry. We have only the slightest chance to escape being annihilated during the next five to ten years. Our science is in a state of total perversion. Everything humans are capable of inventing is first of all and with the highest priority applied to the arms race. 95% of human creativity is channeled into this insanity. We are suicidal maniacs."

The legends of a prehistoric "war in heaven" appear to have a basis in fact. The craters on the Moon and Mars can not all be explained in terms of meteorites or volcanos, because many of them are in precise geometric patterns, such as parallelograms, crater chains and crater pairs. The geometric distribution of the craters cannot be convincingly attributed to chance. These patterns are duplicates of the patterns projected for use in saturation bombing of large areas in modern nuclear warfare. Is our civilisation on the brink of making the same irreparable mistake that totally destroyed a previous high civilisation?

The legend of Vishnu's laser-loaded invincible disc may be both a memory and a preview of a periodically recurring celestial visitation, an event which does in fact historically take place, with far-reaching consequences for humanity, radically affecting the development of our species.

The ostritch-with-its-head-in-the-ground attitude of our authorities towards UFO phenomena has also characterised their attitude towards LSD, and is directly responsible for the disastrous social situation so aptly summarised by Dr. Stanislav Grof in his brilliant *LSD Psychotherapy* (Hunter House, 1980):

The repressive legislation in regard to psychedelic drugs has succeeded in terminating almost all legitimate scientific research, but has been quite ineffective in curbing unsupervised self-experimentation. It is nearly impossible for the average professional to get a license for psychedelic work and a supply of pharmaceutically pure substances, but black market samples, frequently of problematic quality, are easily available to the teenage generation . . . LSD is a catalyst or amplifier of mental processes. If properly used it could become something like the microscope or telescope of psychiatry. Whether LSD research continues in the future or not, the insights that have been achieved in LSD experimentation are of lasting value and relevance. . . . LSD is a tool of extraordinary power; after more than twenty years of clinical research I feel great awe in regard to both its positive and negative potential. Whatever the future of LSD psychotherapy, it is important to realize that by banning psychedelic research we have not only given up the study of an interesting drug or group of substances, but also abandoned one of the most promising approaches to the understanding of the human mind and consciousness.

In most of the civilisations of antiquity, a hierarchy of initiates was the custodian of the potions made from the powerful hallucinogenic "plants of the gods", which were dispensed to neophytes only after careful and extensive preparation, in order to minimise negative effects. What our contemporary authorities have done is to create a situation which is precisely the opposite of this, and which maximises the negative effects. This could be corrected by legally allowing responsible and qualified researchers, such as Dr. Grof and his colleagues, to resume their activities.

In antiquity a species consciousness coexisted with a tribal consciousness and an embryonic individual consciousness. As individuality became more and more developed, the species consciousness faded more and more into the background, like a broadcasting station being "jammed" by a more powerful station, becoming the "still small voice" reported occasionally by mystics. Even further in the background than the species consciousness is a planetary consciousness, a composite of the brain waves of all the species living in this planet's biosphere, including the Schumann Resonance in the ionosphere, which is the brain wave of this living earth itself. Contact with planetary consciousness was sometimes achieved by oracles, such as the one at Delphi, but when genuine contact failed it was frequently faked. However, with modern equipment it would be possible to measure an individual's brain wave attunement to the Schumann Resonance, and thereby establish whether such contact is genuine or faked.

Furthest back of all is cosmic consciousness, a composite of the consciousness of all forms of life on all the stars, including the macro-consciousness of galaxies, which are also living creatures. We each have this cosmic consciousness, concealed within the deepest and most ancient portion of our systems: our DNA code. The angelic alphabet in letters of fire, of which all forms of life are created, our father/mother ancestral source and common point of origin, the omnipresent Old One: DNA has found expression in terrestrial human terms in systems such as the runes of Odin and the Enochian archetypal characters, series of highly condensed symbols of elemental meaning, as well as in elegantly eloquent scientific equations.

Responsibly conducted LSD research may be the most effective tool available to us for bringing the DNA code to conscious awareness. Making conscious contact with our own DNA and activating its latent potential is our skeleton key to communicating with extra-terrestrial or other-dimensional entities, no matter what their point of origin. It is the pearl of great price we didn't know we had, the foundation stone which the builders rejected.

Under exceptional circumstances, any one of the deeper levels of consciousness may surge to a crescendo that overwhelms the relatively recently developed individual consciousness, resulting in a seemingly irrational eruption that may be interpreted (depending on one's point of view) as divine guidance or prophetic utterance or poetic inspiration or diabolical heresy or insanity. Of course, in a civilisation which systematically represses awareness of any level deeper than the tribal one (patriotism), such manifestations tend to be automatically categorised as insanity. In Aztec Mexico, anyone who objected to witnessing human sacrifice was automatically considered to be insane, and therefore next in line for sacrifice. Ken Kesey's classic *One Flew Over the Cuckoo's Nest* dramatically demonstrated how the repressive system works in our contemporary society.

As Professor Petit so aptly pointed out, we humans are behaving like suicidal maniacs.

From the point of view of the Watchers, do government officials who are responsible for dumping nuclear waste into the circulating waters on which all forms of life depend have a right to survive? Once radioactivity is released into the environment, it can't be taken back or neutralised. The process is irreversible. Nuclear waste has a half-life of approximately 714 million years, whether it be buried on land or dumped in the sea. During the first part of that cycle, the radioactivity increases instead of diminishing as the years go by. One solution would be to shoot the waste into outer space, but the amounts already produced are so huge that there is no way we could get more than a tiny fraction of it off the planet by this method with our present technology. No one can say with any precision how much waste has been disposed of during the last 40 years by the U.S., the U.S.S.R., and other nations possessing nuclear technology that used the easiet and cheapest method: clandestine dumping into the ocean in steel drums. Although no precise estimate can be made, it is obvious that the amounts must be enormous. The probability that the quantity is sufficient to destroy all life on this planet within the next 35 years, as the steel drums break open through normal corrosion and their contents seep unavoidably into all water everywhere, raising its radioactivity beyond the lethal level, is very strong indeed. So even if we manage to avoid nuclear war, the small groups of power brokers that make the major decisions in our civilisation have in their ignorant arrogance already signed humanity's death warrant. Government officials made this "mistake" (!) through stupidity rather than on purpose, but that does not diminish the extent of the tragedy or their responsibility.

If all the nations responsible for dumping nuclear waste into the oceans were to agree without delay to collaborate as a team, using their submarines and navies to search the ocean floor and retrieve as many of the steel drums as possible, giving this project tip-top priority above all other projects, humanity would at least stand a chance of survival. What are we going to put first: corporate profit margins, or the survival of the human race?

Unfortunately, this question has already been answered. Since at this decisive moment in history, the citizens of the United States have seen fit to re-elect by a landslide majority a bellicose Administration that habitually turns a blind eye to pollution of the environment, that uses hypocritical double-talk to justify its sabotage of all attempts at arms control (as if any new weaponry that can be used defensively could not also be used offensively, and we had a monopoly on righteousness), that antagonises our allies and multiplies our enemies, recklessly escalating already intolerable international tensions to flash-point, and that is totally dedicated to producing even more nuclear waste in the maximum amounts possible, there is nothing we can do, except to prepare ourselves for Doomsday.

There is nothing we can do, except to renew the ancient covenant between the children of the Earth and the children of the stars, each of us sending a telepathic S.O.S. Mayday call for help to save the planet's biosphere. Whether one thinks of it as a prayer, a mental message, or a psychic telegram makes no difference. What is essential is for each of us to send as whole-hearted a call as possible to positively-oriented forms of intelligent life from elsewhere. No equipment is necessary. They are telepathic, and they are out there. Because it is their nature to respect freedom of choice, they will not intervene unless the collective signal we choose to send is strong and clear.

Does any one species have the right to exterminate all other forms of life on its planet while committing nuclear suicide?

Has humanity's ancient Great Goddess, the Earth Mother, ignored and poisoned by her own children, who have even forgotten that she is alive, sent distress signals through space? Are those distress signals what the UFOs have come in response to? Has Mother Earth asked to have her face cleaned? Have we been transforming our planet into a cancer cell in the body of the galaxy instead of making it the garden of the universe? Perhaps the Christian, Islamic, Hebrew, Mazdean and Hopi traditions of Judgment Day refer to the day when the Earth is once more "relieved of its heavy load".

APPENDIX

AS WE GO TO PRESS

This was taken from *Pursuit*, vol. 18, no. 4 (Journal of the Society for the Investigation of the Unexplained, P.O. Box 265. Little Silver, NJ 07739.)

The Westchester Wing
by R. Perry Collins

The wave of UFO activity characterized as the "Westchester Wing" has carried on into 1985, although the magnitude of the wave seems to have diminished. There have been several unusual incidents which serve to highlight covert federal interests not only in "coverup" attempts but also in active pursuit of the object(s). It has become increasingly obvious to investigators that the federal government not only is almost frantically attempting to explain away and deny the phenomenon, but also to tap the efforts of those less restricted (civilian) investigators. This has, at times, led to some humorous situations. At one point, in a conversation with Bob Girard about the implications of this surveillance, I jokingly said that I really had no problem with it, as I belonged to the "KSP." Bob asked what that was. I calmly replied that the KSP was the "Krypton Special Police," assigned to investigate the investigators of UFO investigators. Whoever was listening in overreacted as our line was immediately cut and I was left with a dead phone.

Lt. Lesnick, tired of being followed whenever he went to interview witnesses, decided to get even. He had his followers tailed. For several weeks up to five cars played Keystone cops across the Connecticut and New York countryside. Phil Imbrogno, amazed, watched a helicopter slowly drifting over his residence as an individual inside pointed a camera at him. Quickly, Phil ran for a camera to point back at them. Heedless of this merriment, the "Wing" continued appearing, making friends among the populace and causing alarm to the establishment.

The implications of all this, and the details of the actions of both the UFOs and the people involved with them provides us with a rich field of information. There is a great deal to learn here, not only about our "visitors," but about ourselves. When I say

257

"making friends among the populace" I mean it literally. In many cases involving this "Westchester Wing," as with other UFO appearances over the years, there is evidence of what we call "psychic" interaction between the witnesses and the object. There have been many cases, some of which will be detailed here, where this interaction took place. For instance, the object has been noted to recede in distance when witnesses became fearful, come closer when they desired a better look, and respond to witness viewing positions with maneuvers and displays of lights. The object has hovered over residences of families who had noticed it slowly following them home. It has even hovered at less than 500 feet altitude a short distance from homes until whole families gathered to watch. Then, slowly cruising directly over, it displayed itself with breathtaking effects and beautiful lights. The wing-shaped arrays of light are multicolored, strong but with a soft glow and are almost entrancing. These lights are turned on and off, again in direct correlation to the presence of witnesses. Someone, it seems, is saying hello.

Someone is also paying very close attention to our nuclear weapons storage areas. Someone is providing periodic demonstrations of ability to quickly and easily nullify ballistic missile installations, anti-aircraft missile launches and jet aircraft interception attempts. This activity has been going on for years but it is only recently that investigators have been able to get solid information about it and to make that information more available to the public. The wave of activity involving the "Westchester Wing" comes at just this time of growing public awareness. This UFO wave has been identified by J. Allen Hynek as one of the largest and most consistent displays in history. It has been centered over one of the most affluent and influential population centers in the nation. We must ask ourselves whether or not all this can be coincidental.

There have been numerous appearances of the "Wing" in 1985, but, as stated, the reports have decreased in number. I shall concentrate on three specific events of note; a very dramatic incident over the Indian Point nuclear facility, a sighting over Meriden, Connecticut involving an untraceable military helicopter and an unusually well-planned example of efforts to divert attention from the real phenomenon. These cases will provide a focus for what seems to be the fading of this particular wave of UFO activity. As other investigators, particularly Jacques Vallee, have noted, UFOs generally seem to present themselves with periodic waves in both time and location. This wave may now have served its purpose: the reinforcement of the almost mythological reality of the UFO phenomenon.

The three examples shall detail some reactions of established social groups, primarily those concerned with government and national security. Before going into depth with those examples, let's look more closely at the reactions of local groups and individuals, especially those individuals who observed the "Wing" at close range. Many police officers who were witnesses to the low over-flights of the UFO were adamant in their statements. They agreed that what they saw was not a plane or groups of planes. One officer reported a very large, structured craft which glided silently over his cruiser, stopped, rotated on its axis, and moved slowly over his position again. Many other patrolmen who had seen only the formations of planes were just as convinced that the whole thing could be explained as aircraft. In early 1983, when the UFO overflights began, the first explanation offered was that the sightings could be explained by the presence of ultralight aircraft. Just as this was being publicized as untenable (largely through the efforts of Phil Imbrogno), the formations of Cessna aircraft began to be noticed. It is important to note that these formations of aircraft had not been widely seen nor reported in the media until more than a month after the first reported UFO sightings over Yorktown, NY. Since that time there have been many reports, both of a very large, low, dark object variously illuminated and of close formations of light aircraft, flying at five to seven thousand feet, displaying non-regulation lights. Many witnesses, some of them pilots themselves, reported having seen both displays. They agreed that there was no confusing the two.

While the majority of the population in the areas where the highest number of reported sightings has seen nothing, a significantly large minority has viewed and reported definitely seeing an unusual object(s). Throughout the summer and fall of 1983 and well into 1984 the UFO wave gained momentum. Local media reports, witness reports and intensive investigation by Lesnick and Imbrogno became the talk of many social gatherings. It became fashionable to discuss the subject and debate the pros and cons of its real nature. Local newspapers did yeoman service in presenting many of the aspects of the situation. Independent radio and television stations followed the activity, often inter-viewing Lt. Lesnick and Imbrogno. The "V"-shaped displays of lights continued. Those who saw them were often professional people whose articulate reports were difficult to discount. It became easier, as reports came in, to separate the planes from the UFO. Often the witnesses themselves knew the difference.

The area where these reports were most concentrated included Westchester, Putnam and Dutchess counties of New York and Fairfield County in Connecticut. These four counties are closely clustered around New York City. The media there receive much more national attention and were reluctant to get involved with the whole subject. City journalists who spoke to investigators said they frankly didn't know what to think. There were several times that major television networks mentioned the reports. These came after evenings where the witnesses numbered in the thousands. But these were isolated dates and the networks made no effort to follow up or clarify their brief airings. All but one of the major newspapers of the city made little or no effort to publish the numerous reports. The New York *Times* published two well written items discussing the activity. These appeared on April 17, 1983, near the beginning of the true UFO wave and on September 11, 1984, as the wave continued but as reports of the aircraft became more numerous.

The reports of low overflights of the large, structured UFO often referred to strong thoughts and feelings by the individuals involved. Often the UFO seemed to respond to these thoughts and in some cases to initiate them. Many witnesses noticed more direct interaction than the obvious light displays and maneuvers. Bill Hele works as meteorologist for the National Weather Corporation at Westchester Airport. On the evening of March 24, 1983, he was driving along the Taconic State Parkway in Westchester County, NY when he saw the object. "I've been around aircraft all my life and I can honestly say I've never seen anything like it," he stated. "I had the feeling of being stared at, analyzed and rejected. It wasn't a dangerous feeling, but I had the feeling of being examined from head to toe. There was a series of lights, maybe a half dozen in a row, with one or two hanging on the end like a pendant. They went out for 15 to 20 seconds and reappeared with no sound. There was no shadow, no silhouette, no nothing. Just lights, but they were changing multiprismatically. We're talking a magnitude of a quarter mile long or longer of lights . . . It caught me by total surprise." Hele's experience was mentioned in the Sept. issue of *Omni* magazine and again in the Hartford *Courant* of Aug. 16, 1984.

As the sightings continued, there were more people who noticed an almost "psychic" interaction with the object. Approximately ten percent of the witnesses reported definite correlations between their thoughts and the actions of the "Wing." On March 17, 1983, between 7 and 10 pm, several hundred people in the area of Brewster, NY watched as a large "V"-shaped array of lights cruised low over the town and nearby Interstate 84. One witness, Dennis Sant, got an extremely good look at it. He and his family were coming home from church when they saw the object hovering near their home. As they got closer to the house, it seemed to disappear. Thinking that was all there was to see, they went inside. Soon Sant felt an impulse to go back outside and walked out his front door. As he glanced in the direction of nearby I-84, he saw a large "boomerang"-shaped object hovering silently less than 200 feet over the highway. It had red, white, blue and green lights on its "wings" and a large yellow light in the middle. People on the road were stopping, exiting their cars and staring at it. Sant remembers wishing he could get a better look. Immediately after his thought, the craft made a sharp turn and slowly moved directly towards him. It lost altitude until it was about thirty feet from him and less than 100 feet up. Now it stopped and resumed hovering for approximately one minute. Then it began slowly moving over his back yard, emitting a soft hum. Sant was able to jog almost directly under it and saw a dark, grey metallic structure. The object again stopped and hovered and Sant backed away from beneath it. As his family and neighbors watched, it suddenly shot down a brilliant beam, illuminating the entire yard for approximately thirty seconds. It then slowly moved away towards the north, gaining altitude.

Many more such "interactive" cases could be presented here, but I prefer to discuss one with which I am most familiar— my own. I too got a good look at the "Wing" in late August of 1983. Several hundred people saw the object that night over a cluster of Connecticut towns that included New Haven, Orange, Milford, Bridgeport, Monroe and Stratford. I interviewed many of them on tape. We all saw the same thing and many of us had similar reactions. I was home alone that night on the third floor of my residence in the north end of Bridgeport, near St. Vincent's Hospital. Strangely enough, just before I saw it, I was reviewing some notes I'd made after speaking with Lt. Lesnick about the wave of "Wing" reports. Deciding to take a break, I walked to my north window.

Suddenly three lights appeared, seemingly low over the rooftops to the northwest. I told myself I was seeing a light plane, but immediately dismissed the idea as the lights were too widely spaced and were drifting very slowly to my left. Just as I became intensely curious, the lights went out. Hoping to see them again, I moved to my bedroom and the west window. As I looked out, directly over my neighbor's house, the lights reappeared. They were much closer now, stationary and about twenty to twenty-five degrees above the horizon. I was amazed. Here I was, a man whose hobby is UFOs, apparently seeing one. The lights sat there, the left one red, the middle one green, the right one blue. Abruptly, I began speaking aloud, "If you are what I think you are, tell me somehow that I'm not hallucinating." The lights seemed to react; the green slowly faded out, came back on and then they all faded. Immediately I received a strong impression to move back to the north window. The impression was so abrupt and so clearly not my own thought that I started to resist it even as I began to move to the next window. Excitement and curiosity overcame me, however, and I quickly moved to the forward room and leaned out the open window. An immense, wing-shaped array of lights greeted me. Later I calculated that the object supporting the lights must have moved sideways and forwards at least one-quarter-of-a-mile in the few seconds it took me to move from the west to the north window. It was now almost directly overhead, between myself and nearby St. Vincent's Hospital. It was moving slowly, silently, apex forward, directly to the east. I had several reactions. I was conscious of a very focused and somehow logical presence, but my mind was only secondarily aware of this. I had worked as a quality control engineer and had grown up in an Air Force family. I first realized that this "wing," if that was what it was, could not be an airfoil. It was moving too slowly to hold itself up. I was also busily engaged trying to line up reference points, judge how many hand widths it took up, etc., so that I could later trigonometrically figure out its actual dimensions. It seemed very large and very low. For approximately 20 to 30 seconds it drifted over and then suddenly the lights dimmed and went out. I strained to see a shape or a structure, but could not.

In all the excitement, I hadn't thought to find a camera. I quickly walked to the phone, noting the time from the wall clock and called Lt. George Lesnick. After a brief talk, I walked outside and towards the area where it had "disappeared." I spent a long time, at least half an hour, standing in an open area, wondering, hoping it would come back. It had definitely impressed me, "psychically" and otherwise. As I previously mentioned, I spent a good deal of time on the phone that night, calling local police and airports, finding that many others were also seeing it.

There are numerous other examples of the interactive nature of this wave of UFO activity. In July of 1984 I interviewed a family of four living in the suburbs of Danbury, Connecticut. The husband had been leaving work later than usual and was moving out of the parking lot when he noticed some odd looking lights in the nearby sky. At first he paid little attention to them, thinking only that a plane was flying around at low altitude. As he drove home (a trip of several minutes) he began noticing that the lights seemed to be pacing him. Still he took little notice until he pulled into his driveway and got out of his car. He then could clearly see a huge array of colored lights drifting slowly towards his house. Calling his wife and children, they all gathered on the back porch just as the object came directly over them. It was clearly triangular in shape and as it moved overhead it executed an abrupt ninety-degree turn without slowing or showing a turn radius. The husband described the turn, "The tip of the triangle was moving in the direction of flight when the thing seemed to slowly rotate on its central axis, so that the tip was finally pointing ninety degrees from where it started. Then, without any change in speed, just as the tip completed its rotation, the thing just moved off in a completely separate direction, back over the front of my house." The couple had spoken to only a few close friends about the incident and seemed relieved to hear that many other people were having similar experiences in the area. While this case doesn't necessarily show interaction of a "psychic" nature, there certainly appears to have been a specific display for a specific group of witnesses. The family felt no fear of the object and it displayed no hostility. Again we can say it seems someone, using a clearly unknown and very impressive technology, may be saying "hello" at such a level so as not to disturb society as a whole. The aparently immense craft has yet to land in the center of town in broad daylight. Human nature and our current cultural consensus could conceivably make such an event an unmanageable chaos. Whoever is "saying hello" presumably knows us well and seems to be showing great care in letting us get gradually and comfortably acquainted with it or them.

We should attempt here a closer approximation to the actual structure of the object displaying the lights. "Westchester Wing" is a term I coined simply because most of the reports were coming from Westchester residents and most of the reports described a wing or boomerang-shaped display of lights. Only a relatively few reports refer to a structure. The most common descriptions of the structure itelf are: huge, dark metallic grey, a grid or lattice underneath, tubular attachments and circular attachments. Descriptions vary as to the actual outline of the object or objects. Phil Imbrogno has deduced from computer studies of reported times, areas, durations and frequencies that we may be dealing with as many as three different UFOs, all with similar characteristics.

One witness I interviewed gave some pertinent clues about the ambiguity of the actual shape or structure of the unknown object. The report came from a professional woman living near Goshen, Connecticut. Between 9:00 and 10:00 pm, on September 17th, 1984, she was driving along a fairly deserted road outside of Goshen when she saw a long string of glowing white lights paralleling her car just over the treetops on the side of the road. She slowed to get a better look and as she did so the lights moved directly over her car, changing in shape to resemble a very large "horse-shoe." They remained hovering like this for approximately two minutes. A pickup truck approached from the opposite lane and continued on down the road. As it disappeared, the lights seemed to "uncoil" and form a "V" shape, which then very rapidly moved away to the south. The woman was convinced that the lights were all attached to one object as their relative distance from one another never varied, only their configuration. Within an hour of her sighting, reports were received from several hundred people in the areas of Southington and Southbury, Connecticut, approximately thirty miles away. From all the available reports of these definitely unidentified objects, we can deduce only two possibilities. Either there are several structurally different UFOs or there is one very large UFO which appears to change shape using a variable lighting display.

The first of the previously mentioned three incidents of 1985 on which we'll focus actually took place in the summer of 1984, but only came to public attention in January of 1985. On January 12, 1985, two newspapers run similar headlines. They were startling and controversial. "NUKE PLANT GUARDS REPORT HOVERING UFOS" appeared in the *Journal-News* of Nyack, NY "UFOS

— DID ALIENS BUZZ INDIAN POINT PLANT?" Read the *Reporter Dispatch* of White Plains, New York. Again it was through the tireless efforts of Phil Imbrogno that these incidents came to light. Both articles said basically the same thing. The stories were presented fairly, with both sides of the question aired. Plant authorities basically denied and downplayed the incident. Imbrogno stated that on July 24, 1984, a huge "V"-shaped object slowly descended to within 300 yards of the nuclear plant. Guards became alarmed, shotguns were issued and nearby Fort Smith was alerted. John Branciforte, security coordinator at Indian Point, stated: "He (Imbrogno) could possibly be making it up or he took what they (witnesses) gave him and stretched it out. I think people are going to publish stories on hysteria and misinformation. As far as I'm concerned, it's pure speculation."

The real story, related by Lt. George Lesnick, sounds almost like science fiction. Lesnick was with Imbrogno when they investigated the incident. They interviewed six of the fifteen guards involved. They found more than twenty other witnesses in residences near the installation. And they found definite indications of a coverup, of jobs threatened, of an almost frantic effort to keep the real story from surfacing. Whether or not federal authorities were involved wasn't determined, but certainly responsible officials denied the known facts and even came close to slander. From all that I know of the case, it seems some of the officials, uninformed of the real nature of the events, simply tried to explain it away on the basis of their own preconceptions. As in many UFO cases, there seems to have been two types of coverup: official denial of the facts by those who should be aware of them and denial of the facts by those whose access to them was not direct. The second is a manifestation of our desire to create and maintain a comfortable cultural consensus, whereas the first is purposeful deception and is not so easily forgiven.

George Lesnick had worked as a police officer for the town of Fairfield, Connecticut for twenty-nine years, rising to the rank of Lieutenant before retiring in July of 1985. He is a healthy, robust, straightforward man who had received numerous recommendations for his police work. He had been instrumental in saving lives, solving kidnap cases and generally serving his community as a dedicated and professional police officer. His comments and investigations on a case are those of a professional investigator. He does not "stretch facts." If George is not absolutely sure of his material, he does not speculate.

It is with this in mind that I relate the events that actually led to the January headlines in those New York papers. I spoke with George several times to get the facts of the incident straight. In October of 1984, George, Phil Imbrogno and J. Allen Hynek were being interviewed on a late night radio show in New York. Lee Spiegel of NBC had all three men on a telephone hookup to discuss the now twenty-month-long wave of UFO activity involving the "Westchester Wing." After the show, the investigators received fifteen calls. One came from a man who George named "Deep Throat." He was a security officer at the Indian Point nuclear facility. He had something he wanted to talk about with the investigators. A time and a place were arranged for an interview. No one but Lesnick, Imbrogno and the guard knew of the meeting. The officer indicated he would have several other guards with him.

George and Phil arrived at the meeting to find six guards from the plant and, surprisingly, lawyer Peter Gersten. Accompanying Gersten was the same woman who had interviewed me the year before, posing as a MUFON investigator. She was accompanied at that time by an FBI agent, sitting quietly at the next table, unnoticed by myself but under surveillance by local plainclothes police. George later informed me that he, too, had been invited to that first meeting, but had declined.) As the two investigators entered the diner that had been set up as the rendezvous, they noticed Gersten and his friend and somewhat surprised, began to talk with them. "Deep Throat" came over and introduced himself and indicated where the other five guards were sitting. At this point Gersten seemed to try to take over and manage the meeting, inviting everyone to sit at his previously reserved table. Lesnick interrupted and insisted on separating the witnesses, so as to get a clearer look at how their stories compared. He took three and Phil took three, leaving Gersten and his friend somewhat at a loss.

The story that came forth was startling but not so unfamiliar to those aware of how authorities at higher levels react to the presence of UFOs at "sensitive" installations. To be fair I attempted to contact the woman involved. It took some time, but I found her Connecticut address, mailed her a letter and got no response. I drove to her house, dropped a note asking her to call me. She did call, but quickly denied being aware of any FBI involvement and hung up before I could ask about her being at the Indian Point meeting. Maybe she's being set up, maybe she's actively involved, but certainly she pops up under unusual circumstances asking informed questions about UFOs. She is not an investigator for MUFON as she told me. This I confirmed through Marge Christensen, MUFON state coordinator for Massachusetts. Perhaps I am mistaken. Perhaps she has a sincere interest in UFOs. Having met her, I would say her interest is sincere, but then so is the interest of the FBI—they just don't seem to be able to admit it.

All six guards related the same basic story. Phil and George questioned them for nearly two hours. On the evening of July 24, 1984, a huge, V-shaped object, displaying two rows of bright, glowing lights, slowly approached the nuclear plant. It descended to an altitude of less than 500 feet and approached the facility to within 100 yards. The second shift security officers at first could not believe it. The object then stopped and hovered over them, emitting a low humming noise. The men became nervous as the object continued to hover and someone gave the orders to issue shotguns. Fifteen guards were involved and as the object remained stationary they became very nervous. Another order was issued to contact nearby Fort Smith. As the now thoroughly shaken guards watched, the object continued to hover almost directly overhead. After approximately 15 minutes the object slowly drifted away and then abruptly accelerated upwards and to the northwest. The security officers interviewed were all relieved that no one had ordered them to fire upon the craft, but admitted that they were keyed up enough that they would have, had it been deemed necessary.

The two investigators made appointments with some of the witnesses to meet again, and "Deep Throat" called them several more times. In his last call he said he could no longer talk or meet with Lesnick or Imbrogno, as his job was in jeopardy. Neither of the investigators could reach any of those they had interviewed earlier. They were simply told by powerplant authorities that the men were unavailable for comment and could not come to the phone. When asked about possible films from the plant's security cameras, the same officials replied that the cameras had not been working that night due to a technical malfunction. Lesnick was told the cameras "weren't loaded" at the time. As a professional police officer, he found this explanation difficult to believe. Considering the current protests about nuclear power faculties, and the resultant activity of demonstrators that appear around such plants, a "malfunction of security cameras" is not likely. Security at sensitive installations has also been intensified due to ongoing threats of terrorist activity.

The second incident of note took place over Meriden, Connecticut early in April of 1985. At the time I was working as a technical supervisor at an engineering company in Meriden. Many of my fellow employees knew of my interest in UFOs and would occasionally drop in to my office to discuss the subject. That morning, as I was walking towards my work area, a secretary approached me to relate a UFO sighting she, a friend and her friend's father had experienced less than nine hours before. As I briefly questioned her it became apparent that what she had seen fit the "V"-shaped-object category. The three witnesses had seen the object moving slowly, apex towards the ground, near the junction of the Merritt parkway (Highway 15) and I-91 (Interstate Highway to Hartford). Since this was near our plant, I took the opportunity to drive over to the area at coffee break. As I looked around for powerlines or other features, I suddenly noticed a very low-flying helicopter of unusual design. I am fairly familiar with aircraft but could not at first identify this one. It appeared to be a military aircraft of gunship design. Stopping my car, I got out and viewed the aircraft through binoculars. It seemed to be making a sweep of the area and was at less than 300 feet altitude. As it made a second pass near my position, I could clearly see it, indeed, was of a military-gunship design, painted dark blue and showing commercial NS numbers in red. I noted the numbers and returned to work as the helicopter slowly moved away to the north at the same low altitude.

Back at the office, I had little time to really think about it, but I was almost sure that there was a connection between the UFO sighting of the previous evening and the appearance of the unusual aircraft. Around two that afternoon, an engineer coworker dropped by to tell me that he and his wife were sure they had seen a UFO early that morning. It turned out to have the same characteristics as the one seen by the secretary, but it was seen six hours after hers and was not moving slowly at all. In fact, the engineer and his wife were at first convinced they were watching a low-flying delta-winged bomber except that after very quickly traversing the Meriden area, it had stopped abruptly and hovered, again over the area of the highway junction. The helicopter had arrived no more than five hours after the sighting. This was too much for me to ignore, so I called the Bridgeport Air Registry Service and gave them the NS numbers I had noted. I asked who might be flying the craft that day over Meriden. After several minutes they replied that I must be mistaken because the only helicopter with that registry number was owned by an individual in Torrance, California. Now I really became curious. What was a very expensive military helicopter doing low over Meriden, Connecticut, flying a search pattern in exactly the same area as of a UFO report only hours old? What private individual could afford it, get clearance to buy it, ship it from coast to coast and then casually use it to seemingly track UFOs? This was too much.

I didn't give up, but I eventually did find myself, basically, chasing my own tail. I called the Sikorsky Aircraft plant, the Army National Guard in Hartford, the State Police, the Coast Guard at East Haven, the New Haven airport, the Hartford airport (all in Connecticut) and finally another investigator in Long Island. I got nowhere. Nobody had heard of, seen or had any record of such a helicopter. Finally I called Torrance, California and asked for the number of the man listed as the registered owner. There were two listings for that name. I called them both. The first man laughed and said he sure would like to own a helicopter, but he didn't think he could handle the payments. The second politely said no, he didn't fly and that I must be mistaken. I struck out. Whatever happened, three things stand out: the reported UFO apparently was our old friend, the "Wing;" the helicopter was almost an unusual as the UFO itself; the coincidence of the UFO and the gunship being in exactly the same area within hours of each other is difficult to explain. Almost as an afterthought, I might add that military helicopters of gunship design are not usually painted dark blue and they definitely do not display civilian registration numbers in bright red paint. You can draw your own conclusions!

The third incident of note in 1985 really didn't involve the "Westchester Wing" directly, but it certainly gives a very clear example of the extreme efforts being made to dismiss and explain away the wave of UFO activity. It began in February of 1985. I was being interviewed by Jim Montavalli, managing editor of *The Fairfield Advocate*, about the UFO activity. I had contacted him, presented him with the evidence I had gathered, and asked if he was interested in an article for his paper. I found Jim to be an interested and unbiased man, and he ran an enthusiastic three-page article on Feb. 20th. I impressed upon him the fact that the two most informed and active investigators of this UFO wave were Lt. Lesnick and Phil Imbrogno.

Montavalli contacted them and arranged for an hour-long television interview on his weekly program "What Do You Think?" The show was well advertised for a week in advance and was presented live on WUBC, Channel 12 from 8:00 to 9:00 pm on the evening of March 20th. Just as the show ended and everyone was leaving an apparently immense ring of slowly moving lights came on directly over the Bridgeport studio. From Bridgeport the formation of unusual lights moved over New Haven and into central Connecticut, putting on a display seen by many hundreds of people. I saw them while on Route 34 near New Haven and watched them carefully as they moved over New Haven and then inland.

The display lasted approximately seven minutes from my position and very nearly caused several accidents as drivers pulled over to watch. Alas, it was not a UFO. It took me several minutes, but as the formation turned over New Haven, I realized they must be aircraft. There were eight of them, and their precision was almost perfect until the turn. Then four of the planes drifted slightly apart from the other four before reforming. The next day headlines throughout Connecticut loudly condemned these formation-flying fools for nearly causing accidents on highways throughout the state. Demands were made for an FAA investigation. The pilots were never found. The origin of the aircraft remains a mystery. That they were aircraft is certain. Paul Estefan, administrator of Danbury, Connecticut Municipal Airport, dispatched a plane to track the lights and the pilot tracked them to two airports in New York state. But Estefan refused to name the airports, saying that the pilots had not really broken any laws.

Was it really a coincidence that these planes put on a display that began just as the Channel 12 show ended? Was it really a coincidence that immediately after Lesnick and Imbrogno presented the evidence of two years of solid investigation, the perfect and easily accepted explanation casually flew over? Was it really a coincidence that this aircraft formation flew over the exact area where the TV show was being seen? From years of patient inquiry into the UFO phenomenon, I can assure you it all was not.

UFOs have profoundly alarmed those at high levels of national security in almost all of the countries of our planet. They have effortlessly rendered ICBM sites ineffective, easily evaded interception attempts by the most advanced aircraft of the United States and the Soviet Union, destroyed antiaircraft missiles launched at them with a technology far beyond our own. They have, at the same time, made a distinct and almost mythological impression on people throughout the world. They have not displayed overt hostility towards individuals, have not landed and disrupted our society and have shown no inclination to do so as yet. We may evolve into a unified world which peacefully moves out to explore our solar system, our universe. In such a case, UFOs may not make open and direct contact for hundreds of years. It may take that long for us to develop socially to the point where we would not be totally disturbed by such contact. We may also attempt to violently commit nuclear suicide, thereby poisoning our world, and killing all lifeforms on our planet. It would be a human decision. In such a case, somebody may come down and take our toys away, scolding us severely and imposing their own order upon us.

In reaching these kinds of conclusions, I feel that the majority of people in this country presently do not have a firm grasp on the UFO reality. Most simply avoid the subject. The avoidance maneuvers are varied: scientists, in general, see the UFO scene as a can of worms, full of inconsistencies; the media, especially the national media, still treat the subject with tongue in cheek; various authorities, from local police to those up to and including the presidential personnel, simply deny UFOs or explain them away as misidentification of man made or natural phenomena. A significant portion of the population treat UFOs in a semi-superstitious manner, in much the same way religious prophecies are treated. It is important to realize that these attitudes are not symptoms of a "planned coverup," at least for the most part. Habitual attitudes such as these are more the symptoms of the cultural-consensus "reality" within which we all usually function.

The realities of our world are largely our own creation. In trying to understand that concept, in trying to delineate its boundaries, we very often create that reality most comfortable to ourselves and those around us. This process leads to the cultural consensus "reality" which most of us share and support. UFOs, as yet, have not been fully accepted into that reality. People often ask me "Do you believe in UFOs?" My most consistent reply is "No! Do you believe in helicopters?"

UFOs are a reality not subject to our belief systems, although it seems they have initiated numerous "beliefs," "mythologies" and even possibly "religions." UFOs exist. The evidence for that existence is now much too solid to deny. That evidence could be an underlying force behind our rapidly evolving military technology. Deep-seated fears of what we label as the "unknown" may be a factor in our feverish arms race. It is even almost comforting to realize that now, as we peer off into the darkness of our self-created position, we could, if unified, at least have some chance to "battle" those "dark forces of the unknown." Unfortunately, those "dark forces" are largely creations of our own imaginations. Alien invaders haven't yet arrived to enslave us. In fact, I should imagine any advanced life form would be hesitant to try. We are an aggressive and pugnacious species and would make very poor slaves.

The human race is rapidly moving into an age where the nature of "reality" is changing every day. We need to understand that we create and maintain that "kind" of reality where we all pretty much agree on "how things are." The ultimate reality of our existence is still very much of a mystery, even to those scientists who specialize in exploring and defining it. We are part of a matter/energy universe which is only now beginning to be somewhat understood. Small-particle physicists, those closest to what we might call the "ultimate" reality, readily admit that at this stage of the game, they can define our universe most closely with only one word: ineffable. Science and religion are now beginning to find that they may well be exploring the same ideas, the only difference being in their approaches. UFOs are representative of a "reality" which also seems to be "ineffable."

The actual appearance of UFOs to witnesses, the evidence of UFO activity not only perceived by our senses but registered on our technological sensors, is overwhelming. It is best understood when viewed in a semantically-clear fashion. *They are here.* They are seen, tracked on radar, photographed, acted upon, and display actions which are as yet poorly understood. The data available on UFOs indicates the presence of several groups or "groupings" of visitors from other worlds. There are several broad common denominators of these groupings. One of the most consistent of these seems to be a gradual and periodically reinforced series of appearances, labelled "UFO waves." These appearances do not take place on a grand scale; likewise, landings and flyovers generally do not occur at the capital cities of the world. We are not yet prepared to face a culture of beings as far ahead of us as we are of cave dwellers. Anthropological studies show clear examples of the fates of primitive societies exposed to modern man.

Another common denominator of UFO activity is their appearances near majority military centers throughout the world. These appearances are again periodic, almost on a "reinforcement" schedule. Often these appearances coincide with "demonstrations" of the technological ease with which missile bases are electronically nullified, interceptor aircraft easily out-distanced, antiaircraft missiles destroyed at launch. Examples of these kinds of incidents are coming more and more to the public eye.

Perhaps it is time we started growing up. Our visitors, friendly or not, certainly cannot afford to let us come swarming off our planet armed and angry. What would you do if you were up there looking down at a planet whose dominant lifeforms seem to be preoccupied with making bigger, better and deadlier devices to either kill themselves or to keep each other from killing themselves? It would seem our visitors have been extremely patient. Perhaps they can help. Perhaps not. Perhaps they are angelic, attempting to help only indirectly. Perhaps they are demonic, attempting to move us onward towards "Armageddon." Perhaps they are neither.

Here we sit, our halos held up by our horns, for the most part unaware of the real nature of our visitors. Perhaps that nature is unimportant. Perhaps more important is our perception of their nature. Perhaps, just perhaps, we can help ourselves. With the awareness that the universe is not our enemy, that it is just the opposite, we might possibly move into a future of tremendous potential. We are growing up. Hopefully we shall share our movement into racial maturity with others who seem to have already evolved towards social and racial sanity. Again, it is our choice. We are, after all, fairly intelligent, especially when we're not chasing each other through the treetops.

Addendum

I finished this article and submitted it to PURSUIT in early

September of 1985. Since that time there have been two clear cases of the unknown object seen low over populated areas of New York and Connecticut. There was also a sharp rise in the number of isolated reports of unusual lights in these months. Most of these reports could not be attributed to aircraft activity. A summary of these reports is given here; it seems as if this resurgence is a clear indication that this wave is not finished.

The first incident of note came to light through Peter Gersten's UFO Hotline (914-739-6830). On the evening of September 12th, from 9:00 to 10:30 pm, an unusually large number of reports came into the hotline. All described an unusual object, studded with lights, low over New York City and surrounding areas such as Yonkers and New Rochelle. Some callers reported the "V" shape. Others said the lights varied in their appearance. Several callers reported that there was definitely a very large object involved as the stars were occulted or blocked from view by its passage overhead. I listened to the report of one woman who, along with her husband, saw the object as its light configurations began to change. Her report was familiar; the process she described was almost exactly the same as that seen by the woman I interviewed in Goshen, CT. The media did not make much comment on this activity. Channel 7 News at 11:00 pm that night mentioned unusual lights seen over the New York City area.

The second incident involving large numbers of people was one I investigated personally. On the evening of October 17th 1985, an estimated two thousand witnesses saw the object as it appeared over Bridgeport, Fairfield and Danbury, Connecticut. As it moved over these towns it was seen, by separate witnesses, to "change shape" from a "V" to a straight line and back to a "V." The witnesses, some of them police officers, again referred to rows of large lights that defined the shape of the object. It moved very slowly, rotated on its axis and accelerated very rapidly. It was described as "larger than an airliner at low altitude" by witnesses I interviewed. Visiting the Fairfield and Bridegeport, CT police departments, I found that there had been a very large number of calls that night from people concerned about the object.

I decided to call the hotline and put my findings on record. The hotline, established more than a year ago, was a direct result of UFO activity in the area and received reports, replaying some of the more dramatic ones for several days. The report from the night of the 17th was recorded on the 19th and played back on the 20th to the 22nd. It gives a clearer idea of the nature and magnitude of the incident:

"Thursday, October 17th—"V"-shaped white, red, green and blue lights were first seen over Main Street, Bridgeport, CT at approximately 8:35 pm. The "lights" moved slowly north to the area of St. Vincent's Hospital, stopped, hovered for three to five minutes, then rapidly accelerated away to the north. It apparently turned to the east and was next seen hovering over Fairfield University, Fairfield from 8:45 to 8:55 pm. Again stopped, hovered, "V" unfolded to straight line. Altitude verified at less than one thousand feet by "trigging out" witness positions and angles of observation. All witnesses agree the size of the display was larger than a large jet airliner. After hovering over Fairfield, while viewed by police officers, object rotated on its own axis and moved away. Reports came in from Trumbull, Monroe and then Danbury. Shortly after 9:00 pm, over Danbury, police chief John P. Basile saw it with over thirty other witnesses. Also seen over Bethel and New Fairfield areas and then Candlewood Lake. Articles on page four of the Bridgeport *Telegram* of Friday, October 18th and page 13 of the Danbury *News-Times* of the same date. Approximately three hundred calls to the Fairfield Police Department, calls also to the Danbury police, local radio stations and newspapers. Estimated number of witnesses, two thousand."

There can be no doubt that something unknown is evident. Other reports that came to my attention were as follows:

September 11th, 1985: Single witness, female, reports that while walking dog in Trumbull, CT at 11:30 pm, saw large group of red lights moving low over position from north to south. Reported by personal acquaintance.

October 7th, 1985: A Bridgeport fireman, thirty years old, while bicycling from Bridgeport to Florida (local newspaper coverage) reports seeing low-flying "V"-shaped object followed closely by several military helicopters. Witness reports that this was near the coast of Virginia, about 9:00 to 10:00 pm and object and choppers moving south to north. Reported by personal acquaintance.

October 16th, 1985: Two witnesses, female, report seeing a "V"-shaped object low over beach near West Haven, CT, between 11:30 and 12:00 pm. Report also cites "mild sunburn" as a result of "being under the thing." Interviewed one witness by telephone, unable to follow up and clarify "sunburn" aspect.

October 16th, 1985: Newburg, NY, reports of unusual lights over area, reported by UFO hotline.

October 18th, 1985: Between Atlantic City and Newark, NJ, over Garden State Parkway between 11:00 and 12:00 pm, single witness reports seeing "V"-shaped object with white lights and large central red light. Reported by personal acquaintance.

October 31st, 1985: Report of a "close encounter of the third kind" at 3:30 am in Ossining, NY. UFO hotline, no clarification.

What we have been calling the "Westchester Wing" continues to be seen. Its appearances continue to frame questions of its origin and purpose. We all, each in our own way, have much to learn in probing for answers.

R. Perry Collins is an aerospace engineer and part-time physics teacher living in Connecticut. He has been an active UFO investigator and researcher for a number of years.

There was another sighting of the "Westchester Wing" on May 29, 1986. As usual, the authorities attributed it to pranksters in ultra-light aircraft. However, as it hovered, then went suddenly from a dead stop to high speed, a maneuver that ultra-light aircraft are not capable of, it appears to have been a genuine UFO.

In Sweden on April 17, 1986, there was a sighting of a large UFO (about 450 feet long) that contained an interesting detail: as a normal passenger airliner approached the vicinity, the UFO emitted a sort of steam, and was covered by a cloud by the time the airliner came over the horizon, which dissipated after the airliner had disappeared over the opposite horizon.

Ozires Silva is President of Embraer, the largest manufacturer of aircraft in Brazil, and is also President of the government-owned petroleum corporation, Petrobas. Being at the head of both of these important corporations, he is one of the most influential men in Brazil. San Jose de Campos is the high-tech center of Brazil's military-industrial complex.

On May 19, 1986, Mr. Silva had a conference with the President of Brazil, Jose Sarney, at Brazilia, at which the Minister of Aviation, Brigadier General Octavio Moreira Lima, was also present. Mr. Silva then took his private jet to San Jose de Campos. At 9 pm the pilot of Mr. Silva's jet had begun his descent to land, when the control tower informed him that there were three UFOs in his flight path. The pilot canceled his approach, and, with the permission of Mr. Silva, attempted to pursue the objects, but gave up after 13 minutes, as the UFOs were traveling at such high speed that he was unable to catch up with them. The pilot saw two of the objects visually, and described them as very bright red lights, which could not be confused with stars or known types of aircraft. Three jet fighters were scrambled. One of them picked up the three UFOs on radar at 9:45 PM, and pursued them until 10:15 PM, when he gave up further pursuit because his fuel was running low. At that time, ground radar at several different air bases reported UFOs. Radar scopes were saturated with an enormous number of UFOs. Three more jets were scrambled. Some of the pursuers found themselves being pursued. One jet reported being chased by 13 objects that were very small, approximately the size of ping-pong balls. The 13 objects temporarily paced the jet, taking positions near its right and left wings. They were intensely luminous, red and white and green, traveling at speeds estimated by the military jet pilots as varying between 160 and 1,350 miles per hour.

Three days previously, on May 16, a civilian pilot flying near Brazilia had reported having been followed for 460 miles by small luminous objects. On the second and third days following the incident. May 21 and 22, larger UFOs, of the sizes usually reported, were witnessed and photographed over other parts of Brazil.

The Minister of Aviation, Brigadier General Octavio Moreira Lima, confirmed that the events of May 19 had actually taken place, and ordered that an investigation be made of them.

Sources:
> *News-Times*, Danbury, CT, May 30, 1986.
> *Ostersund-Posten*, Ostersuna, Sweden, May 6, 1986.
> *Globo*, Rio de Janeiro, May 22 & 23, 1986.

Translation credits:
> Robert Pratt and Wendelle Stevens.
> Reuter News Agency, May 23, 1986.
> United Press International, May 24, 1986.

Credit:
> UFO Newsclipping Service, Rt. 1 Box 220, Plumerville. AR 72127.

The on-site injection well at Kerr-McGee's plant near Gore, Oklahoma, has now been shut down, following concerted action by concerned citizens, spearheaded by Native Americans for a Clean Environment. However, Kerr-McGee has applied for an on-site waste dump, consisting of 25 acres of pits that go down to only 10 feet above the water table, and that do not have any lining whatsoever, simple pits of raw earth. The waste is to be dumped into them without being put into containers. If the permit is approved, the 25 acres will probably be enlarged into a multi-state dumping ground.

At present, waste is being stored in open pools, which overflow after heavy rain. Massive chronic leakage has been reported from one such pit since 1974, and although widely discussed among government agencies, no corrective measures have been taken.

The Oklahoma Water Resources Board, of which Robert S. Kerr is a member, issued a permit to Kerr-McGee that allows the Gore plant to legally dump 11,000 pounds of nuclear waste per year into the Illinois River at its confluent with the Arkansas River. This permit expired in 1982, but Kerr-McGee continues to dump its waste into the river anyway. N.A.C.E. protests to the authorities about this situation are met with evasive double-talk.

The license of the plant has been amended 28 times by the Nuclear Regulatory Commission without the knowledge or participation of the public. Its safety record demonstrates that accidents and leakages occur persistently but rarely reach the news media.

In 1982, the NRC gave Kerr-McGee a permit to test nuclear waste as a fertiliser, so long as they tested it on their own property. Kerr-McGee was given a tax write-off (reported as 80%) to buy up thousands of acres of farmland in Sequoyah, Haskell and Muskogee Counties, and has been spraying them from planes with "treated" nuclear waste ever since. After all this time, there has been no evidence of any potential value as a fertiliser. N.A.C.E. maintains that this is just one more disposal scheme, disguised as an experiment. Multiple health problems are spreading among the people living in the vicinity of the plant.

Jacinta and Francisco Marto, and Lucia dos Santos, who saw the vision of the Blessed Virgin Mary at Fatima, Portugal, in 1916. The phenomena witnessed by a crowd of over 70,000 people at the Catholic miracle of Fatima in 1917 strongly resemble descriptions of modern UFO sightings. See Chapter One. (*Fortean Picture Library*).

UFOs photographed in Balcarce, Argentina, July 19, 1974 by Sr. Antonio Le Pere. (*UFO Photo Archives*).

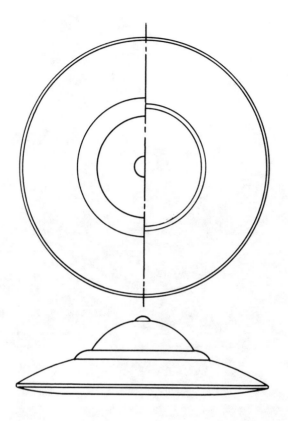

Late in the afternoon of July 19, 1974, at Balcarce, Argentina, a low-domed, circular disc-shaped metal-looking flying object approached and paced an automobile being driven along route 226 near that city by Sr. Antonio Le Pere, a local resident. It was near 18:00 hours when Le Pere noticed the intruder keeping pace with him from a position only a few hundred meters to his left, and barely 10 meters above the ground there. Le Pere slowed his automobile as he worked on his camera and readied it to take a picture, and he snapped two good clear color photographs of the strange object before it started climbing and flew away. Le Pere took the pictures through the rolled down window on the driver's side of the car, shooting over his left arm holding the steering wheel.

The object was of a coppery-brownish smooth finished reflective material like metal, or something between a metal and ceramic finish, but it was of a strange color for familiar metals. It had a raised dome on the top surface of the craft, and seemed to have a reddish glow either on the rim edge or surrounding the rim very closely to the ship. The strange machine flew a steady course and was quite obviously under intelligent control.   (*UFO Archives*).

There are many different types of UFOnauts. These small, 3-4 foot tall extraterrestrials are some of the most common type which have been reported. This particular type is often seen carrying weapons, taking soil samples or otherwise investigating the environment. Reports state that these extraterrestrials are often extremely hostile, and are seen mostly in rural locations. (*Loren Coleman*)

UFO photographed over Trindade Island, South Atlantic Ocean, January 16, 1958. (*Fortean Picture Library*).

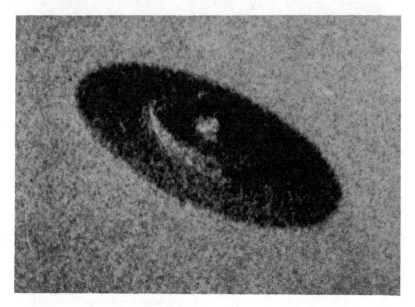

UFO photographed at Barra da Tijuca, Brazil, May 7, 1952. See Chapter One. (*Fortean Picture Library*).

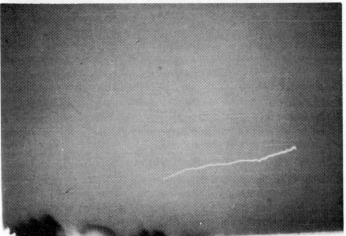

Top: Photo by Dr. Harley Rutledge of a single ball of light, a portion of a 20 second exposure on Polaroid film. The motion is right to left. A duplicate exposure taken with another camera at the same time revealed an entirely different image.

Bottom: Farmington, Missouri, 1973. After noting three stars through binoculars in a vertical, straight line, Rutledge took a 15 second timed exposure of the bottom star which appeared to "jiggle". Immediately after taking the photo, the star simply disappeared. See Chapter One. (*Dr. Harley Rutledge*).

UFOs photographed over Conisbrough, South Yorkshire, England on March 28, 1966. see Chapter One. (*Stephen Pratt/Fortean Picture Library*).

UFO photographed by George J. Stock, Passaic, New Jersey, July 29, 1952. See Chapter One. (*Fortean Picture Library*).

15th century Italian fresco: The Legend of the Cross by Piero Della Francesca (1409—1492) which is on the wall of St. Francis of Arezzo Church in Tuscany, Italy. (Reproduction shown here by F. Lagarde)

15th Century Italian fresco is from Mount Athos Monastery in Greece, date unknown, showing St. John dictating the Apocalypse to a young disciple. In the upper lefthand corner is a part of a luminous sphere, from which rays are converging toward the head of St. John. In the upper righthand corner is a typical UFO shape, which emits a converging beam.

Replica of Olmec statuary head at National Museum of Anthropology, Mexico City, Mexico. The Olmec culture is among the earliest known in the Americas. The Olmec preceded the Maya, the Toltecs, and the Aztecs in Mexico. The giant stone heads are carved out of black basalt and weigh about 40 tons each. The nearest places where black basalt could be quarried are between forty and seventy miles away. See Chapter Two. (*Dennis Stacy/Fortean Picture Library*).

Tiny figure of a man sitting cross-armed and cross-legged on a ledge found in a cave by gold prospectors near Casper, Wyoming in 1932. He was dark bronze in color, very wrinkled, and no more than 14 inches high; of an extremely great age, historically speaking, and of a type and stature unknown. When an x-ray was taken, a skull, spine, ribcage and bones, almost exactly like those of a normal man were clearly discernible. Closer study established that the creature weighed about twelve ounces, had a full set of teeth, and was probably about sixty-five years old when he died. See Chapter Two.

Top: This engraving (1582) shows the English magician Dr. John Dee, astrologer to Queen Elizabeth; alchemist, mathematician and geographer, who together with his friend Sir Edward Kelly is said to have invoked famous dead people. Dee along with Kelly, obtained access to the construction of the Enochian system of magickal skrying in the 16th Century. See Chapter Two.

Left: Portrait of Dr. John Dee.

Enochian	Title	English
	Un	A.
	Pe	B.
	Veh	C or K.
	Gal	D.
	Graph	E.
	Orth	F.
	Ged	G.
	Na-hath	H.
	Gon	I, Y, or J.
	Ur	L.
	Tal	M.
	Drun	N.
	Med	O.
	Mals	P.
	Ger	Q.
	Don	R.
	Fam	S.
	Gisa	T.
	Vau	U, V, W.
	Pal	X.
	Ceph	Z.

Enochian Alphabet

A copy of the Enochian Alphabet compared to the English alphabet. To obtain magical spells, an Angel pointed to the letters on a chart, and Kelly would pass on this knowledge to Dee. Each word was written backwrds, as it was considered too dangerous and powerful to write the words correctly. See Chapter Two. (*Enochian Magic by Gerald Schueler, Llewellyn Publications*).

THE HOLY TABLE

Dee and Kelly devised a Holy Twelvefold Table containing seven different talismans, as shown in Figure 1. This table is covered with Enochian writings. In the center is:

O I T
M L U
L M L
O O E

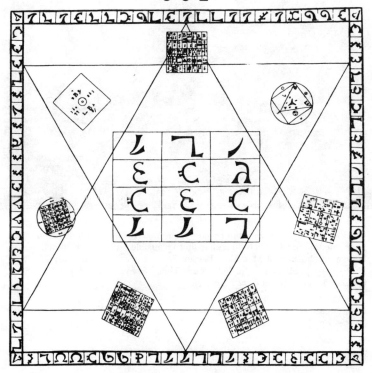

Figure 1. The Holy Table

See Chapter Two. (*Enochian Magic by Gerald Schueler, Llewellyn Publications*).

An example of spontaneous human combustion, a rare but persistently recurring phenomenon for which it is difficult to find a plausible explanation. Spontaneous human combustion of Mrs. M.H. Reeser, St. Petersburg, Florida, July 2, 1951. Photograph published in St. Petersburg Times & Evening Independent. See Chapter Three. (*Fortean Picture Library*).

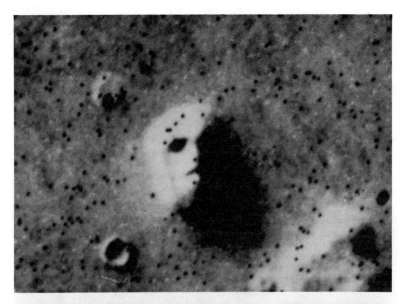

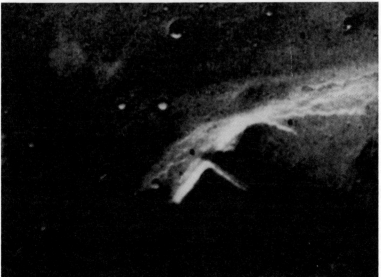

Martian Face & Pyramid
Picture of gigantic, one mile long Sphinx-like stone face, taken from Viking
spacecraft which orbited Mars in 1977. Ten miles away from the Martian face is
found a rectangular pyramid which dwarfs our Great Pyramid. It has precisely
defined sides and corners, one of which points due Martian north. See Chapter
Three. (*NASA photo*).

Charles Fort, 1874-1932. Famed pioneer of research into unexplained phenomena during the 1920's. See Chapter Four. (*Fortean Picture Library*).

Loch Hakel Cup-Marked Stone

Sutherland, Highland Region, England. In Chapter Five the mysterious Gypsy explains "the devil's hoofprints" by saying that "The Measure-Marker was left idling. . . . Marker is like a low-power stonecutter." The clusters of cup marks found on rocks in different parts of the world were made by a similar and more powerful instrument. The cup marks come in clusters because the UFOs have a tendency to wobble and oscillate as they hover.

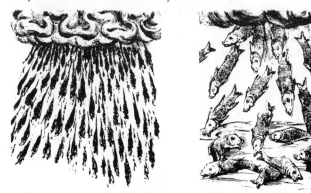

Ancient Signs in the Sky

Long before there was any talk of flying saucers, the ancient chronicles told stories of unknown celestial objects. In the 16th century these incidents were reported: a rainstorm of blood in Lisbon in 1551, and a rain of fish from the sky. See Chapter Four.

CREDITS

Russian UFO incident at Gorki: *Le Matin*, Lausanne, Switzerland, June 2, 1984.

Case involving Premier Wran: *Sunday Telegraph*, Sydney, N.S.W., Australia, Sept. 8, 1985.

English cases involving Oxford, Windsor and Prince Charles: *Times*, Oxford, Oct. 4, 1985; *Daily Express*, London, Feb. 5, 1986; *Windsor, Slough and Eton Express*, Feb. 7, 1986; *Sunday Mirror*, London, March 2 and 9, 1986; *National Enquirer*, March 18, 1986.

Case involving USAF Lt. Col. Halt: *News of the World*, London, Oct. 2, 1983; *Ipswich Evening Star*, Suffolk, article by Paul Durrant, Oct. 3, 1983; *The Guardian*, London, Jan. 5, 1985.

Concerning Stonehenge/Glastonbury Tor/Midsummer Hill isosceles triangle: "Landscape Geometry in Southern Britain" by Michael Behrend, Institute of Geomantic Research, 1975; *The Ley Hunter's Companion* by Paul Devereux and Ian Thomson, Thames & Hudson, 1979.

French Trans-en-Provence case: *Liberation*, Paris, Nov. 14, 1983; *France-Soir Magazine*, Paris, Nov. 19, 1983, article by Jean-Yves Casgha; *France-Soir*, Paris, Jan. 4, 1984, article by Francois Corre.

Strange aspects of the death of Pope John-Paul I: *In God's Name* by David A. Yallop, Bantam, 1984. Also *L'Autre Monde*, issue no. 26, Paris, 1979.

UFO phenomena preceding the death of Pope John-Paul I: *Review Record*, Miami, FL, Dec. 19, 1978; *Jacksonville Journal*, Jacksonville, FL, Sept. 17, 1978.

UFO/earthquake link and Shemya UFO/earthquake incident: *Tacoma News Tribune*, Washington, April 7, 1978; *Space-Time Transients and Unusual Events* by Michael A. Persinger and Gyslaine F. Lafreniere, Nelson-Hall, Chicago, 1977.

Fletcher Reel NASA press conference: *Wisconsin State Journal*, Madison, WI, Oct. 10, 1982, article by Rose DeWolf.

Concerning the Palaeolithic UFO shapes: article by Aime Michel in *Flying Saucer Review*, Nov./Dec. 1969.

Concerning the San Lorenzo Olmec site: "Suggestive Hallucinogenic-Derived Motifs from New World Monumental Earthworks", an unpublished manuscript by Marlene Dobkin de Rios, Ph.D., Dept. of Psychiatry and Human Behavior, University of California, Irvine, CA.

Concerning the Olmec compass: "Lodestone Compass: Chinese or Olmec Primacy?" by John B. Carlson in *Science*, 189-760, 1975. Copyright by the American Association for the Advancement of Science, 1975. For this item, and the following three items, also: *Ancient Man: A Handbook of Puzzling Artifacts* by William Corliss, Sourcebook Project, Glen Arm, MD 21057, 1978.

Concerning 1932 excavations at the Monte Alban site: "Recent Discoveries in Mexico and Guatemala, Anonymous, in *Nature,* 131:101, 1933.

Concerning the Cuicuilco pyramid: "Cuicuilco" by Ron Willis in *INFO Journal,* 3:1-7, 1973, P.O. Box 367, Arlington, VA 22210.

Concerning dwarf and giant skeletons in Tennessee: *The Natural and Aboriginal History of Tennessee* by John Haywood, first published in 1823, was republished in 1959 by McCowat-Mercer, Jackson, Tenn. Also *The Rebirth of Pan* by Jim Brandon, Liberation Press, P.O. Box 69, Dunlap, IL 61525, 1984.

Concerning the changes in Venus and the Assyrian army reduced to ashes: *Worlds in Collision* by Immanuel Velikovsky, Doubleday, 1950.

Concerning the Voynich manuscript: summarised from articles by Michael Daiger ("The World's Most Mysterious Manuscript", *Occult,* Jan. 1976); Frank Smyth ("The Voynich Manuscript", *The Unexplained,* issues 70 and 71); Alfred Werner ("The Most Mysterious Manuscript", *Horizon,* Jan. 1963).

Concerning Black Elk: *Black Elk Speaks* by John G. Neihardt, Morrow, New York, 1932 (current edition by Pocket Books); "The Wisdom of the Contrary: A Conversation With Joseph Epes Brown" in *Parabola,* Vol. IV. No. 1, 150 Fifth Avenue, New York, NY 10011.

Concerning UFO sightings in Europe 1819-1842: article by Marie-Therese Hartmann in *La Savoie,* Albertville, France, Feb. 3, 1984.

Concerning UFO reports from U.S. Midwest in 1897: *Kansas City Star,* Kansas City, MO, Feb. 17, 1985.

Concerning transient Martian anomalies: *Flying Saucers From Outer Space* by Major Donald Keyhoe, Holt, 1953; *Mysterious Universe* by William Corliss, Sourcebook Project, Glen Arm, MD 21057; personal communications from Richard Heiden of the Aerial Phenomena Research Organisation and from Lucius Farish of the UFO Newsclipping Service, Rt. 1 Box 220, Plumerville, AR 72127 (an indispensable source of information, through whom I obtained nearly all the newspaper articles referred to in this book).

Concerning UFO photo cases presented: UFO Photo Archives, P.O. Box 17206, Tucson, AZ 85710.

Photo Credits
Janet & Colin Bord, Fortean Picture Library;
UFO Photo Archives;
Loren Coleman
Dr. Harley Rutledge;
Leonard H. Stringfield;
NASA.

STAY IN TOUCH

On the following pages you will find listed, with their current prices, some of the books and tapes now available on related subjects. Your book dealer stocks most of these, and will stock new titles in the Llewellyn series as they become available. We urge your patronage.

However, to obtain our full catalog, to keep informed of new titles as they are released and to benefit from informative articles and helpful news, you are invited to write for our bi-monthly news magazine/catalog. A sample copy is free, and it will continue coming to you at no cost as long as you are an active mail customer. Or you may keep it coming for a full year with a donation of just $2.00 in U.S.A. ($7.00 for Canada & Mexico, $20.00 overseas, first class mail). Many bookstores also have *The Llewellyn New Times* available to their customers. Ask for it.

Stay in touch! In *The Llewellyn New Times'* pages you will find news and reviews of new books, tapes and services, announcements of meetings and seminars, articles helpful to our readers, news of authors, advertising of products and services, special money-making opportunities, and much more.

The Llewellyn New Times
P.O. Box 64383-Dept. 010, St. Paul, MN 55164-0383, U.S.A.

•   •   •

TO ORDER BOOKS AND TAPES

If your book dealer does not have the books and tapes described on the following pages readily available, you may order them direct from the publisher by sending full price in U.S. funds, plus $2.00 for postage and handling for orders of $10 and under. Orders over $10 will require $3.50 postage and handling. There are no postage and handling charges for orders over $100. UPS Delivery: We ship UPS whenever possible. Delivery guaranteed. Provide your street address as UPS does not deliver to P.O. Boxes. UPS to Canada requires a $50 minimum order. Allow 4-6 weeks for delivery. Orders outside the U.S.A and Canada: Airmail—add $5 per book; add $3 for each non-book item (tapes, etc.); add $1 per item for surface mail.

FOR GROUP STUDY AND PURCHASE

Our Special Quantity Price for a minimum order of five copies of *EXTRA-TERRESTRIALS AMONG US* is $29.95 Cash-With-Order. This price includes postage and handling within the United States. Minnesota residents must add 6% sales tax. For additional quantities, please order in multiples of five. For Canadian and foreign orders, add postage and handling charges as above. Credit Card (VISA, Master Card, American Express) Orders are accepted. Charge Card Orders only may be phoned free ($15.00 minimum order) within the U.S.A. by dialing 1-800-THE MOON (in Canada call: 1-800-FOR-SELF). Customer Service calls dial 1-612-291-1970. Mail Orders to:

LLEWELLYN PUBLICATIONS
P.O. Box 64383-Dept. 010 / St. Paul, MN 55164-0383, U.S.A.

THE GOBLIN UNIVERSE
Ted Holiday/Colin Wilson

Throughout history, we have been confronted with things that fail to fit squarely into our self-conceived reality. Many times we find them frightening. Even modern science is fearful and rejects those things for which it presently does not have any explanation—things like monsters, UFOs and the many things that go bump in the night.

It is the world of mind that is the Goblin Universe—goblin only because of our own limitations. And it is this greater universe that is the place of magick, of psychic phenomena, of ghosts and poltergeists, UFOs and the Men in Black, dragons and yetis and the Loch Ness Monster, of prophecy and retrogression and other mysteries.

Ted Holiday and Colin Wilson explore this amazing world with accounts of Ted Holiday's personal experiences and his search for a 'unified theory' to open our perceptions to the full universe. Wilson sees the problem in terms of the built-in nature of the human brain and our lack of training in its use.

Wilson and Holiday examine a wide range of 'occult' phenomena and explore the technologies by which we may expand our world.

0-87542-310-8, 272 pages, 5¼ x 8, photos. $9.95

CRYSTAL POWER
by Michael G. Smith

This is an amazing book, for what it claims to present—with complete instructions and diagrams so that YOU can work them yourself—is the master technology of ancient Atlantis: psionic (mind-controlled and life-energized machines) devices made from common quartz crystals!

For as little as $10.00 you can easily construct an "Atlantean" Power Rod that can be used for healing or a weapon; or a Crystal Headband stimulating psychic powers; or a Time and Space Communications Generator; operated purely by your mind.

These Crystal Devices seem to work only with the disciplined mind power of a human operator, yet their very construction seems to start a process of growth and development, a new evolutionary step in the human psyche that bridges mind and matter.

Does this "re-discovery" mean that we are living, now, in The New Atlantis? Have these Power Tools been re-invented to meet the needs of this prophetic time? Are Psionic Machines the culminating Power To The People to free us from economic dependence on fossil fuels and smokestack industry?

This book answers "yes" to all these questions, and asks you to simply build these devices and put them to work to help bring it all about.

0-87542-725-1, 250 pages, 5¼ x 8, illus., photos, softcover $9.95

THE MESSAGE OF THE CRYSTAL SKULL
By Alice Bryant & Phyllis Galde

The most fascinating, mysterious artifact ever discovered by mankind. Thousands of years old, yet it is beyond the capabilities of today's technology to duplicate it. Those who have touched the skull or seen photographs of it claim increased psychic abilities and purification. Read this book and discover how this mystical quartz crystal skull can benefit you and all of humankind. Famed biocrystallographer Frank Dorland shares his research of the skull.

0-87542-092-3, mass market, 200 pages, illus., photos $3.95

CRYSTAL SPIRIT
by Michael G. Smith

Crystal Spirit is the book thousands of people have asked for after reading the popular *Crystal Power* by the same author. Now that the fad appeal of crystals is wearing off, we can use crystals to experience the deeper essence of ourselves—to facilitate our self-awareness, self-growth, and self-understanding.

Crystal Spirit contains timely and hard-to-find information on:
- New types of crystal rods
- Crystal pyramid devices
- The crystal pipe from Native American traditions
- Ki and Chi energy through crystals for martial artists
- Health and exercise with crystal wristbands

The book begins with explanations of crystals of the ancient past and how to reconstruct your own: the Trident Krystallos, Atlantean Crystal Cross, Crux Crystallum. The book ends with the introduction of the new crystal pipe based on traditional Native American practices and the science of Universal Energy. The crystal pipe, which came into being during the Harmonic Convergence of 1987, is a new tool for the beginning of a new earth cycle. Between these two chapters is a wealth of information and instruction on other crystal inventions, all of which are inexpensive and simple to construct and use, that are beneficial for earth healing and individual development.

0-87542-726-X, 208 pgs., mass market, illustrated $3.95

PSYCHIC POWER
by Charles Cosimano
Although popular in many parts of the world, *Radionics* machines have had little application in America, *UNTIL NOW!* Charles Cosimano's book, *Psychic Power*, introduces these machines to America with a new purpose: to increase your psychic powers!

Using the easy, step-by-step instructions, and for less than a $10.00 investment, you an build a machine which will allow you to read other people's minds, influence their thoughts, communicate with their dreams and be more successful when you do divinations such as working with Tarot cards or Pendulums.

For thousands of years, people have looked for an easy, simple and sure way to increase their psychic abilities. Now, the science of psionics allows you to do just that! This book is practical, fun and an excellent source for those wishing to achieve results with etheric energies.

If you just want a book to read, you will find this a wonderful title to excitingly fill a few hours. But if you can spare a few minutes to actually build and use these devices, you will be able to astound yourself and your friends. We are not talking about guessing which numbers will come up on a pair of dice at a mark slightly above average. With practice, you will be able to choose which numbers will come up more often than not! But don't take our word for it. Read the book, build the devices and find out for yourself.

0-87542-097-4, 224 pages, mass market, illus.   **$3.95**

LIFE FORCE
by Leo Ludzia
A secret living energy—as ancient as the Pyramids, as modern as Star Wars. Since the beginning of time, certain people have known that there *is* this energy—a power that can be used by people for healing, magick, and spiritual development. It's been called many names: Mana, Orgone, Psionic, Prana, Kundalini, Odic force, Chi and others.

Leo Ludzia puts it all together in this amazing book *Life Force*. This is the first book which shows the histories and compares the theories and methods of *using* this marvelous energy. This *FForce* is available to us all, if only we know how to tap into it. Ludzia shows you how to make devices which will help you better use and generate this *Life Force*. This specialized information includes easy-to-follow-directions on: how to build and use pyramids, Orgone Generators such as those used by Wilhelm Reich, and how to make and use the "Black Box" designed and used by the genius inventor T.G. Hieronymus.

0-87542-437-6, 220 pgs., mass market, illus.   **$3.95**

THE TRUTH ABOUT WITCHCRAFT TODAY
by Scott Cunningham

The Truth About Witchcraft Today, is the first real look at the facts about Witchcraft and the religion of Wicca. For centuries, organized religions have perpetrated lies about the ancient practice of Witchcraft, and to this day, many misinformed people think Wicca involves worship of the Devil, sex orgies, and drug use—it just isn't so! As Cunningham plainly states, the practice of magic is not supernatural or Satanic—Witches and folk magicians are only utilizing, through timeless rituals, *natural energies* found within the Earth and our bodies to enrich life by creating positive change.

If you are completely unfamiliar with Witchcraft, and have wondered exactly how magic works, this book was written for you! In a straightforward, easy-to-understand manner, Cunningham explains the differences between folk magic, ritual magic, ceremonial magic, and religious magic. He describes the folk magician's "tools of power"—crystals, herbs, candles, and chants—as well as the ritual tools of the Wiccan: the athame, cauldron, crystal sphere, and pentacle, among others. He also provides an excellent introduction to the practice of magic by delineating two simple folk magic spells, a circle-casting ceremony, and a complete Wiccan ritual.

ISBN: 0-87542-127-X, mass market format, 224 pgs.,   **$3.95**

THE SPACE/TIME CONNECTION
Leo F. Ludzia

Reality is not what you think it is. This fascinating book will shatter old misconceptions about the true nature of reality. You will learn about the mysterious "4th dimension" of time that is used by humanity but misunderstood.

Here are the latest scientific findings from the worlds of modern physics and mind science. Written in a fast and easy-to-understand format, it presents a model of humanity, mind and the universe that is disturbing to what we have been told is real, but is somehow familiar.

From reading this book and doing the easy exercises included, you will be able to obtain *anything you desire!* No longer will you be a victim of fate. You can gain in self-confidence, and change your life forever.

0-87542-449-X, 200 pgs., illus., mass market format   **$3.95**

THE LLEWELLYN ANNUALS

Llewellyn's MOON SIGN BOOK: Approximately 400 pages of valuable information on gardening, fishing, weather, stock market forecasts, personal horoscopes, good planting dates, and general instructions for finding the best date to do just about anything! Articles by prominent forecasters and writers in the fields of gardening, astrology, politics, economics and cycles. This special almanac, different from any other, has been published annually since 1906. It's fun, informative and has been a great help to millions in their daily planning.   **State year $3.95**

Llewellyn's SUN SIGN BOOK: Your personal horoscope for the entire year! All 12 signs are included in one handy book. Also included are forecasts, special feature articles, and an action guide for each sign. Monthly horoscopes are written by Gloria Star, author of *Optimum Child*, for your personal Sun Sign. Articles on a variety of subjects written by well-known astrologers from around the country. Much more than just a horoscope guide! Entertaining and fun the year round.

State year $3.95

Llewellyn's DAILY PLANETARY GUIDE and ASTROLOGER'S DATE-BOOK: Includes all of the major daily aspects plus their exact times in Eastern and Pacific time zones, lunar phases, signs and voids plus their times, planetary motion, a monthly ephemeris, sunrise and sunset tables, special articles on the planets, signs, aspects, a business guide, planetary hours, rulerships, and much more. Large 5¼ × 8 format for more writing space, spiral bound to lay flat, address and phone listings, time zone conversion chart and blank horoscope chart.   **State year $6.95**

Llewellyn's ASTROLOGICAL CALENDAR: Large wall calendar of 52 pages. Beautiful full color cover and color inside. Includes special feature articles by famous astrologers, introductory information on astrology. Lunar Gardening Guide, celestial phenomena for the year, a blank horoscope chart for your own chart data, and monthly date pages which include aspects, lunar information, planetary motion, ephemeris, personal forecasts, lucky dates, planting and fishing dates, and more. 10 x 13 size. Set in Central time, with conversion table for other time zones worldwide.   **State year $7.95**

Llewellyn's MAGICKAL ALMANAC
Edited by Ray Buckland
The Magickal Almanac examines some of the many forms that Magick can take, allowing the reader a peek behind a veil of secrecy into Egyptian, Shamanic, Wiccan and other traditions. The almanac pages for each month provide information important in the many aspects of working Magick. Each month, following the almanac pages, are articles addressing one form of Magick, with rituals the reader can easily follow.

State year $9.95

RUNE MIGHT: Secret Practices of the German Rune Magicians
by Edred Thorsson

Rune Might reveals, for the first time in the English language, the long-hidden secrets of the German rune magicians who practiced their arts in the beginning of this century. By studying the contents of *Rune Might* and working with the exercises, the reader will be introduced to a fascinating world of personalities and the sometimes sinister dark corners of runic history. Beyond this, the reader will be able to experience the direct power of the runes as experienced by the early German rune magicians.

Rune Might takes the best and most powerful of the runic techniques developed in that early phase of the runic revival and offers them as a coherent set of exercises. Experience rune yoga, rune dance, runic hand gestures (mudras), rune singing (mantras), group rites with runes, runic healing, runic geomancy, and two of the most powerful runic methods of engaging transpersonal powers—the Ritual of the Ninth Night and the Ritual of the Grail Cup.

The exercises represent bold new methods of drawing magical power into your life—regardless of the magical tradition or system with which you normally work. No other system does this in quite the direct and clearly defined ways that rune exercises do.

0-87542-778-2, 192 pgs., 5¼ × 8, illustrated **$7.95**